DEAL AND DISTRICT
AT WAR

David G. Collyer

ALAN SUTTON PUBLISHING LIMITED

First published in the United Kingdom in 1995 by
Alan Sutton Publishing Ltd · Phoenix Mill · Far Thrupp · Stroud
Gloucestershire

British Library Cataloguing in Publication Data

A catalogue record for this book is available from the British Library

ISBN 0-7509-1025-9

Typeset in 11/13 pt Bembo.
Typesetting and origination by
Alan Sutton Publishing Limited.
Printed in Great Britain by
Butler & Tanner, Frome, Somerset

Contents

Acknowledgements

Particular thanks are due to the following: Harry Adnitt; Pam Andrews; John Annal; William H. Austen; Roy Baker; Bill Barry; K.C. Bartlett; Stephen P. Batambeau; H. Beauchamp; George Bennett; Rodney Betts; Stan Blacker; Alice Bond; W.H. Bourne; Alice Bradshaw; Bernard Burgess; Emily Burgess; Joe Burke; Glyn Casey; Roy Catherick; Percy Cavell; M.W. Cole; Leonard Collyer; Leslie Collyer; George Cornwell; Ron Crier; E.W.G. Cummings; Bert Curling; Albert Daniels; Irene Davies; R.L.J. Eames; Marjorie Fenn (Kemp); Mrs N. Finnis (Clark); Edgar Gee; Don Gill; Charles Grant; Peggy Griffiths (Oatridge); Mary Guy (Evans); 'Tom' Hackney; Len Hale; Martin Hall; Zena Hambrook; P.J. Handley; Olive and Stuart Harlow; Marilyn Hayward; Kathleen and Lew Hilson; R.J. Hollyer; Alfred Holmes; Peter Hoskins; Joan Islemonger (Hayward); Alan Johnson; E.H. Johnson; Peter Kalla-Bishop; Jesse Kidgell; Bernard Kimpton; Harry Lane; Barbara Leigh; Charles Lumsden; John Lythgoe; J. Mahonie; Thelma Mansell; Emily Martin (Callighan); J.G. Martin; Arthur McAulty; Heinz Mollenbrok; Fred Newton; James Nice; Mary Osbourn; Ken Owen; Patricia Parker; Ken Patterson; Mabel Pedler; Eileen Phillips; Jack Pickup; Percy Ponting; Les Poupard; Ron Read; John Rolfe; G.C. Salisbury; R.S. Shelford-Bidwell; R.S. Senior; G. Silkstone; Vic Skinner; Ron Somers; Peter Spittal; Mary Steenhouse; Peter Stewart; Roy Stout; Dick Sullivan; Jim Sutherland; C.P. Turl; Cynthia Turner; Eva Turton; Helen Ward; Ron Warren; Bob Waugh; Nick Weeks; Mrs R.G. Wells; C.A. White; John Whitehouse; H. Williams; John Wilson; Les 'Timber' Wood; Jim Woodward; Stan Wyatt.

My grateful thanks are due to all the other people who have assisted me with this book, whether their contributions have been included or not, and also to all those who have loaned or donated photographs, especially Mr Barry Hollis, Photographic Manager of South Eastern Newspapers; Norman Cavell; Mr F. Challinor; Mrs Nora Davies; W.L.A. Fenn; Mr Paul Grundy; Mrs Doris Hirst; A.E. Jordan; Mr R.W. Moss; Royal Marines Museum; Mabel Pedler; Mr T.W. Senior; Mrs Doris Speares; Mrs R. Summerton; Mrs Vi Wagner and Mrs Jill Watson.

I would like to acknowledge the kind assistance of Mr Martin Hall, who not only gave permission to quote from his late father's book *Sea Surgeon*, but also contributed some personal reminiscences of his own. I would also like to thank the Public Record Office for permission to quote from the *War Dispatches* of Lieutenant-Colonel C.D. Fellowes; Mrs Ruth Nicol, curator of the St Margaret's Bay Local History Society, for permission to quote from a series of articles she wrote for *Bygone Kent*, based on the entries in their local ARP logbooks; and Mrs Robson, editor of the Tilmanstone parish magazine, for permission to use extracts from various issues containing reminiscences from the Second World War in the village.

Introduction

Deal's preparations for war had started as early as 1935, after the representatives of East Kent coast towns had been advised by the Home Office to prepare a passive defence scheme against unprovoked attack on their areas. The town councils of Deal and Sandwich, and the rural district councils of Eastry and Dover, started by forming Air Raid Precaution (ARP) committees to plan policy and recruit personnel. Recruitment of personnel began with a radio appeal for volunteers. By August 1938 ARP services had been developed by all the local authorities in their own areas. At this time the services were divided into various sections such as Wardens, Report and Control, Rescue, Casualty and Decontamination. The last section was established to deal with victims of a poison gas attack. The ARP services were backed up by the Red Cross and St John Ambulance Brigade. There were also Rescue Parties, initially known as First Aid Parties, but this name was misleading because they dealt not with casualties but with the immediate repair and security of buildings. The Auxiliary Fire Brigade, the Women's Voluntary Service (WVS) and the Police completed the overall organization that was set up to deal with casualties and damage affecting the civilian population in the event of an attack. (Fire-watching was a later addition.)

In small communities such as Deal and Sandwich the ARP officials had the great advantage of knowing most of their staff personally. Training of the new recruits commenced and stockpiles of equipment were built up. Much of the pre-war ARP training took place at the Civil Defence Training School based at Betteshanger Park, where up to 200 volunteers were processed every two weeks. Much of the activity was not taken altogether seriously by the local population, and the exercises and parades of ARP personnel were regarded with amused detachment; that is until the outbreak of war in September 1939. Then it all became much more serious. Buildings were allocated as Control Centres, First Aid and Wardens' Posts, and people were recruited to man them, and also to serve in the Rescue, Demolition and Repair Parties. Borough and village fire services were co-ordinated, as were medical services, involving local practitioners, the St John Ambulance Brigade and Red Cross personnel, many of whom were part-time volunteers.

Alderman E.J. Dobson, Mayor of Deal, and Lieutenant-Colonel Prescott-Westcarr, Mayor of Sandwich, and the chairmen of the rural district councils were appointed titular heads of the War Emergency Committees which had overall responsibility for both the ARP organization and the Auxiliary Fire Service and its administration. The town clerks of boroughs acted as the administration officers. The Wardens' service proved to be the most popular with volunteers – St Margaret's ARP had no fewer than eighty-nine persons on its roster during the first few months of the so-called 'phoney war'. After the Dunkerque evacuation, however, a large number of people left the area, and the ARP organizations were reduced to a hard core of personnel who remained for 'the duration'.

Deal Borough Fire Brigade, under the command of Mr Lionel Denne, had three

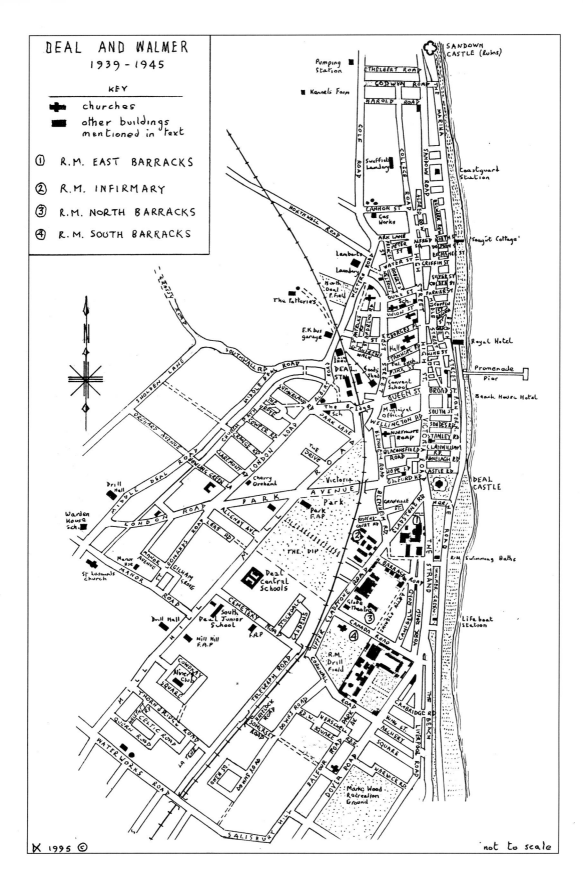

DEAL AND WALMER
1939 - 1945

KEY

✠ churches

▬ other buildings
mentioned in text

① R.M. EAST BARRACKS

② R.M. INFIRMARY

③ R.M. NORTH BARRACKS

④ R.M. SOUTH BARRACKS

SANDOWN CASTLE (Ruins)

not to scale

K 1995 ©

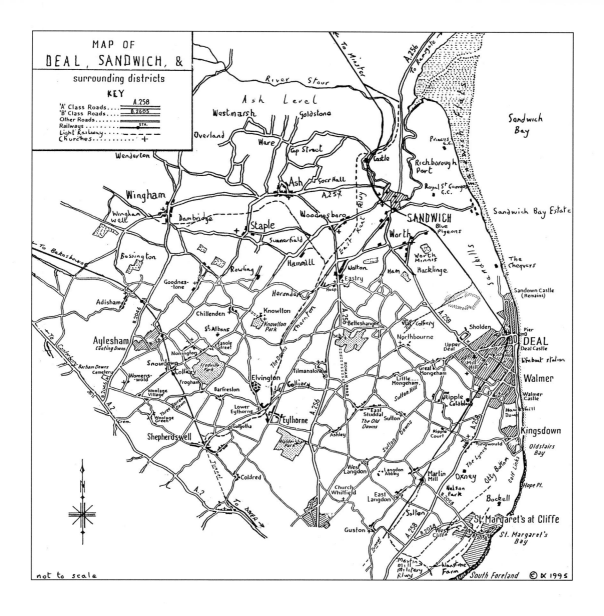

MAP OF
DEAL, SANDWICH, &
surrounding districts

KEY
'A' Class Roads.... A.258
'B' Class Roads.... B.2605
Other Roads.......
Railways..........
Light Railway..... STA.
Churches.......... +

not to scale   © CK 1995

stations, the main one being at Deal Town Hall. The others were initially at Warden House, Upper Deal and at Denne's Yard on Dover Road in Walmer. However, the former was a private school and when the owner reclaimed his premises, the Warden House station was moved to a site near the Brickmaker's public house in Mill Road. This site had previously been used by Mr Davis for his motor engineering business; his son Godfrey now became the station clerk at the new fire station. In the later stages of the war the Denne's Yard station was also moved, into the former RAF Walmer Nissen-hutted camp in Granville Road.

During the Munich Crisis of September 1938, Deal and Sandwich ARP organizations had both taken their duties seriously. Gas-masks had been issued to the civilian population, as the greatest fear at that time was a repeat of the horrendous casualties caused by gas attacks in the trenches of the First World War. Everybody was issued with a gas-mask, and for a while people carried them everywhere they went. Adults had the standard black type, which was carried in a cardboard box on a string over one shoulder, and had a canvas waterproof cover. There was an 'all-in-one' type for small babies, which was operated by hand-bellows, while older children had the 'Mickey Mouse' type. The children's masks were available in different sizes, and were exchanged as they grew older. Civil Defence workers had a stronger type of gas-mask, which was carried in a canvas bag on the chest, while rescue workers had the Army type which was even more robust. Civilians were frequently exhorted to carry their gas-masks with them at all times, with slogans such as 'Take care of your gas-mask and it will take care of you!'.

In the event of a gas attack, it would have been necessary for the survivors to carry out 'clean-up' operations on those who had become contaminated, the procedures for which were contained in the leaflet issued by the Ministry of Home Security. To supplement the cleansing stations, such as the ones in Cemetery Road and at Lambert's Laundry in Western Road, Deal, local villages were covered by a special mobile personnel gas cleaning unit. This was based at Temple Ewell and visited ARP posts to demonstrate the methods of dealing with persistent gas contamination. The unit itself consisted of a lorry with a water tank and heating apparatus, at the back of which was a canvas enclosure suspended from a steel frame. Inside this were six spray nozzles fed with heated water at 120°F (40°C), the temperature being adjustable to suit weather conditions. Casualties would be required to strip before entering the enclosure, and to wash thoroughly using the soap provided in hanging containers. All the ARP personnel were required to have a working knowledge of this apparatus, and it was planned to provide a second unit later 'to cover both sexes'; fortunately neither of them were ever needed.

Trenches and shelters were excavated, but not always in correct places, for example, those on the Marina promenade which were undermined by the sea and became flooded. Cellars were strengthened, and sandbags were placed in and around the entrances and windows of hospitals and public buildings; again the hasty installation led to problems later on, as at Deal's War Memorial Hospital, where a hastily erected blast wall started to collapse. The Deal area was lucky in having available a ready supply of pit props and shoring timbers from the local collieries. There was also a ready supply of sand at the North End, as Mr Victor Skinner remembers, which was very useful when workers were required to assist with the filling of sandbags at Kennel's Farm. Victor lived at the Hare and Hounds public house in Golf Road. Blackout practices were undertaken during the annual air defence exercises, and thus was born that immortal phrase 'Put that light out!' Some wardens took their job a little too seriously, and in the process did nothing to foster good relations with residents in their area; Kath Hilson (née Upton) recalls:

> We lived in St Patrick's Road, and one night there was a knock on the door, and there stood Mr Bransby, our ARP Warden who told my mother we were show-ing a light. My mum asked where it was, so he asked her to go outside. They went round into Union Street and, still not seeing any light, Mum asked him again where it was. He pointed to a little chink of light in one corner of a win-dow. Mum never forgave him, and she wouldn't speak to him after that!

One fear connected with the influx of refugees from the Continent was that enemy agents would infiltrate the defences and provide a 'fifth column', but it had already been recognized that there were some local residents who were more than sympathetic to the Nazi cause. Mrs Pam Andrews recalls that William Joyce ('Lord Haw-Haw') spent some of his summer holidays at St Margaret's Bay, which perhaps accounted for his uncannily accurate reports of events in this part of the country. 'Spy' stories and rumours circulated, mostly concerning people in the community who were thought to have acted 'suspiciously' or were just 'foreign-looking'. Most of the rumours were totally unjustified, but some of the suspicions turned out to have some foundation in truth. Kath Hilson recalls:

> Mrs Chapman lived in a big house on the corner of St Patrick's Road, opposite the coal yard. Up in the attic there was always a light show-ing, and my Mum and all of us used to think she had left it on because she was helping the Germans. People used to reckon she was a bit of a spy because she was a German lady.

And John Rolfe remembers:

> A farmer at Tilmanstone was thought to be a Nazi sympathizer as all his tractors and farm machin-ery had been imported from Germany. As it turned out he was interned for the duration of the war. There was also a rumour going around that when the authorities searched his house, they found a radio set hidden up one of the chimneys.

ARP warden at Betteshanger Park. Before the outbreak of war, fortnightly training courses for up to two hundred ARP personnel were held at the Betteshanger Park Mansion near Deal. Those who scoffed at these precautions soon changed their tune in September 1939.

C.S. Drake with his collection of aircraft souvenirs. Every boy in the East Kent villages who owned a bicycle would pedal off to the site of each aircraft crash, hoping to arrive before the Police, Home Guard or military authorities, and thus secure some souvenir.

The villages around Deal were also busy preparing for war. At St Margaret's Bay provision of a shelter for civilians was soon under discussion by the ARP committee, as was noted in their war diary:

> On 27 October Wardens Groves, Hornsby and Leese met with the representatives of the Civil and Military authorities to discuss the provision of a public air raid shelter for the village. It would be for the benefit of 'any inhabitants who might be in the streets when a raid occurred'. The probable cost was put at £250, and it was decided that its use would be such as not to warrant the expenditure! There was an ARP shelter in Street Farm Garage which the public were allowed to use in an emergency and Mr Groves had one built under the garden of the Cliff Hotel.

Until the advent of the Anderson and Morrison shelters villagers had to make do with whatever protection their own homes could offer.

The ARP held regular practice sessions for rescuing, evacuating and treating casualties, sometimes using volunteers, including the local schoolchildren, to act as 'casualties'. John Rolfe was part of the Eastry contingent on one occasion:

> Just before the war started, we schoolchildren plus a few adults were involved in an ARP exercise in which we acted as air raid casualties, being bandaged up with 'broken' arms and legs etc. After this had been done, we were all taken over to Snowdown Colliery in one of Tritton's Coaches, where a St John Ambulance Brigade official inspected us to see if we had been bandaged up correctly. I had a 'broken arm' bandaged tightly across my chest; it wasn't very comfortable, and I was glad when I was free. We were then all given a cup of tea and sent home!

As many village children were not evacuated, they were around to see and hear what was going on, both on the ground and overhead. The lads used to cycle out to visit almost every aircraft that crashed or force-landed to collect souvenirs, despite many warnings from the police not to pick things up at crash sites. At Ash John Wilson took full advantage of his father's connection with the Home Guard to visit the sites of crashed aircraft:

The Ash Home Guard was sent out to guard crashed planes, but we lads used to cycle miles when we knew an aircraft had crashed – it was a race to try to get there before the police or military, and we would pick up anything we could as souvenirs. I used to have lots of bits and pieces which I had collected; you might not believe it, but our garden shed had more ammunition in it than the Home Guard had at first!

Deception was another important aspect of the war effort in the area. A plan code-named 'Fortitude South' was intended to convince the enemy that the threat of invasion would come from the Kent coast, and to divert attention from the real preparations taking place further to the west. There were schemes to divert enemy bombers away from targets such as airfields, which involved 'Starfish' sites, where decoy fires would be lit when bombing attacks were made on airfields at night. John Wilson recalls that deception plan for Manston had another 'spoof' diversion:

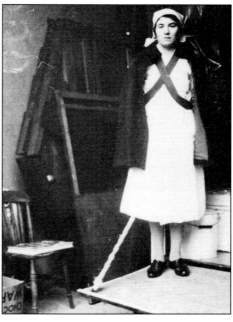

Nurse Vera Bryant in the back of the ambulance. Formerly the cashier at the Regent cinema, Vera trained at Deal Hospital before being posted to the Nelson Hall ARP depot early in 1940, where she served until May 1942.

> There was also a dummy aerodrome on the Monkton Marshes between here and Manston aerodrome, and I can remember seeing a flashing light on top of a four-wheeled RAF trailer being towed around at night to fool the Germans into bombing those isolated marshes in error, instead of the real aerodrome.

Apart from E.C. Pain's *Deal and Walmer in the War of Liberation, 1939–45* very little has been published so far on the Deal area during the Second World War. The first part of this book is based partly on the war diaries compiled by Miss Vera Bryant (Mrs V.H. Dadd), who was a nurse based at the Nelson Hall ARP depot in Deal. Her son John, who has now inherited the diaries, wished to see something of his mother's wartime service on record, and this book is a tribute both to her and to all the other volunteer workers in the East Kent area who served their country, in whatever role. Other quotations are taken from the official St Margaret's ARP logbooks. Further background information has been gathered from interviews or correspondence with local residents, or those who served in the area, both in civilian occupations and in the Armed Services, many of whom are now members of the White Cliffs Veterans' Association.

David G. Collyer
July 1995

Glossary

AA	Anti-aircraft		IB	Incendiary Bomb
AFS	Auxiliary Fire Service		JG	Jagdgeschwader (Luftwaffe fighter squadron)
ARP	Air Raid Precautions			
ASR	Air Sea Rescue		KG	Kampfgeschwader (Luftwaffe bomber squadron)
ATS	Auxiliary Territorial Service			
CD	Coastal Defence (artillery); also Civil Defence		LDV	Local Defence Volunteers
			Lt	Lieutenant (British) or Leutnant (Luftwaffe Pilot Officer)
CHL	Chain Home Low (radar)			
CO	Commanding Officer			
DCRE	Dover Command Regional Engineer		MC	Military Cross
			MGB	Motor Gun Boat
DFC	Distinguished Flying Cross		ML	Motor Launch
DSM	Distinguished Service Medal		MV	Motor Vessel
DSO	Distinguished Service Order		NAAFI	Navy, Army and Air Force Institute
ENSA	Entertainment National Services Association			
			NCO	Non-Commissioned Officer
FAP	First Aid Post		NFS	National Fire Service
F/O	Flying Officer		PM	Parachute Mine
FOC	Fire Operational Control		P/O	Pilot Officer
Fw	Feldwebel (Luftwaffe Sergeant)		RA	Royal Artillery
Gefr	Gefreiter (Luftwaffe Lance Corporal)		RNR	Royal Naval Reserve
			SH	Shell
HAA	Heavy Anti-aircraft		SS	Steam Ship
HE	High Explosive		Staffel	Luftwaffe squadron
HMD	Drifter		Uffz	Unteroffizier (Luftwaffe Corporal)
HMT	Trawler			
HQ	Headquarters		UXB	Unexploded Bomb
HSL	High Speed Launch		WLA	Women's Land Army
Hpt	Hauptman (Luftwaffe Flight Lieutenant)		WVS	Women's Voluntary Service

CHAPTER ONE

August–December 1939

Wednesday 30 August
(Noted inside the front cover of St Margaret's ARP logbook): Received from Dover RDC – one thousand sandbags for First Aid Post; one thousand sandbags for Warden's Post.

Thursday 31 August
The following personnel called-up for full-time paid ARP service, and reported for duty at West Street depot:
Rowe S. (Deputy Ambulance Officer); Jordan A.C. (c/o Personnel); Baker A.; Clements; Davies G.; Foster R.; Giles J.; Jordan S.; Neeve F.; Neeve H. Nurses: Cooper, Harvey and Tucker; Foster and Giles night duty.
I was attached to the Walmer Baptist FAP as nurse, mornings only, as volunteer.

Friday 1 September
Mortuary taken over as HQ Post. Equipment received. Rota duties prepared. Walmer Baptist FAP almost full of equipment.

Blackout regulations now came into force. It became an offence, on penalty of a severe fine (or even imprisonment for persistent offenders), to show a naked light or have an unscreened window after dark. The police, helped by special constables, had to investigate all reports of lights showing after dark. The blackout was intended to prevent identification of built-up areas from the air, thus hindering enemy aircraft navigation. It was also, especially along the coast, intended to foil any attempt by 'fifth columnists' to signal to enemy craft offshore. This may seem somewhat fanciful, but was proved to have been necessary when it was later discovered that German 'sleepers' had been installed in many coastal towns and ports, ready for their anticipated enemy invasion. Another 'counter-espionage' measure was the removal of several large motor-boats from Deal beach, some of which were sold.

The first Royal Navy operation in the Dover Straits was to lay a mine-barrage across the narrowest part of the Channel to prevent U-boats by-passing the Goodwins.

Sunday 3 September
Air raid alert 11.20hrs–11.35hrs.

Everyone listened to Chamberlain's speech at 11.00 a.m., hoping war can be averted, but no use. Chamberlain had just said 'England declares war on Germany at 11 o'clock' when the sirens blew for the first time in earnest – we had only had them before for practice purposes. What a fright we all had, scared stiff! We had been trying to finish our gas room off, and we nearly fell off the table with shock, but the All Clear came a few minutes after. What a relief it was, everybody talking nineteen to the dozen.

   12.30hrs: St Margaret's ARP night duty at Central Control.

Training at the Royal Marines depot at this time was Mr G. Smith, who recalls the effect of that first siren on the residents of Walmer:

> When the air raid sirens sounded for the first time, I remember seeing women and children running past Jubilee Gates in Dover Road, screaming and crying. I also watched the trainee soldiers in full kit, marching through the gate, with the Royal Marines band playing. I gathered they were going to form a battalion to go to France. We took great delight in digging up the officers' lawns in front of the barrack-rooms to fix up our Lewis machine-gun emplacements.

The main Observer Corps Post in Deal was at the North Deal pumping station, with a sub-station on Hawksdown at Walmer. Henry T. Arnold and Guy Farrant served as chief observers. John Wilson recalls that as well as plotting enemy aircraft that crossed the British coast to enable the RAF to intercept them, the Corps personnel at Ash also provided a facility for British aircraft returning at night:

> Jack Foat, the local butcher, was in charge of our first post, which was in the field opposite the end of Cherry Garden Lane. One night, early in the war, we came past there and noticed a lot of flares set up in a nearby field. When Dad asked about this, Jack told him that they were set out in a 'V' to help our aircraft find RAF Manston.

Wednesday 6 September
Air raid alert 06.50hrs–07.10hrs.
   I was on duty at Walmer Baptist; you wouldn't know we could move so fast. Shutting all the windows, filling hot-water bottles, etc and some very amusing incidents.

Another lady serving at this First Aid Post was Miss Eileen Phillips, as part of the Civil Nursing Reserve:

> I served at Walmer Baptist Church Hall and later at the Victoria Park Clinic FAP when it was opened, until I was evacuated to Ilfracombe in June 1940 with my mother. Dr Boulden and Dr Neil used to come and give us lectures, as did Mr Lionel Denne from the Deal Fire Brigade. Amongst the others I recall were Miss Ryder Richardson and Miss Bower and a Miss Cook of the St John Ambulance Brigade. Miss Bower looked after Revd Peasgood, who was Chaplain to the Fleet and also the Royal Marine chaplain at the start of the war.
>   I can also remember being caught out at Deal Town Hall during an air raid with a group of children who should not have been there – there was some trouble about that incident.

Some 1,500 school-age children were evacuated from London and the Medway towns as an emergency measure, and arrived in the area; the local Reception Committees were hardly overwhelmed as they had been prepared for around 3,500. However, about ten days later some 500 of them were re-evacuated from the area owing to a lack of secondary school places. Children from Gillingham went to Sandwich, while Roy Catherick recalls there were other refugees at Ripple:

> During the first part of the war, I attended Ripple Primary School until in June 1940 I had to move to Deal Central School. While I was at Ripple I can remember that we had some German-Jewish children sent there, also the refugees from London at the start of the war. My mother was very keen to have one of the London children stay with us, as our family originally came from South London, before arriving at Great Mongeham.

Sunday 17 September
Dr Hall visits SS *Rupert de Larrinaga* (Sp) off Deal.

Tuesday 19 September
Dr Hall visits SS *Svanejell* (Nor) freighter.

Sunday 24 September
Dr Hall called to SS *Norruna* (Sw) in The Downs; patient landed to hospital.

Tuesday 26 September
I was transferred from Walmer Baptist to Victoria Hospital FAP to start my training; reported for duty 06.00hrs.

Thursday 28 September
Dr Hall called to SS *Delfshaven* (Du); fireman brought ashore to hospital.

Saturday 30 September
Dr Hall visits SS *Delfshaven* again; Captain ill. Later he was called to liner *Noordam* (Dt); patient landed to hospital.

Thursday 5 October
Party test at Cemetery Road. Busy at hospital, quite a lot of ships laying off here.

Dr James Hall FRCS, OBE, the famous 'Lifeboat Doctor', boarding a ship from one of the motor boats which often took him out to urgent medical cases on board vessesl anchored in The Downs.

Friday 6 October
Early a.m.: SS *Mahratta II* aground on Fork Spit (cargo of tea, hemp and jute). Tugs used to try to re-float her. *Lady Beaty* ferries seventy-eight crew to the tug *Challenger* and some to tug *Skipjack*; *Mahratta* broke up the following afternoon.

The wreck of the *Mahratta* brought an unexpected windfall for Phil Johnson's father, who was walking along the North Deal seafront on his way back from 'Flint' Robert's pub the Rose and Crown:

> He heard a bumping and a 'swoosh' on the beach, and looking down saw a chest of tea bumping along the sea wall. As he was near to the Coastguard Station, father popped in to report this find. He was told to go back again and 'If it's a piece of wood, you can take it home.' This he did, and my mother dried the leaves in the oven, as the chest was lined with tinfoil to keep the tea-leaves moist, and then shredded them so they could be used; that kept us going for cups of tea for a considerable time.

Sunday 8 October
Submarine U-12 sunk by mine off Goodwin Sands.

The first victim of the newly laid minefield was of particular interest to Telegraphist William J. Fogg, who was serving on board the Royal Navy survey vessel HMS *Franklin*:

> We were involved in the incident when the wrecked U-boat U-12 was found stranded on the Goodwin Sands, the day after using depth charges from our

The wreck of *Mahratta II* on the Goodwins. Like her namesake, which was lost in very similar circumstances in 1909. *Mahratta II* became yet another victim of the infamous Goodwins in May 1940. Her cargo of hemp, jute and tea provided a lucky windfall for at least one local resident.

escort on a contact. We buoyed the wreck and then the naval experts arrived to salvage what they could in the way of confidential books, etc.

A further task was surveying a safe navigable path for convoys through the Goodwins.

Tuesday 10 October
Civilian casualty treated. Lecture at Walmer Baptist Hall attended. Mrs Dyer came up to the Royal Cinema, where I was cashier, to see if I could start on the Mobile Unit tomorrow morning as full-time personnel. Mr Carey released me at once. Mobile Unit stationed at 'Linwood' in Mill Road.

Thursday 12 October
Lecture attended. Joined Mobile Unit with Miss Cook as Sister-in-Charge.

Friday 13 October
Inspected Nelson Hall: Dr Kirk, Dr Neil and Captain Soames provisionally agree tenancy. Started my duties with Mobile Unit at 06.00hrs.
Submarine U-40 sunk by British mine off the Goodwins.

The U-40 was not the only vessel that encountered the infamous Goodwin Sands, as stoker 'Nobby' Clark, then serving on board the mine-layer HMS *Plover* remembers:

> We had joined up with a Dutch mine-layer, the *Williem van der Zan*, and came south to Sheerness, loaded up with mines, to do a night run in the Straits of Dover. But I'm afraid that we both finished up on the Goodwin Sands at 11 o'clock at night (I had the middle watch below). By now it was clear moonlight, and we thought that 'Jerry' must see us and start shelling. Two tugs came out of Dover, but could do nothing – we floated off at 6 o'clock the next morning.

Saturday 14 October
Learning where all the drugs etc are kept on the Mobile.

Tuesday 17 October
Anti-aircraft gunfire from ships in The Downs.

Thursday 19 October
Dr Hall in Walmer lifeboat to tanker *Mirza* (Du) – aborted.

Friday 20 October
Dr Hall called to Greek freighter; appendix case landed to hospital.

Sunday 22 October
Air raid alert 12.10hrs–13.20hrs.
  Prepared coffee, tea, and filled hot water bottles but they were not needed, so we were drinking coffee nearly all day.

Tuesday 24 October
Submarine U-16 stranded on Goodwins after hitting a mine.

Wednesday 25 October
Dr Hall called to SS *Buccari* (It); landed patient, could not find SS *Silvano* until re-launched after midnight.

During November 1939 local building contractor Mr R.L.J. Eames was busy converting the emergency mortuary buildings at Mill Hill into the HQ Post for the ARP.

Wednesday 1 November
Mr G. Davies appointed ARP Company Officer; A.C. Jordan appointed Stores Officer. Lecture by Dr Davies attended.

Saturday 4 November
SS *Nicholaos M. Embiricos* (Gk) hit mine and sunk near East Goodwins light-vessel.

The large number of ships lost to magnetic mines laid from Heinkel He-115 seaplanes or Dornier Do-22 flying-boats resulted in some measures being taken to try to catch the planes while on the water laying their deadly cargo. One of those who was given the task was Leading/Seaman James Clayton-Pearson, attached to 'Contraband Control' at Ramsgate:

> One Saturday night two seamen and myself boarded a trawler with a Lewis machine-gun and ammunition. During the night a very thick fog came down, so the skipper anchored off Deal, for when the Royal Marines went to Sunday Divisions, the sound of the band came over the water loud and clear. We had just put the Lewis gun on a stand to show the skipper and the crew how it was to be used, when we heard the engines of a plane, and by the sound it was carrying a heavy load. The skipper wanted me to shoot in the direction of the noise, as it sounded almost overhead, but it would be a waste of ammo in that thick fog.

Monday 6 November
Dr Hall visits Dutch coaster, two crew both ill, but her skipper refuses to land them – ship sails during night.

Tuesday 9 November
Mines washed ashore.

Serving on board HMS *Plover* was Quartermaster 'Jacky' S. Fisher who recalls that not all of these mines stayed where they were laid:

> All the mines we laid were 'anti–submarine', set to explode around 90ft below the surface. Several of them broke adrift and became 'floaters' after stormy weather. Once we had the job of collecting a couple which had been washed up on the beach around Deal. One we towed back to the *Plover*, the other was well up on the shingle, so it was loaded on to a 'lorry RN' and returned to Dover.

Sunday 12 November
Civic Service at Victoria Baptist Church, Revd Ivor J. Wensley being Mayoral Chaplain to Alderman E.J. Dobson.

Wednesday 15 November
Dr Hall called to liner SS *City of Edinburgh* to land an appendix case to Deal Hospital.

Friday 17 November
Dr Hall called to SS *Slava* (Yg); appendix patient landed to hospital; later made fruitless search for SS *Maihar* during afternoon.

Saturday 18 November
SS *Simon Bolivar* (Du) aground on South Goodwins.

Sunday 19 November
Call from SS *Montferland* (Du); patient landed for kidney-stone operation to Deal Hospital. Later in day visited SS *Perrakia L. Cambanis* (Gk); patient with same symptoms, and so landed for X-ray (acute lumbago).

Monday 20 November
Air raid alert 18.57hrs–20.20hrs.
   Anti-aircraft fire seen in clear sky; later it was reported that an enemy raider was repelled over East Coast.
   Dr Hall visited MV *Tiba* (Du); seaman with a broken ankle landed for treatment at hospital.

Wednesday 22 November
RN Trawler *Aragonite* struck by mine and sunk opposite Deal Coastguard Station while mine-sweeping; the crew rescued by tugs; attempted to tow her ashore but she finished up on the sandbank off North Deal; four RN ratings injured – landed to Deal Hospital.

Saturday 25 November
Dr Hall visits MV *Helvig* (Dn); found his patient had been treated by doctor from SS *Mito Maru* (Jp) anchored nearby.

Sunday 26 November
Dr Hall called to SS *Rixby* (Br) on lifeboat to fireman with gall-bladder trouble.

Monday 27 November
Search in fog for SS *Springdale* (Br); Dr Hall finds AB with tuberculosis – landed to Deal hospital; also visited SS *Astrid* (Bel) to treat eye injury to ERA.

Tuesday 28 November
Allocation of twenty-seven beds received: Nelson Hall (7); Cemetery Road (7); Victoria Park (13); hold for further instructions.
    Form received for ARP uniforms.
    Dr Hall called to SS *Corte Real* (Pt); serious heart case landed to hospital but died – interred in Deal Cemetery.

Thursday 30 November
After fruitless search Dr Hall finally finds SS *Igor* (Gk); chief engineer seriously ill – treated on board.

Friday 1 December
Call to SS *Kelbergen* (Du); elderly fireman with stomach cancer – chose to remain on board for return to Holland. Also visited SS *Veerhaven* (Dt) to find four seamen sick on board.

Saturday 2 December
Trawler *Atlantic* calls Dr Hall to treat crew member with septic finger.

Monday 4 December
Dr Hall visits SS *Frangoula B. Goulandris* (Gk); landed fireman with infected bladder to Deal hospital.

Tuesday 5 December
07.00hrs: Dr Hall receives call to SS *Manzoni* (It); captain had suffered heart-attack, but ship had departed for Rotterdam.
    P.m.: Revisited *Veerhaven* to collect one patient.
    'Freddy' Upton's boat breaks down; towed in by the Pilot cutter.

Wednesday 6 December
One party from Nelson Hall depot came to us at 'Linwood' Mobile Unit, to give us Practical Test for nurses. One party to exercise with Kingsdown First Aid Post.
    Dr Hall called to British vessel flying ENL [Death on board] flags, so took Police Sergeant Jarrett with him.

Friday 8 December
General Steam Navigation Co. SS *Merle* mined and sunk off North Sands Head. French coaster *Dinard* mined inside the Goodwins, foundered near Deal pier.

Local motor-boats, including 'Darky' Budd's *Britannic*, rescued a dozen of the *Dinard*'s crew who were taken to Deal hospital. Mary Osbourn was one of hundreds of people who watched the sinking of this vessel:

> The *Dinard* was a huge French boat that had been mined out to sea, and you could see the French sailors with their red and blue pom-poms on their tam o'shanters, running about on deck.
>   I think she must have been hit while in a convoy because she came round from south of the pier and she seemed to be trying to beach at the North End. While we were watching her, she just got lower and lower in the water. I couldn't believe my eyes, as when she hit the beach bank she laid over on her side and all the sailors were running about on the top of the hull; the boatmen and the Walmer lifeboat, were circling round getting as near as they could to rescue them. Then, all of a sudden, she rocked a bit again and then she rose up, almost out of the water, bows first and then went down again by the stern. As she was a coal-fired boat with steam engines, the boilers exploded and all the steam rushed out.

A few days afterwards, Mrs Mary Osbourn witnessed the sequel:

> She came up again on an even keel, with her masts and funnels and deck all upright. I was amazed and asked Mr Roberts how this could happen and he explained that as she had gone down on her side by the bank, the tide against the bank would have kept pulling her round so that eventually she had to come upright.

Saturday 9 December
Dutch coaster *Celebes* visited by Dr Hall.

Sunday 10 December
Early a.m.: Belgian steamer *Kabinda* sank inside Fork Spit, and broke in half after bales of cotton had been discharged to lighten the load; some men still aboard – all rescued by Walmer lifeboat.

Sunday 17 December
09.30hrs: Siren test – gas works siren failed to sound.

The air raid sirens in Deal were located at various points around the town. There was one at the gas works in Cannon Street; one at the main fire station behind the Town Hall and another on the water tower in St Richard's Road. Yet another siren was situated at the East Barracks at Walmer, but it caused some confusion when it first sounded, since it went off before the official civilian warning had been issued. After

The Belgian steamer *Kabinda* was wrecked on the Goodwins on 12 December 1939; her sister ship, *Kalabo*, was also involved in a collision, leading to the loss of the steamer *Flanders*.

some negotiation between the Deal ARP War Emergency Committee, and the Commandant of the Barracks it was agreed that the Royal Marines would follow civilian practice, and only sound the Red Alert.

Sunday 18 December
French mine was reported floating in St Margaret's Bay.

Tuesday 20 December
One party to Mobile Unit at 'Linwood'; practical test for nurses. One party to exercise with Post K and Kingsdown FAP.

Wednesday 21 December
Demonstration given with full personnel to control centre staff and others, showing action taken on receipt of air raid messages, etc; and action messages from control.

Thursday 22 December
Tug *Napier* came to grief off Ramsgate.

Saturday 24 December
Decorated Nelson Hall; we helped to decorate hospital and Linwood.
   10.00hrs: Dr Hall visited Dutch coaster *Libra* to treat ship's cook.
   P.m.: Call to tanker *Jenny* (Nor); heart-attack patient landed to hospital, but died a few

days later; on his return Dr Hall was called to coaster *Ora* (Br) – patient injured in fall; landed to Deal hospital.

Sunday 25 December

I was on duty at hospital on Christmas night, but gee, didn't we have a spread!
Crew member of *John Hopkinson* (Br) insisted on landing to have X-ray of injured thumb; rest of the crew enjoyed a run ashore.

Monday 26 December

11.00hrs: attended a sherry party this morning at Linwood.

Wednesday 28 December

Long search in snow for *Pietro Campenella* (It) to fireman with pneumonia – examination tug assisted by landing him.

CHAPTER TWO

January–August 1940

The old Manor House in Manor Road, Upper Deal, was the local St John Ambulance Brigade Headquarters during the early months of 1940. There were also some changes in the distribution of ARP posts during this time as the deacons at Walmer Baptist Church requested the use of the Sunday School Hall, so the FAP was removed to the old Forester's Hall in North Barrack Road. This building was much more suitable, with the added attraction for the nurses of rooms nearby offering sea views. Miss Zena Hambrook, one of the nurses, recalls:

> We had the upstairs front room over Mr Snow's bookshop on The Strand as our rest-room. Whatever time of day or night the siren went, we had to report for duty at the First Aid Post.
>
> All the District Nurses were recruited into the Civil Nursing Reserve, and I served for the first six months of the war, but after the town had been evacuated, there were not enough people left in Deal to justify keeping us on, so we were transferred to the Mobile Unit.

The first vehicle with which the Mobile Unit was equipped was a rather ancient motor-bus that had been converted to an ambulance, but this was not considered entirely suitable, and steps were taken to replace it with a small lorry. Mrs Mabel Pedler also remembers why this vehicle was required:

> The Mobile Unit was attached to the Park Avenue FAP and we were fully equipped for the treatment at the site of incidents of patients who were too badly injured to be removed to hospital by ordinary ambulance. From the Victoria Park FAP a number of us were also sent to the Deal Memorial Hospital when required.

Since the outbreak of war, Walmer lifeboat had been launched some twenty-six times and had saved forty-five lives, while assisting vessels which had been in collision or had been mined in the RN Contraband Control area. During the winter of 1939/40 the Walmer lifeboat was launched a further forty times, to save eighty-five lives. The illnesses dealt with by Dr James Hall were many and various, ranging from a call to the tug *Arcadia* to land two serious gastric cases, to the skipper of a Dutch steamer who demanded to be landed with 'influenza' after a near-miss from a mine. In fact this 'mine' turned out to be only a cushion. More useful items seen floating off Deal were cases of margarine from the *Dunbar Castle*.

However, many mines were washed into The Downs anchorage, and also came ashore along the beach, including one which arrived opposite the Walmer lifeboat house. Dr Hall remembered this particular mine being 'sold' by Perce Cavell, the Walmer lifeboat mechanic, to his eldest son for 5*s*. There were several ways of dealing with these magnetic mines; one way was to tow barges filled with scrap-iron

Mobile Unit nurses with their original transport. The first vehicle allocated to the Park ARP centre Mobile Unit was this ancient bus, which was garaged at the old Laundry behind 'Linwood' in Mill Road. When a more suitable form of transport was found by the local ARP Committee, the old bus was pensioned off.

Mobile Unit nurses at Park FAP. Ready to rush to the aid of casualties who were too badly injured to be moved to hospital, the nurses of the Park ARP centre's Mobile Unit answered many calls throughout the war years.

through The Downs, so that the mines could be exploded without significant damage to shipping. Another method was by air – Vickers Wellington bombers from RAF Manston detonated the mines harmlessly by passing a strong electric current through wiring rings mounted beneath the fuselages.

Wednesday 3 January
Pilot cutter *Prudence* sank after collision with SR mailboat. AB with sprained back landed for treatment. Dr Hall was visiting vessels to treat fractured jaws and ribs in days of alternate snow, fog and rough weather.

Thursday 4 January
Dr Hall on fruitless visit to *Olaf Bergh* (Nor) – passed RN launch with his patient aboard en route.

Saturday 6 January
SS *Cedrington Court* sank off North Goodwins, ten minutes after an explosion; thirty-four crew saved.

Monday 8 January
SS *Dunbar Castle* wrecked near North Goodwins after striking mine. Forty-eight passengers, including Mr L.H. Walter of Clanwilliam Road, and 150 crew. Some were landed by lifeboats, or at Deal pier by the coaster *Loanda*; ambulance crews assisted.

Tuesday 9 January
All personnel assisted at pier, landing the *Dunbar Castle* casualties; nurses prepared beds, and made tea and coffee, and cut and buttered bread, but survivors were taken to Gordon Blain's. One party to Walmer lifeboat, to attend casualty with fractured jaw.

Friday 12 January
Badly burned cook from *Dunbar Castle* died in hospital.

During this week the new purpose-built ARP post at Victoria Park was made ready to receive casualties, and one of those to serve there was Miss Peggy Oatridge who lived at Wellington House, Mill Road, just across the way.

> During the 'Phoney War' I did a first aid course and so I had to report to the FAP in Victoria Park in case there was a raid. I was the 'Instrument Nurse' but I wasn't really trained to do this. Of course nothing was happening then, so we got bored.
> At the back of our house was the old Lambert's Laundry, closed before the war started, so the FAP had their mobile ambulance garaged down there.

Tuesday 16 January
Walmer lifeboat rescued twenty-two crew from the Italian *Permuda* after it ran aground on

North Goodwins. Brake light-vessel badly damaged in same gale. Three lifeboats attempted to pull the *Permuda* off the sands.

23.00hrs: Injured survivors from *Permuda* landed by Walmer lifeboat which was then re-launched on a fruitless search for *Swainby*.

Fairey Battle N2258 of No. 253 Sqn belly-landed at Wingham Barton Manor after suffering engine failure in a snowstorm.

Wednesday 17 January
Lifeboat called to take Dr Hall to coaster *Camroux IV* (Fr); skipper with heart failure after influenza; landed on 18th after the weather abated.

Dutch tug from Rotterdam pulled *Permuda* off the Goodwins and beached her opposite Walmer lifeboat house.

Thursday 18 January
Permuda repaired; surveyed and passed OK – departed.

Sunday 21 January
05.30hrs: Irish vessel *Rynanna* aground on East Goodwin. Injured crew members landed by Walmer lifeboat.

Tuesday 23 January
Walmer lifeboat rescued thirteen more crew of SS *Rynanna*, still aground on East Goodwins, by crossing the sands on the high tide.

Saturday 27 January
Dr Hall called to tanker *Mamura* (Dt) in Trinity Bay after it struck a mine, to treat minor injuries; revisited skipper of *Montferland* to report on a patient while on his way back.

Sunday 28 January
TA searchlights were deployed along the coast to locate mine-laying seaplanes. St Margaret's unit got cut off by snow, and the CO's relief attempt failed after the car got stuck on Bay Hill.

Monday 29 January
Mine washed through Deal pier before striking *Nora* (Dt).

One of the best remembered events of the early war years was when the 350-ton Dutch 'schuit' *Nora*, carrying a cargo of straw boards, was struck by a mine and crashed through Deal Pier. A large hole was blown in her stern, injuring several of the crew, and blowing one of them into the water. Two salvage tugs managed to tow this vessel inshore about fifty yards south of the pier, but on a rising tide and with a south-westerly gale blowing up, this was a recipe for disaster.

The *Nora* lay there, almost completely submerged, for some time, but the rising tide gradually lifted her from the shingle ridge, and as the tide gathered strength, the

This photograph clearly shows the extent of the damage caused to the pier by the wreck of the *Nora*. Hundreds of people watched the drama unfold on Deal seafront on 29 January 1940. In the background are RN Contraband Control vessels.

The wreck of the *Nora* stranded on her side after damaging Deal pier. The Dutch schuit *Nora* had demolished a section of Deal's Victorian pier (in the background, left) after she had been beached to the south of it on a rising tide and with a south-westerly gale imminent.

danger to the pier became all too apparent. The very few people who happened to be on the pier were shepherded ashore in good time to witness the drama unfold, along with others who had gathered to watch, including Mrs Mary Osbourn:

> The sea was getting rough, and suddenly she broke anchor and started to drag herself slowly along towards the pier. She hit the pier with some force, and the next big wave pushed her under the decking, which lifted up like a pack of cards; the noise of her grinding and bumping as she broke through the piles I shall never ever forget – it was ghastly. After she had broken through the tide swung her round and she turned on to her side. All the effects were pouring out as she had a large hole in her side.

Wednesday 31 January
Dr Hall called to SS *Prinz Mauritz* and *Quaric Number Two*; on the former ship the casualty had already been treated by the Ramsgate doctor, and latter ship did not exist on Lloyd's Register.

Thursday 1 February
Some of the *Dunbar* survivors have gone home; one died at six this morning; only one here [Deal Hospital] now.
   Another death at sea, this one on SS *Aldebaran*. Dr Hall and Police Sergeant Mummery attended; the casualty had fallen down a shaft; his body brought ashore.

Friday 2 February
Inquest into death on SS *Aldebaran* held by Deal coroner.

Sunday 4 February
Dr Hall visited a ship flying the wrong flag (it should have been flying 'Pilot required'), and looked for the *Kirkwood*, which was requesting a doctor, but it had sailed on to Gravesend; later called to an old tanker.

The reason for Dr Hall's many fruitless trips in bad weather is explained by his son, Martin:

> It is worth remembering that there was no radio contact between the Coastguard and the lifeboat in those days; let alone with the more usual motor-boats that took Dr Hall out. The only communication was either by flag signal (in good visibility) or with an Aldis-type lamp flashing Morse Code, which Father (a DIY enthusiast) had cobbled together using a bicycle headlamp on a pole wired to a 6-volt car battery. The same goes for the merchant ships themselves, which relied on flag-hoists of the international sign 'W' meaning 'I require medical assistance'.

Monday 5 February
Dr Hall visits SS *Blommersdijk* (Dt) in thick fog; treated 4th Engineer with rust scale in his eye.

Tuesday 6 February
Dr Hall called to MV *Dinteldyke* to treat similar case.

Wednesday 7 February
Dr Hall visits MV *Libra* to treat 2nd Engineer with cracked ribs and spinal injuries; brought ashore for X-ray.
   P.m.: Visit to SS *Prinz Willem III*; it was a suspected case of malaria, so he took his house surgeon along, but the patient had influenza.

Friday 9 February
Dr Hall called to treat an Indian stabbed in a fight on SS *Lake Geneva* (Est); he was taken to hospital and police enquiries started.

Saturday 10 February
Gallia (No) mined and sank in The Downs. Weather still cold.

Dr Hall was called to SS *Antverpia* (Bel) at the Goodwins Fork buoy and decided to take his eldest son Martin with him as a treat for his seventh birthday. Martin recalls:

> What an unexpected thrill! Mother had asked me earlier what I would like for my birthday lunch. I asked for roast chicken and ice-cream. Father was called to go to sea and he took me with him in the motor-boat assigned for the trip. We arrived alongside the Belgian steamer *Antverpia*. A bowline was tied round my waist and I had my first experience of climbing a rope-ladder up the ship's side. While Father dealt with the medical case I was taken along to the galley and given a freshly cooked pancake (an enormous one) by the third mate. So lunch was a little late, but I still enjoyed the chicken and ice cream, when we finally got back home.

Monday 12 February
19.30hrs: *Flanders* sunk out here.

The Belgian steamer *Flanders* sank in The Downs after being run down by the Belgian steamer *Kalabo* (sister ship of the *Kabinda* which was wrecked on the Goodwins) and sank two miles off shore; her crew of forty-five were rescued, and the ship's pet pig Adolph was saved by the RN patrol boat.

Tuesday 27 February
18.00hrs: Collective exercise – supply patients for Post 7.
   Some fifteen members of HMS *Exeter*'s ship's band arrived at Deal Railway Station on a visit to the depot.

Saturday 2 March
08.15hrs: Corporation employee Mr A. Redsull sent for someone to examine his shoulder.

H. Neeve reported the man had a dislocation, and he had put his arm in a sling. Phoned for an ambulance to take patient to hospital.

Sunday 3 March

Eight Italian ships with 60,000 tons of coal detained in The Downs, but later allowed to proceed. [Italy was then neutral.]

Wednesday 6 March

14.30hrs: Supplied three patients for Mobile Unit practice held at Mongeham.

Friday 8 March

19.30hrs: Lecture for staff at Forester's Hall.

Saturday 9 March

Collier *Ashlea* on the Goodwins; the destroyer *Beagle* and tugs tried to assist. The German M/L *Schiff II* was seen laying mines off the North Foreland.

Will Dadd and Vera Bryant's wedding, St George's Church, Deal, 26 February 1940. Many of her ARP colleagues attended and lined the entrance when they emerged as man and wife.

HMS *Exeter*'s band at Deal station, 28 February 1940. These members of the Royal Marine band serving on board HMS *Exeter* arrived at Deal for Warship Week as the RN School of Music band had been evacuated to Malvern the previous year.

Monday 11 March
15.11hrs: Ladies held bandaging practice in conjunction with nurses. *Meriton* sunk out here.

Tuesday 12 March
07.30hrs: Mrs Pearce of Nelson Street asked for somebody to go and look at Mr Pearce. F. Neeve reports Mr Pearce is dead. Phoned for Dr Hutchinson.

Wednesday 13 March
The destroyer *Keith* damaged her ASDIC [echo locator] system by grounding near the South Goodwins buoy; to Chatham for repairs.

Monday 18 March
Steamship *Tina Primo* lost in The Downs.

Wednesday 20 March
Phobos (Dt) was wrecked near North Goodwins, and *Bryant* was sunk by a mine. The destroyer *Brilliant* stood by while tugs rescued her crew.

Saturday 30 March
Late afternoon Dr Hall called to Belgian steamer; a fireman had hung himself, so he went accompanied by Sergeant Jarrett.
   Call to *Orion* (Dt); trimmer with septic hand. He was landed to hospital.

Sunday 31 March
Dr Hall called to SS *Regulus* (Fn); master with suspected appendicitis.

Monday 1 April
Coroner's inquest on the fireman from the Belgian steamer; master and two ship's officers come ashore to attend.
   Dr Hall visited SS *Pandia* (Fn); mate with eye abscess; while there he witnessed German mines being dropped from an aircraft, almost on top of the vessel.

Wednesday 3 April
Major O'Callaghan gives a demonstration of sending out First Aid Parties, etc. for Control Centre.

Thursday 11 April
18.18hrs: Two parties supplied for Post 4 exercise. One party did not go out. Telephonist on duty was Miss Garrett; Nurse Dadd was with the Stretcher Ambulance, and Mrs Smith, Mrs Marsh and Mrs Godson were on duty with their own cars.

Tuesday 16 April
14.30hrs: A. Cave and S. Harris patients for Mobile Unit.

Wednesday 17 April
18.00hrs: Examinations held for anti-gas certificates. All the candidates passed.
  German seaplanes laying mines in The Downs.

Thursday 18 April
Nelson Hall depot supplied patients for Post 9 area. This was cancelled by Mr Ford owing to weather conditions.

Saturday 20 April
LMS railway steamer *Mersey* sank off Ramsgate after a mine explosion – eight crew members landed; one was killed and another died on the way to hospital; twelve others missing, presumed drowned.

Sunday 21 April
Germans repeat mine-laying operations off Ramsgate. Dr Hall visited Panamanian vessel; some mines exploded while he was treating three Greek seamen.

Nelson Hall personnel with their laundry van ambulance. All sorts of vehicles were used to transport injured patients to hospital, including this van belonging to Swaffield's Laundry. Vera is holding a blackboard on which is written 'Dunbar Castle – cold, cold wind' – they had helped to rescue the survivors of the *Dunbar Castle* who landed at Deal on 9 January 1940.

Monday 22 April

Norwegian steamer *Bravoer* hit by a mine while anchored near *Break* light-vessel; four crew members rescued by Deal motor-boats; mate and chief engineer were landed by 'Darky' Budd, who was delivering provisions nearby.

Tuesday 23 April

SS *Lulworth* sunk after explosion near North Foreland; captain and mate killed, eight crew injured, remainder landed.

Wednesday 24 April

10.12hrs: A. Baker and S. Jordan attend ARP office, disinfecting gas-masks. *Rydal Force* lost on Goodwins.

Saturday 27 April

Girasol sunk in The Downs.

Tuesday 30 April

Miss Walford used the Main Hall at Nelson Hall ARP depot for distributing 'gas helmets' for babies and 'Mickey Mouse' children's gas-masks. Trestle table and chairs to be issued.
    German mine-laying aircraft active in The Downs.

In May 1940 Mr Eames started work on the construction of static water basins (circular concrete storage troughs) at several locations. The first ones were built

The wreck of SS *Lulworth* on the North Goodwins. The *Lulworth* sank near the North Foreland after an explosion that killed both her captain and chief officer, and injured eight of her crew. The injured men were rescued with the remainder of the ship's complement.

at The Beach, Walmer; in Victoria Park; in the Stanhope Road car park; in College Road; and in Station Road, Walmer; these were followed by others in Telegraph Road and Canada Road. In the following months, Mr Eames worked on the air raid shelters in Mockett's Yard at Upper Deal and then Mill Road School; meanwhile the temporary shelters at the Parochial School were being demolished.

Wednesday 1 May
14.16hrs: Dutch vessel *Helder* aground at Kingsdown.

Thursday 2 May
17.00hrs: Two Parties for Post 6, two Party cars; two ambulances – Nurse Tucker and Nurse Harvey.

Friday 3 May
German mine-laying aircraft active in The Downs. Dr Hall summoned from hospital to MV *Helder* (Dt); steward with bronchitis landed to hospital.

Saturday 4 May
23.59hrs: Enemy aircraft seen over Deal, heavy ack-ack [anti-aircraft] fire from the direction of the sea was heard. (Seaplane mine-layer?)

Staff at the Nelson Hall depot with their ambulance. Left to right: M. Tucker, E. Bashford, D. Harvey, Vera Dadd. They are in full uniform, complete with kit-bags and tin hats.

Two of Vera Dadd's colleagues at the Nelson Hall ARP post were 'Dot' Harvey (left) and 'Marge' Tucker, who befriended Vera while her husband Will was away serving in the Royal Navy.

Monday 6 May
Royal Netherlands Navy vessels took shelter in The Downs after the German invasion of Holland.

Thursday 9 May
Dr Hall visits *Stureborg* (Sw); fireman with acute middle ear infection landed to hospital for twenty-four hours.

Friday 10 May
RN Contraband Control abandoned after the invasion of Holland and Belgium; many vessels dumped their cargoes and departed for the colonies; some bananas dumped by *Montferland* were recovered by boatmen.

SS *Aurora* (Du); assistant engineer with epileptic fit treated on board by Dr Hall.

A Hurricane N2333 of No. 3 Sqn based at Merville force-landed at St Margaret's having got lost while pursuing a He 111 bomber.

A Bristol Blenheim of No. 600 Sqn crashed at West Cliffe Road at St Margaret's after its crew had baled out; reason unknown.

Hurried redeployment of anti-aircraft guns was undertaken, as Peter Erwood discovered when he returned from his week's leave on the following day:

I returned to duty on Saturday and found that the unit had moved to a new green-field site near Deal [Sholden?] with our two 3in ack-ack guns. A few days later, enough of us to man another 3in gun site were moved a few miles nearer to Ramsgate [Hacklinge?], where, after another couple of days, two of the most unbelievable antiques were delivered to us – they were probably the first AA guns ever made.

To cap it all, we were given the interesting news that there was no other Troop between Pegwell Bay and Dover, so that in the event of an invasion, the defence of that line was down to us as well. With six rifles and a dozen or so pickaxe handles, the chances of any spirited resistance seemed rather on the thin side.

Our officers instructed us that should paratroops land, we were to rush at them with the pickaxe handles, stun them and grab their guns. Luckily the situation did not arise, as on 20 May we were all rushed back to the Dover area.

Saturday 11 May

Dr Hall visited SS *Oranje Nassau* (Du); master injured during their escape from Flushing; he was landed to hospital for X-rays, but was back on board that evening. Then to HMS *Nautilus* for the sole survivor of the Dutch torpedo boat *Johan Nassau* who had been injured in a fall from the bridge; taken to hospital.

Sunday 12 May

Most Contraband Control vessels now departed; *Zeffiro* (It) left after colliding with a British steamer; mate with internal complaint – Dr Hall made his 99th mercy call to treat him.

Afternoon call to a British tug; the chief engineer and radio officer suffering from food poisoning.

Monday 13 May

Dr Hall called to SS *Sparta* by lifeboat during north-easterly gale; AA gunfire and aircraft heard when ashore; several patients including the pilot of the Boulogne supply boat *Firth Fisher* with an injured back sent to hospital.

Tuesday 14 May

Anthony Eden broadcast an appeal for 'Local Defence Volunteers'; volunteers flocked to Deal police station, and were formed into D Company 8th (Cinque Ports) Battalion.

The Deal Gas Company staff formed an LDV (later Home Guard) platoon, and were responsible for guarding the gas works at night, as well as keeping a fire watch in case of incendiary bombs being dropped. Leslie Collyer recalls going on his first LDV patrol:

'A' Company, Deal Gas Works Home Guard platoon, photographed in the grounds of the Cannon Street gas works. My uncle, 'Les' Collyer, (back row, right), was the chemist at the works.

At first there were two of us, Bob Lovelock and myself marching around the works – he carried the .38 duck-gun with one bullet in his pocket. He wasn't allowed to put the bullet into the gun and fire it without permission from the Lieutenant (our governor Mr White) who in turn had to obtain permission from the Divisional Officer, and so on; I carried a pickaxe handle! We had no uniforms, just armbands with LDV on at first.

The villages also had their own LDV forces and used what facilities were available to them. At Eastry, this consisted of a shed in the back garden of Walton Villa; according to Mr R. Martin, one of the first volunteers:

We then moved to a barn which stood on the site of the new fire station, and then our last home was in Aumbry Cottages in Church Street.

In the early days, I was entrusted with the bolts for our four [Lee-Enfield] rifles just in case anything went wrong during the invasion. In that case our first line of defence was to have been at Wingham. On one occasion we were sent up to Durlocks railway station to guard a train-load of ammunition.

Thursday 16 May
Destroyer *Verity* relieves *Whitshed* on North Goodwin patrol. Three large Belgian steamers anchored in The Downs, but with only a total of 200 refugees on board. An assortment of shipping seen in The Downs. Up to ten or more casualties were being treated by Dr Hall, sometimes after he had been operating all day at Deal Hospital; his house surgeon volunteered to help.

Friday 17 May
Dr Hall visited *Pontrieux* (Fr); French naval ratings, women and children refugees on board; one rating with compound fractures of both arms was sent to hospital, others patched-up.

Saturday 18 May
Dr Hall called to visit *Leka* (Nor) but found that she had already sailed. To *Pontrieux* again, where he decided to land some of the injured men, and a woman with fractured collar bone.
   The Royal Air Force requisitioned Staple Station for the delivery of materials for a dummy aerodrome near Manston.

Sunday 19 May
Destroyer *Whitshed* attacked while on North Goodwin patrol, and claimed one enemy surface vessel sunk.
   Early morning visit to a Naval trawler by Dr Hall to collect the body of a Spitfire pilot killed by AA fire; body landed. His parachute was given to Dr Hall who was nearly shot as a 'spy' by a RM sentry while walking up the beach to his home!

The 397 London schoolchildren were now re-evacuated to South Wales, and members of the Wiltshire Regt arrived to take up Coastal Defence. Installations of scaffolding, girders and mines formed the beach defences, with narrow gaps left in the scaffolding for the launching of fishing boats. Percy Cavell, a former mechanic of the Walmer lifeboat who lived on the Strand, remembered being kept awake at night by the noise of pile-drivers installing lengths of railway line into the promenade to form an 'anti-tank' barrier.

Monday 20 May
The mayor appealed for CD [Civil Defence] volunteers at a meeting held in the Odeon.
   Destroyer *Malcolm* attacked by three enemy aircraft while on North Goodwins patrol. Dr Hall visited SR mailboat to treat a mixed bag of patients, among whom were a British major general injured in a car smash, an RAF flight sergeant wounded in the arm and an RN officer with pneumonia.

Tuesday 21 May
Five French destroyers – *Cyclone*; *Mistral*; *Sirocco*; *Frondeur* and *Fougouex* – took shelter in The Downs to escape the bombing of Dunkerque. HMS(T) *Burnie* suffered near-misses off the North Foreland.

Wednesday 22 May
P/S *Brighton Belle* sank after colliding with a wreck in The Downs.
   12.00hrs: Six hospital ships in The Downs.

During the following week the hospital ships were attacked by German aircraft. Mary Osbourn recalls:

> Some of the troops were landed at Deal but not very many. There was quite a big boat with a big red cross painted on it anchored to the north of the pier, and that was machine-gunned two or three times. I was in the teashop, and we could hear the noise of gunfire, so I ran outside to look. That boat had a lot of wounded men on and they took some of them off in boats and ferried them to hospital.

Friday 24 May
The North Goodwin, 'Gull' and 'Wreck' buoys re-aligned for the evacuation. During the next ten days, there was increasing Dunkerque traffic, so a passage was cleared to the east of the Goodwins for two-way traffic.

Saturday 25 May
F. Neeve sent to High Street to render first aid to Mr Hill; Neeve reported that Mr Hill had fractured his wrist, and he had taken him to hospital.

Sunday 26 May
Spitfire L1031 of No. 19 Sqn force-landed on Walmer beach with engine failure after a Bf109 attack off Calais. Flying Officer M.D. Lyne taken to RM Infirmary with injured knee.

A sketch of Spitfire L1031 after it force-landed on Walmer beach. F/L Michael Lyne managed to glide his Spitfire home across the Channel after an attack by enemy fighters off Calais.

More familiar to fishing parties in pre-war days, 'Darky' Budd's motor boat *Britannic* was one of several boats which carried Dr Hall on his missions of mercy. She also went to Dunkerque on 28 May 1940 but was lost during the evacuation.

Deal's contribution to the evacuation from Dunkerque were ten beach boats, including the motor-boats *Gipsy King* (George Riley); *Lady Haig* (Harry Meakins), which was damaged; *Rose Marie* (Freddy Upton) and *Golden Spray* (Fred Roberts); plus *Moss Rose* (Tommy Adams) and *Britannic* (H. and J. Budd), both of which were lost during the evacuation. Two of the ship's lifeboats from SS *Dunbar Castle*, which had remained on the beach since their arrival, were also towed across. One of those who watched them depart was Mary Osbourn:

> It was a wonderful sight – I shall never forget it. It was a quarter to eight in the morning when they left. The Revd Daniels from St George's Church came up to the seafront with two or three fellows from the choir. They came along to the pier as the boats set off and we all sang 'Eternal Father, strong to save' as they were going out to sea. Everybody was crying, it was awfully sad, but then Revd Daniels put his arms up to the heavens and said 'May God go with you!' and we all felt the same.

One of the most controversial aspects of the evacuation was the role played by the local Kent lifeboats. While the crews of the Margate and Ramsgate boats sailed for Dunkerque without question, other lifeboat secretaries, whose responsibility it was to authorize launchings, did not consider that the risk of damage to their vessels was justified and refused to allow them to go. The Royal Navy was therefore ordered to requisition all the remaining lifeboats, man them with volunteers and then dispatch them to assist in the work of ferrying troops from the beaches out to larger vessels offshore. In the case of the *Charles Dibden* the secretary's fears of damage were proved right, as her mechanic Perce Cavell remembered:

> The Walmer lifeboat was damaged at Dunkerque when she ran on to a sub-merged lorry and was holed below the waterline. She had to be taken off service, and I helped take her away to Oulton Broad in Norfolk where she was repaired, but she did not come back on station until the following year.

The local residents were not aware of Operation Dynamo for some days, but most guessed that something big was going on as most of the motor-boats from the Deal beach were missing. When the operation got under way, two of the main evacuation routes for vessels passed through The Downs, and large numbers of ships, of all sorts and conditions, passed through or anchored off Deal. The smoke from the burning oil storage tanks at Dunkerque Harbour on the horizon marked the destination of many vessels that returned more than once to rescue the remnants of the British Expeditionary Force, French troops, and a few civilians.

Monday 27 May
Dr Hall called to *The Marquis* (Br); there were troops, Belgian refugee families, and some Luftwaffe POWs in the hold; this vessel had been shelled and attacked by enemy MTBs; the crew, including one Belgian Army agent, had been injured by shells; the police met the casualties on landing.

MoD vessel *Corfield* reported that a French patrol boat had hit a wreck near Deal Bank buoy; it was towed to Dover by the drifter *Comfort*.

Dover destroyers patrolling North Goodwins to Wandelaar fighting against E-boats.

A Bristol Blenheim IV R3703 of No. 53 Sqn damaged by a fighter attack was abandoned by its crew, and crashed at Chillenden. P/O Aldridge and A/C Trafford were both injured; but Sgt Macrae was unhurt.

An important role was played by the local Coastguards who assisted not only with monitoring the vessels involved in the evacuation; but also in reporting enemy aircraft; summoning rescue craft for ditched pilots, and keeping a weather eye open for any invasion threats. During this year Auxiliary Coastguard stations were opened at Walmer, the Guilford Hotel at Sandwich Bay, and at Shingle End.

Tuesday 28 May
Destroyer *Windsor* with several hundred troops aboard was attacked by enemy aircraft; she arrived in The Downs with twenty or thirty casualties and damage from near-misses.

Dr Hall visited 'Q'-ship alongside the Southern Guard ship, to attend to a Royal Artillery major on board with machine-gun bullets in both legs. He also visited the tug HMS *Sun V* after a collision with a destroyer resulted in a brain injury to a leading seaman; he was landed and taken to hospital. HMS *Delta* was visited during evening, one sick seaman landed.

A Bristol Blenheim 'E' of No. 235 Sqn ditched off the Goodwins; its crew all picked up.

Spitfire FI L1011 of No. 610 Sqn force-landed at East Langdon for reasons unknown; but its pilot, F/O W.H.C. Warner was unhurt.

Wednesday 29 May

F. Neeve assisted at Forester's Hall loading survivors from a ship wrecked by a mine into ambulances.

Dr Hall called to SS *Yewdale* in the lifeboat; it was near the *Dinard* wreck buoy; many wounded aboard (seventy-four plus several dead) who had been treated by an RAMC captain aboard. The master was advised to make for Ramsgate and was escorted there by the Walmer lifeboat.

Avro Anson I K8773 OY-X of No. 48 Sqn shot down by Bf109; ditched off Deal. A/C Harding had shot down one Bf109 and had damaged two others; P/Os Allington, Wharry and A/C Dilnutt were all picked-up OK.

Avro Anson N5065 of No. 500 Sqn shot down by Bf109s returning from a raid on coastal targets; it ditched off Walmer. P/O Leeson, Sgt Hoskins, LAC Cunningham and Cpl Elvidge all OK.

Thursday 30 May

Unidentified Dutch schooner lost off the Goodwins. Ex-Polish destroyer spots periscope off North Goodwins; *Anthony* reported torpedo tracks in the same area; destroyer *Vimy* sighted periscope and conning tower off Goodwin Knoll.

Drifters *Golden Gift* and *Shipmates* ran ashore on the Goodwins; both were re-floated without damage or injury.

Friday 31 May

A Ford ambulance, CK.7702, allocated to this depot.

German mine-layers reported in The Downs again.

The defences against invasion were hastily switched from the east coast to East Kent after the fall of France. Signaller Roy Tarrier recalls that 224th Battery 94th Field Regt RA was at Northbourne Court:

> Our troop of four guns was dug in along the perimeter of the churchyard boundary wall. We occupied an observation post at the Royal Marines camp at Kingsdown. Our first task as signallers was to lay a telephone line from Northbourne to Kingsdown. This telephone line was manned from first light each morning, and again at dusk. Our Battery HQ was also stationed at Northbourne and I well remember doing long stints on manning the wireless link to Regimental HQ at Knowlton Court.

Also helping to guard Deal against invasion was Marine E.H. Johnson, who was then training at the RM depot:

> At the time of Dunkerque I took part in many patrols around Deal and clearly remember being stationed on the roof of a house facing the beach, with another Royal Marine. We had half a dozen hand grenades and fifty rounds of ammunition. I was told, if Jerry came, to guard the spot with my life and at the time I hadn't even pulled a grenade pin in practice.

Saturday 1 June
Blenheim IV R3630 'A' of No. 254 Sqn shot down near the Goodwins in an attack by eleven Bf109s, together with L9481 'O' while trying to drive off Junkers Ju 87Bs. F/O Spiers was the sole survivor from these two aircraft.

Passenger ship *Prague* with three thousand French soldiers aboard was shelled and dive-bombed, and eventually beached off Sandwich Flats.

SS *Ashley* aground on the Goodwins.

Sunday 2 June
Blenheim IV L9476 of No. 53 Sqn, shot-up by LAA and damaged starboard propeller, hit a sandbank off Dunkerque trying to avoid flak, and was obliged to force-land on the Goodwins. F/Lt Brown; Sgt Brooks and A/C Knowles picked up by HMS(T) *Samphire*.

Swedish steamer *Emma* collided with French steamer *Hebe* ESE of South Foreland lighthouse and sank.

Calais and Boulogne lightships anchored off Walmer lifeboat house.

The evacuation of local residents was now started, with some 1,500 local schoolchildren evacuated to South Wales. They were seen off by Mayor Alderman Dobson and other Borough officials, the clergy and townsfolk. The evacuation also caused some problems for the churches in the Deal area, as Mr R.J. Monckton recorded in a history of Victoria Baptist Church:

> With the coming of wartime conditions to Deal, and the threat of invasion, many church members evacuated the town. Others were serving in the forces. The congregation and financial support for the church were both severely diminished. The Minister left to take up a temporary pastorate at Harrow for the duration of the war. The remaining members joined the Methodists and Congregationalists to form Deal United Free Church. The affairs of the Baptist Church were looked after by an executive committee consisting of those remaining in the town.

Monday 3 June
GPO cable-ship *Alert* starts to lift and sever the UK–France telephone cables, including one from St Margaret's Bay to Le Panne.

Tuesday 4 June
Destroyers and drifters on anti-mine patrol off North Goodwins; Transport *Emile*

Deschampes (Fr) torpedoed off North Foreland. At 04.29hrs SS *Leda* collided with the paddle-steamer *Marshal Foche*; at 04.54hrs *Leda* rammed and sank a Dutch schuit one mile off North Goodwins.

The miners on Mill Hill formed their own LDV (Home Guard) platoon based at the TA drill hall (later the Kent's Brush Factory) and miners were later absorbed into other units such as that at Deal gas works, while the three collieries in the area also formed their own LDV platoons; one of the first to volunteer at Betteshanger Colliery was Mr G. Silkstone:

> I missed the first call-up by a few months, and as I was a coalminer at Betteshanger Colliery, I spent the war years in this reserved occupation. However, I joined the LDV as soon as the Government asked for volunteers, and within a few days I found myself in a sand-bagged outpost on the waste tip at the colliery in the dead of night, with only my First World War Canadian Ross rifle and a few rounds of ammunition facing, as I thought, the whole German Army across the Channel.

Thursday 6 June
SS *Harcalo* stranded on the Goodwins. Torpedoes found on beach at half-mile intervals from Prince of Wales Terrace (which was evacuated), North Deal to Sandwich Bay.

Lew Hilson was among those who saw these torpedoes and speculates just where they might have come from:

> This happened when I was still working for Sid White, and on the way to work one day there seemed to be a lot of excitement up on the beach. It was reckoned that a torpedo boat, or most probably one of the German E-boats (or 'Schnellboots') which carried four torpedoes, had fired them at ships anchored in The Downs, but they had missed and had run up on the beach at high tide. I went up to have a look at one of them and they were great bluish-grey things. Nobody seemed to know much about them. I don't remember them being carted away, but somebody must have removed them.

Friday 7 June
No I Party (Nurse Tucker) called to Queen Street (Mrs Millar, broken leg).

Tuesday 11 June
Five-day anti-mining night patrols by Dover drifters from North Foreland to Dungeness and the destroyer HMS *Vesper* from South Goodwins to Dungeness. Sea-fishing is now prohibited, so local boatmen have found alternative work, or joined the RNVR.

Wednesday 12 June
Local doctors organized a rota for emergency hospital duty; GPO switched over twenty-four vital telephone lines on receipt of air raid alerts.

This switch-over was also a signal that an alert was soon to be given, as Martin Hall remembers his father using it as his 'early warning' system:

> Father had been appointed as surgeon to an emergency medical team in Deal, and had the privilege of a telephone line to Deal underground telephone exchange (which only had twenty-four lines) in Stanhope Road, and which was brought into use at night and during periods of air raid alerts. Father recalled that when the main exchange was switched out there would be a faint 'ting' from his own phone, thus he would get a private indication that an alert was due. The Deal postmaster, Mr Pengelly, was a friend of my father (who was also the post office surgeon) and allowed me to visit this underground facility once when I was home on school holidays during the war.

Monday 17 June
20.00hrs: On police request for aid at an accident in High Street (Mrs Wilding had sprained her ankle), A. Jordan, G. Clements and Nurse Harvey took the Ford ambulance.

Tuesday 18 June
F. Neeve called to Middle Street; on arrival back reported that a Mrs Olivier was hysterical. An Austin 20 and a Vauxhall have been allocated here for First Aid Party cars.

It was late in June 1940 that driver Cedric Jones, serving with 'A' Troop Carrying Company RASC was drafted to Deal.

> I was serving with the Transport Company that was stationed in parklands of Womenswold, when our sub-section of six Bedford 3-ton lorries was sent on temporary detachment for the Royal Marines at Deal. They were occupying a small private school situated in a quiet little back road with a high wall on the town side and some tennis courts fairly close on the other side.
>
> We parked our lorries under the trees at the top of the school playing-fields, and covered them with scrim nets of course. We had the use of the wooden changing rooms for a billet.
>
> There was always one lorry on stand-by each twenty-four hours, any time day or night. When there was an alert, we loaded up about fifteen Royal Marines with Bren guns and spare boxes of ammunition, and we took the back lanes leading out of the town to a high point about two or three miles out of town, from where we had a perfect view overlooking Dover, which in those days was pretty well over-shadowed by barrage balloons.

Sunday 23 June
Deal and district has become a restricted area; Identity Cards have been issued.
  Only one small Examination Tug remained in The Downs, anchored opposite Walmer Castle.

Reports that the local Coastal Defence guns were first manned by Royal Marines may well have arisen through the confusion with the elements of the Royal Marines Fortress and Mobile Base Defence Units. The role of the latter was initially to defend port and dock installations, while the former had been pressed into service to help protect coastal areas such as Deal. Among the RMFU ranks was Lieutenant J. Mahoney:

> Warden House at Upper Deal was our area HQ, and Brigadier 'Bobbie' Sturgess RM was in charge, when I spent six or seven months in the partially deserted Deal during the fateful year of 1940 and took over the defensive position in 'Seagirt' cottage.
>
> My platoon had normal infantry weapons and this included the Bren gun. Many nights were spent on anti-boat patrol, watching for lights.
>
> No Coastal Defence guns existed then, the nearest to us being that at Deal Castle, where Captain Boothby was in charge of one 4in gun, mounted on the parapet, I think. On the outskirts of Deal we occupied Tormore School and also maintained a road block at Sholden. I also had responsibilities in Sandwich, where members of 'The Link' [an Anglo-German friendship group] met, and I arrested numerous people, including an Australian film actress, and an MP (whose name I have forgotten). Our billet there was at the Bell Hotel.

Tuesday 25 June
Work started on the first 14in gun-site at St Margaret's on the golf course – golf is still being played!

Wednesday 26 June
Winston Churchill visited the area, inspecting defence works.

Lt Mahoney, BSM Bickwell and Mne Muir on Walmer beach. They were members of the Royal Marine Base Defence Unit which helped defend the Deal area after Dunkerque. In the background stands the old South Eastern Hotel and some of the boatmen's beach huts.

During the last week of June Dr Hall was called on alternate mornings to three coasters, *Buoyant*; *Kindiesel* and *Mad Joe*, moored near the Deal Bank buoy in the middle of a now-empty sea. All had injured crew members who were treated by him on board before they proceeded.

Saturday 29 June
Wellington Mk I had engine trouble on returning from operation and had to force-land near Grove Manor, Woodnesborough. P/O Bull and his crew were unhurt.

At the end of June some 150 certificates were awarded to ARP trainees at Deal, while during the following month, Mr Eames was busy building screen walls to replace the emergency access doors to the air raid shelter in London Road (on the traffic island at Albert Road junction). At Staple, the East Kent railway station was handed back by the RAF, while 'B' Battery 74th Medium Regt RA arrived at Ash. They travelled to Brook House from Sturry, with sixteen AEC Matador tractors pulling eight 60-pounder Mk 1 guns, and an assortment of vans carrying their equipment. Among those who came to Ash with the advance party was Ron Somers, who remembers the scramble for the best accommodation:

> Only our officers were actually accommodated in Brook House, so the quicker witted of the rest of us (including me!) commandeered the old 'hoppers' huts'. Some bedded down in the oast house, while the rest had to stay under canvas. Three of us in our hut draught-proofed the lower parts of the walls with empty sandbags, and decorated the upper part with 'pin-up' pictures.
>
> We hired a radio from a shop in Sandwich and as our hut overlooked the latrines, we christened it 'Bogview', which we painted over the door.

Wednesday 3 July
15.55hrs: Four HEs dropped on Sandwich (31 houses seriously damaged; 60 slightly damaged) and Betteshanger Colliery; one HE fell on 'Hardicot', The Triangle, Kingsdown.

Thursday 4 July
Hurricane I N2619 of No. 79 Sqn shot down over St Margaret's Bay by Bf109s. Sgt Cartwright was killed after he baled out with his parachute alight; his body was recovered by HSL.

Among the Royal Marines in the St Margaret's area at this time was Corporal Peter Spittal, serving with the RMFU in the area:

> We worked on the defences along the coast, putting in the gun emplacements and manning the guns; I remember manning a machine-gun during the Battle of Britain, when there were dog-fights going on all over the Channel, with planes crashing and pilots baling out. One day I was on duty when I suddenly heard the roar of a German aircraft engine just above my head, and it was flying so low I could see the pilot's face. Before I could train my machine-gun on the

aircraft, I'm sure the pilot smiled and waved and then was away . . . I hope he reached home safely.

Friday 5 July
Vauxhall KO7738 transferred from Forester's Hall.

Sunday 7 July
Spitfire I R6711 of No. 54 Sqn shot down by Bf109 near Deal; P/O Campbell slightly wounded; Spitfire I P9390 also of No. 54 Sqn shot down in same area; P/O E.J. Coleman slightly injured.

Monday 8 July
07.30hrs: Messerschmitt Bf109E-3 2964 of 3/LG2 shot down by No. 54 Sqn (Way), and dived into the ground at Buckland Farm near Woodnesborough. Lt Albert Striberny baled out and was captured and made a POW. His aircraft was totally destroyed.
    Trawler *Cayton Wyke* stranded on the Goodwins.

Tuesday 9 July
20.00hrs: Heinkel He 59B-1 D-ASUO of Seenotflugkommando I forced down on the Goodwin Sands by a Spitfire from No. 54 Sqn (P/O J.L. Allen). Fw Maywald, Uffz H. Bartmann, Uffz W. Anders and Uffz E. Schiele captured: POWs.
    Spitfire N3183 of No. 54 Sqn force-landed near New Downs Farm after a collision with Bf109; while Spitfire R6705, of the same Sqn crashed into Sandwich Bay, P/O Garton was killed.
    Night: Six HE on Eastry, minor damage only.

While the beach scaffolding was being erected, access to the beach was granted to local people for two hours each day. Here are Mrs Doris Hickman (now Mrs Hirst), her baby daughter Carole, her sister Kathleen (left) and a friend.

My cousin Harold managed to sneak this photograph of the Heinkel He 59B air–sea rescue seaplane D–AUSO while it was beached at Walmer. It was later towed to Dover Harbour where it was destroyed in a bombing raid.

Glyn Casey recalls the aircraft incident:

> Following an attack on the south east on this day, six German aircraft were reported missing by the Luftwaffe. Several Heinkel He 59 seaplanes were dispatched to search for survivors and one of these ventured too near to a small convoy. Two sections of Spitfires of No. 54 Sqn from Hornchurch intercepted this Heinkel and its escort of about a dozen Messerschmitts.
>
> Meanwhile the other section, led by P/O J.L. Allen attacked the He 59 and hit one of its engines. The seaplane was put down on the water near the Goodwin Sands, and it was stranded there at low tide. It was later towed ashore at Walmer.

When the Heinkel seaplane was first towed ashore it was anchored off Deal pier, and Mrs Mary Osbourn remembers that the crew gave would-be capturers a warm reception when they tried to board it:

> That seaplane came in by the pier, and was anchored off the branch that was used for fishing, but when the boatmen took the Customs men out to it, they were fired upon. However, they eventually captured the crew, and the seaplane was hauled up on the beach at Walmer.

At least one of the Heinkel's crew appears to have been interned in Deal Castle, where my cousin, Len Collyer, was engaged on carpentry work connected with the alterations for the Royal Marine gun crews installing the two 6in Coastal Defence guns on the promenade nearby. Len recalled:

One of the guards at the Castle had acquired a pair of flying boots from one of the seaplane's crew, but because he could not leave his post, he asked me to take them as I had a pass. How to get them past the sentry was the problem, but in those days carpenters used to carry their tools in a large canvas bag so I managed to walk out on successive evenings with one boot each time. The guard had asked us to post them to his home, and when we examined them before wrapping them up, we found that they were marked 'Dunlop – Made in England'!

Wednesday 10 July
Dr Hall called to Walmer beach to inspect Heinkel D-ASUO; tug undertook the tow of seaplane to Dover Harbour.

Sunday 14 July
Hurricane I L1584 of No. 615 Sqn shot down by II/JG51 Bf109s off St Margaret's Bay. P/O M. Mudie baled out badly injured and was picked up by RN vessel; he died in hospital next day.

Thursday 18 July
German aircraft attacked wrecks at the end of the Goodwins by mistake; East Goodwin light-vessel (un-manned since June) was dive-bombed and sunk.

Friday 19 July
HMS(T) *John Gatting* reported a low-flying aircraft in The Downs and the destroyer *Beagle* saw a seaplane take off from the sea off Leathercote Point.

Saturday 20 July
23.17 hrs: Four HEs dropped at Eastry.

With Army units installed in the local villages, there was some need for training and rifle practice to be carried out, and because no permanent rifle-range was available, one was improvised at Eastry. According to John Rolfe:

> The Army had a rifle-range in the siding by the chalk pit near Eastry South station, where they rigged up a moving target with a continuous rope and wheels to move it along. They used to fire Tommy-guns and Sten-guns at the targets, and we used to lay on top of the bank peering over to watch. After the troops had all gone, we used to go down to the range and dig bullets out of the chalk wall behind the target.

Wednesday 24 July
GPO cable-laying vessel *Alert* damaged by bombing and gunfire near South Goodwin light-vessel, along with two trawlers, *Kingston Galetea* and *Rodino*.

Thursday 25 July
Convoy CW8 passing through The Downs was attacked off Dover by enemy aircraft.

13.01hrs: Spitfire I P9387 of No. 54 Sqn crashed near Martin Mill station following combat with 109s. P/O Turney-George unhurt.

Spitfire I R6707 of No. 54 Sqn shot down when on convoy escort between Deal and Dover; F/L B. Way was killed. Spitfire R6816 of No. 54 Sqn was lost to Bf109s off Kingsdown; P/O A. Finnie was killed.

18.40hrs: Bf109E 2010 6+I of 8/JG52 was shot down by No. 610 Sqn Spitfire at Elvington Court, near Deal. Uffz Max Reiss captured; POW.

This aircraft crash was witnessed by miner Charles Grant:

> It hit the power cables from the Power House to Tilmanstone, the aircraft's wings came off, and the fuselage crashed into trees at the back of the Colliery. The pilot had a cut forehead but we would have been ready for him if he had shown any sign of putting up a fight – as we all kept sharpened files down our socks in case of any such encounters.

Friday 26 July

01.00hrs: Nore Command destroyers *Vivacious* and *Walpole* arrived in The Downs en route to reinforce Dover after losses.

Railway cranes arrived at St Margaret's gun-site; the gun mountings and cradles now in place. Dummy guns planned. The Martin Mill military railway is being extended to the new gun-sites.

The old Pearson railway, which ran from Martin Mill to the top of the cliffs by the Langdon battery, overlooking Dover Harbour, was re-aligned and extended. To operate this military line, the 195th Company Royal Engineers was posted to the area, attached to the RM Siege Regt; among them was Sapper John Payne:

> I was a 'blocksman', which in plain English is a railway signaller, although we took on all sorts of jobs relating to the railway. At the time that the German invasion was expected, we were taught to use a signal frame at Martin Mill station. The 'block instruments' were in the Booking Office, while the levers, to my amusement, were situated outside on the platform.

Saturday 27 July

After suffering damage, the destroyer *Walpole* escorts *Vivacious*; and the tug *Lady Brassey* tows *Brilliant* through The Downs at night en route to Sheerness. The oldest RN destroyer *Skate* takes over the Channel Patrol.

Sunday 28 July

Spitfire I P9547 of No. 74 Sqn shot-up over Dover and force-landed on Goodwin Sands. The pilot, P/O J. Young, believed killed. Claimed by Oblt Meuncheberg of III/JG26.

Hurricane I P3622 of No. 257 Sqn seriously damaged by Bf109s over Channel and force-landed at St Margaret's Bay. Sgt R. Forward was slightly injured.

Sergeant Forward recalls:

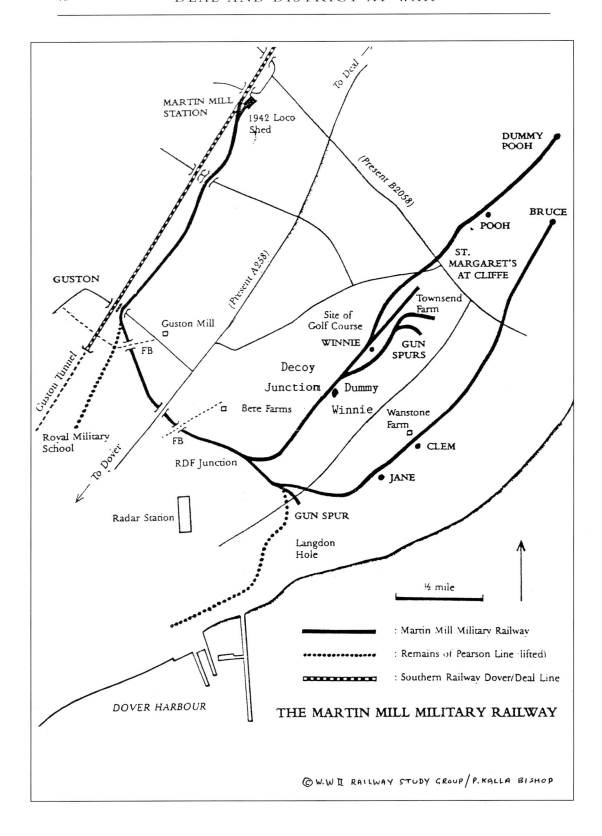

THE MARTIN MILL MILITARY RAILWAY

© W.W II RAILWAY STUDY GROUP / P. KALLA BISHOP

I was shot down from behind, and the Glycol [engine coolant] and petrol tanks were hit. Rather than bale out, although covered in petrol, I decided to force-land. Fortunately I managed to avoid the high tension cables and landed, wheels–up, in a field. I got out, carrying my parachute etc., and walked down the field to a road.

I was picked up by a car and was taken to what I thought was a cottage – it could have been an ARP First Aid Post. I remember being offered a cigarette, but I had to decline this because of the petrol fumes, and I had a glass of milk instead.

Apparently, I was taken by two RN officers to a Naval Dressing Station, a description I had never heard of, so this was not a hospital as such. While the 100 octane fuel was being evaporated, I was told that the body of 'Archie' Finnie [*see* 25 July entry] was upstairs.

Monday 29 July
Spitfire I R6643 of No. 64 Sqn force-landed at St Margaret's Bay after being damaged by return fire from Ju 87's gunner over Channel. Sgt A. Bingham was escorted to the coast by a Hurricane of No. 504 Sqn (P/O Gibson). Aircraft repaired.

Spitfire I N3112 of No. 41 Sqn was unable to return to RAF Manston due to damage caused when F/O McKenzie intercepted a bomber formation over Dover. His cockpit filled with fumes and his canopy jammed, so he was obliged to force-land near Ringwould Mill. Aircraft recovered and repaired.

Afternoon: RM corporal killed by stepping on a mine at Kingsdown.

David Downes's book *Ash*, published by the Ash-with-Westmarsh parish council in 1982, contains some references to the 74th Medium Regt's stay at Ash, including an amusing incident concerning their compulsory rifle practice on the Royal Marine's firing-range at Kingsdown:

> The Medium Battery's look-out tower above Ringleton provided a splendid viewpoint across the Channel for local people agile enough to clamber up to it. Men of the Battery were issued with rifles so as to be able to defend their guns; and taken to the range by the sea at Kingsdown, accompanied by their honorary medical officer. A line of them, including the MO, fired five rounds at huge targets only twenty-five yards away. Between them they recorded only one 'hit' – and that was a shot by the MO. A floating mine close inshore made further firing that day impossible – and no more was ever heard of the need for rifle practice.

Also situated at Ringleton was an underground bunker into which the members of the local Home Guard Auxiliary Unit would have retired if the enemy had made a successful landing. From there they would have engaged in sabotage operations behind the enemy lines for as long as they could hold out. During August secret plans were drawn up for the remaining civilians living in Deal to be evacuated in case of enemy invasion; they would go by bus to the railway station, and thence to Kingston-upon-Thames. Mr R.L.J. Eames was now busy working on an air raid shelter for the ARP post at the Deal council depot in West Street. At Ash, the 74th Medium Regt RA had now dug in completely, and were manning their OPs all night; they were also allocated a Signals Section of 5th Medium Regt RA equipped with a battery of static anti-tank guns at Tilmanstone. Gunner Roy Baker recalls:

> Our duties at this time, because somebody considered that any invasion would come one hour after dawn or dusk, meant long periods of 'standing to', from one hour before dawn to one hour after, and again at dusk, but at all times the gun had to be manned by a skeleton crew on a rota basis. Sleeping on the ground at night in all weathers with only a groundsheet, gas-cape and blanket for protection was fairly tough. No tents or other cover was allowed in case it showed up the position to reconnaissance aircraft.

The German plans for 'Operation Sealion' involved a land attack on the coastal strip between Deal and Ramsgate, largely because of the difficulties of a seaward approach! Ash was to be one area from which there would be no withdrawal, and therefore all sides of the 74th Medium Regt camp had to be fortified with machine-gun posts and barricades in case of invasion. Roy Baker and his pal Gunner Burton found an ideal source of material to build an observation post at Richborough:

> Material for the purpose had to be scrounged and from experience we found that railway sleepers were ideal. Not far away, and not overlooked, was a small single platform railway station with a shelter, which was only used in the summer by tourists visiting the old Richborough Castle, all constructed with nice big railway sleepers. Four of these sleepers, set in the ground, with others across the top and sandbags built up all round made a fine strong elevated defence post.

The work on installing the Royal Marine Siege Regt's first 14in gun at St Margaret's was completed, and it was christened 'Winnie' in honour of its instigator, Mr Winston Churchill.

Thursday 8 August
Spitfire I L1039 of No. 64 Sqn caught fire in combat with a Bf109 of JG51 and crashed at West Langdon; P/O Kennard-Davis baled out, but died of his injuries. Spitfire K9911 of No. 65 Sqn was also shot down over Deal, Sgt D. Kirton being killed.

Friday 9 August
22.55hrs: Five HEs dropped at Woodnesborough.

Sunday 11 August
Night: Machine-gun attack on The Brambles, Kingsdown (one slightly injured).

Monday 12 August
Two shelling attacks (serious damage not known; slight damage not known; 1 killed, 3 seriously injured; slight injuries unknown).
  First shelling: damage to Campbell Terrace, Campbell Road, buildings in North Barracks;

Shingle Alley; casualties at East Barracks; shrapnel found in roof of Deal post office.
  10.05hrs: Shelling at Worth; railway line hit causing single-line working temporarily.
  17.40hrs: One HE at Nonington.

One of the properties damaged in the first shelling was a garage next door to Lew Hilson's home in Campbell Road, Walmer:

> The shell had hit the Barracks' wall and then ricocheted across to where a few Royal Marines were sitting under the colonnade. Marine Corporal Drake was killed, old Mr 'Taffy' Hyatt lost his leg, and a few other chaps were injured at the same time.
>
> When I got home, I went round the back and saw the damage to the garage and my brother's car which was inside it. All our back room windows had been blown out, so I made my way indoors fearing the worst. But I found my mother standing at the kitchen sink quite unconcerned by it all, calmly peeling some potatoes.

Hurricanes from No. 32 Sqn were ordered to patrol over Deal at 20,000ft when thirty to forty Dornier Do17s and nine Bf109s were sighted. P/O A.R. Barton fired at one of the fighters and saw a large piece break off; this was confirmed by a searchlight unit between Deal and Dover.

Deal's first shelling on 12 August resulted in widespread damage; this is Lew Hilson's brother's car, which was garaged at 79 Campbell Road, Walmer. Windows and ceilings were also damaged in the area.

Tuesday 13 August
Night: Spitfire 1 R6766 of No. 56 Sqn had crashed during night-flying practice at Eastry; cause unknown. P/O F.S. Gregory baled out too low over Deal and was killed.

Wednesday 14 August
Trawler *Elizabeth Angela* sunk by air attack in The Downs; raids on the Dover Balloon Barrage and lightships.
　12.45hrs: Eight HEs at St Margaret's.
　Bf109E-1 4872 of 1/JG26 >+8 shot down over Dover by P/O R.F. Smythe of No. 32 Sqn; crashed and broke up at Coldred, some of the wreckage landing near the Carpenter's Arms. Uffz Gerhart Kemen baled out and was captured, wounded.
　Bf109E-4 of III/JG54 fell into the sea at Sandwich Bay; the pilot was picked up and taken prisoner.
　Bf109 of 4/JG52 shot down in Sandwich Bay, but the body of Oberfw Weiss was washed up at Joss Bay, near Broadstairs.

The St Margaret's ARP logbook for this day contained the following report:

The Church of St Margaret of Antioch had a narrow escape when the four bombs, thought to have been aimed at the site of 'Winnie', landed in the churchyard, just missing the Norman tower and the richly carved west door, leaving a large crater only twenty feet from the door; it blew up about twenty graves. [The depression in the ground remains to this day.]
　This month also saw damage to the ARP post at the Cliffe Hotel, which was vulnerable as it was situated near the Royal Marines' camp at Townsend Farm as well as their guns 'Winnie' and 'Pooh'. On one occasion cannon shells hit the roof of the shed and the hotel itself, coming through the ceiling and landing in a mattress.

Thursday 15 August
We have seen some exciting dog-fights all day.
　14.30hrs: Major air actions, including one over Deal.
　15.23hrs: One HE at Palm Tree Inn, Woodnesborough.
　16.00hrs: Dornier Do17Z-2 of 6/KG3 shot down by S/Ldr J.M. Thomson of No. 111 Sqn on sortie over Thames Estuary; crashed in sea between Deal and Ramsgate. Lt H-E. Walter; Fw Schauer; Uffzs E. Kirchubel and A. Pieronczyk captured unhurt; POWs.
　Spitfire N3189 of No. 266 Sqn shot down off Deal; Sgt F.B. Hawley missing.
　Spitfires N3097 of No. 54 Sqn shot down off the Goodwins, pilot Sgt N.A. Lawrence, and R6981 shot down near Deal, F/L A.C. Deere baled out slightly wounded.

Friday 16 August
We saw an air fight, and saw a Nazi plane forced down near Worth. Mr Howland, one of our drivers, caught the pilot. We all gave him a cheer.
　12.35hrs: Bf109E-3 of 4/JG51 + 6 collided with Spitfire R6768 of No. 266 Sqn flown by Sqn/Ldr R.L. Wilkinson (killed) over Eastry after combat over Deal. Uffz E. Buder baled out and was captured unhurt, after landing near the Deal–Sandwich Road at Worth; POW.

Battle of Britain vapour trails over Deal. Sitting in a deckchair in the back garden of his home in the near-deserted Downs Road, Bill Fenn photographed the evidence of the aerial battles which raged above Deal during the summer of 1940.

One eye-witness to this incident was Mr K.C. Bartlett, who has since sought to gain official recognition for Sqn/Ldr Wilkinson's action:

> I was living at Eastry at the time and I was coming along from Felderland Farm, and had just reached the old Primary School in the road leading up to the church, when this Spitfire swooped down so low that I could feel the wind from the wings as it went past me. The pilot had run out of ammunition while attacking the Messerschmitt, and had tried to ram it, but had missed. The pilot then climbed above the Bf109 and deliberately rammed it. The wreckage of his Spitfire fell at Eastry Court Farm, only about 50 yards from where I was standing at the time.

Another person who witnessed the capture of the German pilot was Mr

Ambulance driver 'Minnie' Howland with Nurse Dadd. Although small in stature (hence his nickname) ambulance driver Mr Howland detained Uffz E. Buder when he parachuted down to land at Hacklinge, near Worth.

E.W.G. Cummings:

> I remember one particularly exciting moment when an enemy pilot landed down the slope, across the Deal–Sandwich road near Upton House, Worth. As we approached, the pilot was gathering up his parachute, but he ignored us lads. Then the 'Rescue Bus' [Deal ARP Mobile Unit's Ambulance] turned up – all painted green with large red crosses on it.

12.40hrs: Spitfire N3240 of No. 266 Sqn crashed at Little Mongeham after being in combat with Bf109s over Canterbury; pilot Sub/Lt H.L. Greenshield RN was reported missing.

12.45hrs: Spitfire I N3095 of No. 266 Sqn shot down in flames at Adisham by Messerschmitt Bf109s; pilot P/O N.G. Bowen was killed.

16.14hrs: Spitfire I K9915 of No. 65 Sqn failed to return from combat over Channel; P/O L.L. Pyman killed off St Margaret's Bay.

16.55hrs: Dornier Do17Z-2 of 3/KG2 intercepted by Hurricanes of No. 111 Sqn off Whitstable, ploughed into the ground near Summerfield Farm at Staple and broke up. (This was probably the one claimed by P/O B.J. Wicks.) Lt H.G. Mollenbrok and Uffz P. Hess baled out, both wounded; Gfr Reinicke and Gfr Golob also baled out, but too low for their parachutes to open, and were killed.

Night: IBS fell near the Downs Road footpath, Walmer.

The only survivors from the Dornier Do17Z which crashed at Summerfield Farm, near Staple, were the badly injured pilot, Lt Heinz Mollenbrok (left) and his navigator Uffz P. Hess; their wounded colleagues including Uffz Golob (right) were killed after baling out at too low an altitude.

One of the survivors who lived to tell the tale of his landing at Staple was the pilot, who recounts what happened after he had escaped from his stricken Dornier:

> The next thing that I remember after baling out is hanging from my parachute straps in a tree, and seeing the barrel of a shotgun being pointed at me. Two men tried to get me out of my harness, and twisted the release box on my parachute harness and then banged it, but it wouldn't go first time, so they gave it a good 'whack' and then lowered me to the ground.
>
> My right arm had been badly injured, and was only hanging from a strip of flesh, the bone having been smashed by bullets when we were attacked. As well as my damaged arm, I had a shell splinter in my lung – in later years this has become infected and it still troubles me even now. These two men helped me into the farmhouse and the mother said to put me on the sofa, but I was losing a lot of blood and I did not want to spoil her furniture. So I asked for a chair on which to sit. She was so gentle and kind as she attended to me, and I have never forgotten her kindness.
>
> After this I was taken to the Chartham Hospital, where I remained for ten days.

Fortunately, Mrs Doris Vickers who rendered first aid, had been a VAD nurse during the First World War, and she was able to draw on her knowledge to patch up Heinz before he was handed over to the Red Cross.

As well as being on stand-by to defend the area inland from Sandwich Bay against enemy invasion, gunners of the 74th Medium Regt RA, including Gunner Roy Baker, were allocated the none too pleasant task of recovering the bodies of the other members of Heinz's crew:

> The evening of 16 August was beautiful, and at about 18.00hrs a party of us was detailed to go out and search for parachutists who it was said, had baled out of a damaged enemy aircraft. We set off, and eventually came to a field in which the corn had been cut and stood in shocks.
>
> Here we found a policeman who told us there were two bodies under some shocks. We lifted some of the sheaves, and under two of them we found the young German airmen, both dead. One had very fair hair, while the other was very dark. We obtained a two-wheeled farm cart, of the type normally pulled by a horse, and placed these two lads on it and wheeled their bodies to an open barn, where we left them in the charge of the policeman.

Sunday 18 August

18.00hrs: Bomb damage and casualties at Deal Waterworks, Gladstone Road, Blenheim Road, Cemetery Road ARP depot and Deal Castle. 30 HEs (14 demolished; 133 seriously damaged; 166 slightly damaged; 4 seriously injured; 2 slightly injured).

One flotilla sent to Blenheim Road; two casualties sent to hospital, both stretcher cases, with Nurse Bashford.

We watched forty-seven bombers come in from the sea in formation; they went Ramsgate way; and a further forty-seven turned over here, heading to Dover. We watched

Bomb damage in Blenheim Road, 18 August 1940. These houses, opposite the Royal Marine Infirmary, were the first of many in this road to suffer damage owing to their proximity to the main Dover–Deal railway line.

The ARP rescue van in Blenheim Road. After their houses were damaged, many residents moved to 'safer' parts of Deal, assisted by the ARP rescue services who helped to salvage furniture etc.

as one plane left formation, and heard the bombs coming, and dived for shelter. I bet we did look funny, all the personnel lying in all sorts of positions on the floor, but Blenheim Road, Ravenscourt Road and Gladstone Road were a mess. Redsull's Furnishing Store in Gladstone Road was burned out.

About 19.30hrs Harvey and I went up on our bicycles to have a look, and a warden stopped us, and took us to a woman who needed medical attention in Ravenscourt Road; she was suffering badly from shock, and the ceiling and windows of her house had come down. We managed to calm her, but had to ring for the doctor who ordered her to hospital, so we waited for the ambulance, and went up with her at 20.10hrs.

22.45hrs: Three HEs and IBs at Elvington, Sutton and Nonington.

22.58hrs: Six HEs at Langdon.

At this time, according to Mr Bernard Kimpton, the only anti-aircraft defences consisted of several light machine-guns positioned along the seafront, on top of the Beach Hotel, the Regent Cinema, and the South Eastern Hotel, on Walmer Green and by the Midland Bank at the end of the Strand; while Peter Hoskins recalls seeing others in the 'Gun Field' at Upper Walmer, and a Bofors gun and balloon in the RM drill field in Cornwall Road.

Wednesday 21 August
16.55hrs: One HE at Sutton.

Thursday 22 August
Germans bombarded across Straits of Dover; a convoy going through was attacked from the air, but no ships were hit.

The bombardment of the Channel and the coastal strip between Deal and Folkestone had been anticipated when German long-range gun batteries were photographed in the Cap Gris Nez area. The first shelling was undertaken by enemy mobile rail-mounted guns, but when the fixed gun-sites joined in the barrage, their locations had already been pinpointed by No. 2 Survey Regt RA, with whom Mr Allan Barratt was serving:

> My OP was at St Margaret's at Cliffe, where we had taken over a house in a road running parallel to the coastline. The back garden ended at the cliff edge, and there was an allotment somewhere nearby as a shell exploded in it, scattering the vegetables everywhere!
> The upstairs bay window looked over towards the French coast, providing an excellent view. With our special instruments we could pick out the movement on the Cap, the clock face and docks at Calais, and the coastal railway. The window sill was extended to provide fixtures for our instruments and the room fitted with tables, wireless sets, telephones, wall-maps, etc., while the owner's furniture was stored away in locked rooms.

The 14in gun 'Winnie' fired three rounds at the Cap Gris Nez battery while Convoy CW9 'Totem' was passing the South Foreland and was being shelled by the enemy batteries. Lieutenant-Colonel Fellowes received orders to fire 'Winnie's first shot:

> There was some confusion as these were shortly cancelled, however, after a great deal of telephoning and arranging for one spotting aircraft to go up, we eventually fired three rounds at the batteries near Gris Nez. I took upon myself the privilege of firing the first round to cross the Channel from England, which landed within 300 yards of the target. Owing to an error in correction, the second round, which was fired by the FOC Dover, fell into the sea; the third, however, was much better. The spotter aircraft was ordered back after this as about fifty enemy fighters came over. We had not been allowed to fire a round to test the mounting or to calibrate the gun, on orders given to me by the Prime Minister, who on a visit to us in July said, 'You are not to calibrate the gun or fire the gun until I find you a target, and I will find you a suitable target.'

The 14in shells fired from HMG 'Winnie' were far too heavy to be man-handled to the breech, so lengths of Ducaville track were laid from the 'ready' magazines situated behind the gun to the derrick-type hoist for loading.

Spitfire I R6708 of No. 54 Sqn was shot down off Deal by enemy fighters. Sgt G.R. Collett killed. Hurricane I P3901 of No. 615 Sqn damaged, possibly by fire from another Hurricane, and had to force-land near Deal. P/O D.H. Hone was unhurt.

Friday 23 August
Unexploded bomb of an old type taken to the home of P.C. Wisenden at Adisham.

Saturday 24 August
08.50hrs: Spitfire I R6686 (perhaps K9975) DW-S of No. 610 Sqn crashed in flames at Hammill, Woodnesborough after being attacked by Haupt Foco (II/JG51) off Ramsgate. Sgt S.J. Arnfield baled out, and fractured his ankle on landing.
   Spitfire I P9389 of No. 54 Sqn crashed in School Lane, Kingsdown, following combat; P/O C. Stewart baled out and was picked up by the Royal Navy.
   10.15–10.40hrs: HEs and IBs fell at Adisham (1 seriously injured; 6 slightly injured).

Les Poupard was the General Foreman at the Hammill Brickworks and lived in the bungalow attached to the work's office. Brick production had stopped in 1939 but the works remained open throughout the war:

> A vast amount of emergency feeding equipment and food was stored. The empty kiln was filled with 300 tons of sugar and the kiln buildings housed some 30 tons of margarine and around 100 tons of corned mutton. Staff were reduced to a skeleton to maintain the buildings and plant for the war effort. Mr Parker, the managing director, was an auxiliary fireman, while the secretary was called up for military service. There was a great community spirit in the country areas.

Situated as it was on rising ground, the area near Eastry Mill at Millbank Cottages afforded excellent views towards the Isle of Thanet, and the Luftwaffe's determined attempts to knock out RAF Manston. On this day several Junkers Ju 88A bombers from KG76 are recorded as being 'shot down off Manston', but in the confusion of battle one managed to slip away inland, only to crash near Eastry:

> We had a 'front line' view of the bombing of Manston from our house during the Battle of Britain. On this occasion we saw a line of dive-bombers attacking the airfield. First of all the plumes of smoke rose from the exploding bombs, then they merged into one black pall of smoke which hung over the airfield.
>
> I was standing in the road behind Millbank Cottages with my Dad and some of our neighbours while the bombing raid was going on over Manston. We saw one aircraft coming from Woodnesborough way; its starboard engine was on fire and it was trailing smoke. As it came over we could see one German standing at the doorway of the bomber, looking out, and then he jumped and we saw his parachute open up.
>
> A crowd of us ran down the field to get a better view towards Heronden to see where his parachute would come down, while Dad went indoors to fetch his Home Guard rifle. Meanwhile the bomber had flown on over the fields and crashed near the railway at Upper Venson Farm. Another crew member baled out over Knowlton Woods, but was killed when his parachute failed to open. The other two occupants of the Ju 88 were killed in the crash.
>
> Dad had thoughts of capturing the man we had seen bale out, but by the time he had reached the spot where this German landed, somebody from Heronden House had driven across the fields in a Ford V8 shooting brake, picked up the German airman and his parachute and driven off with him!
>
> Father heard later that, after being wined and dined at the big house, that evening the airman was driven down to a searchlight at the back of Shingleton Farm. Dad was most disappointed that he had not been able to reach the site where the German landed to prevent his being 'spirited away' that afternoon. I went up to look at where the Junkers had crashed and there was just a big black patch in the cornfield, with bits of aircraft scattered all around.

12.55hrs: Bf109E-4 5587 of 6/JG51 10+ landed at Salton Close Farm at East Langdon due to engine failure (damage to oil system) after combat with fighters during an escort sortie with the Ju 88s attacking Manston. (This could have been the one claimed by P/O Wicks of No. 56 Sqn, but it was also claimed by a No. 264 Sqn Defiant crew.) Obfw Fritz Beeck was captured unhurt by Police Sergeant Wood; POW.

Spitfire I X4102 of No. 610 Sqn shot down by Bf109 at Sibotswold Place, Shepherdswell; P/O D.M. Gray wounded.

14.35hrs: Enemy aircraft blew up opposite South Foreland lighthouse; pilot reported to have baled out and been seen swimming in the sea.

Sunday 25 August
Lord Guilford's two children killed by a landmine on the beach at Sandwich Bay during a family picnic.

Spitfire I K9931 of No. 610 Sqn crashed at Stoneheap Farm, at Northbourne; P/O F.T. Gardiner baled out slightly wounded.

Hurricane P7255 of No. 32 Sqn shot down off St Margaret's; P/O Keith Gilman also killed in N2433 when shot down off Kingsdown.

At this time Gunner Harry Lane was stationed at Kingsdown with the 310th Battery RA:

> We were a coastal battery in those days. We had two 6in naval guns set in the clifftop, also a searchlight on the beach down below, also a rocket gun and several types of anti-aircraft gun. Life went on just the same, two days on and one day off, and entertainment was practically nil in wartime East Kent.
>
> I must mention the WVS at Kingsdown, as all the time we were there they did our laundry free of charge; piles of socks were neatly darned, and when we fetched our washing back there would always be a packet of cigarettes in the middle.

Monday 26 August
Fierce air battle over Straits of Dover.

13.22hrs: Do 17Z-2 1160 of 7/KG3 5K+AR force-landed on the Goodwins at low tide with both engines out of action after being shot up by RAF fighters during a sortie to bomb West Malling; Uffzs Reinhard and Ritzel both missing (presumed drowned) Gfr Huhn dead. Fw Essmert captured; POW.

15.30hrs: Bf109E-1 of 2/JG52 2+ shot up in a surprise attack while on freelance sortie over Ramsgate; crash-landed near clubhouse of Royal St George's golf course, severely damaged; Fw Alfons Bacher captured unhurt, POW. Another Bf109 of 2/JG52, pilot Uffz Hartlieb, force-landed on the Goodwins.

Spitfire I R6758 of No. 616 Sqn shot down by 109s and forced to land at Adisham. P/O Marples wounded in the leg by 20mm cannon shell splinters and was hospitalized.

20.55hrs: Three HEs dropped at Eastry.

Wednesday 28 August
Saw a number of dog-fights.

00.01hrs: IBs dropped over the Eastry area.

09.12hrs: Bf109E-4 1353 13+I of 7/JG26; radiator severely damaged while in combat over Canterbury (possibly by a Hurricane of No. 501 Sqn) while on a bomber escort sortie to Eastchurch; force-landed at Goodnestone House Farm, Goodnestone. Fw Karl Straub was captured unhurt; POW.

12.40hrs: Bf109E-4 5146 of Stab II/JG3 exploded in the air over Kearsney after attack by Sgt J.N. Nowell of No. 54 Squadron; Obfw K. Trebling was killed; reported to have been interred at Eastry Cemetery on 29 August 1940.

16.25hrs: Bf109E-4 0941 of Stab I/JG3 shot down by Sgt R.F. Hamlyn of No. 610 Sqn in combat over Dover (this aircraft is probably the one also claimed by F/Lt P.S. Weaver of No. 56 Sqn). Its engine caught fire so the aircraft was abandoned and crashed at Holly

Lodge, Church Farm, Church Whitfield. Lt Hans-Herbert Landry baled out, and landed badly injured at Guston; he died in hospital on 23 September.

Spitfire P9511 of No. 610 Sqn shot down near Deal.

From the St Margaret's ARP logbooks:

Mr Marsh from Martin was injured falling from his cart when his horse bolted after being frightened by gunfire at Nelson Park at St Margaret's.

Thursday 29 August

01.00hrs: Nonington–Eastry road reported blocked, probably by IBs dropped at 00.01hrs.

Friday 30 August

22.10hrs: Six HEs dropped at Staple.

From the St Margaret's ARP logbooks:

Saturday 31 August

08.30hrs: Fighters engaged in a 'scrap' over St Margaret's. A fire was started near the lighthouse, and sixteen balloons were shot down.

Hurricane I 1830 of No. 253 Sqn shot down at Grove Ferry, the pilot Sqn /Ldr H.M. Starr found dead at Hammill Brickworks, Woodnesborough.

Winston Churchill himself visited the wreckage of Lt Hans Herbert Landry's Bf109, which crashed at Holly Lodge, Church Whitfield. Churchill picked up a cartridge case as a souvenir.

The reason why Sqn/Ldr Starr did not survive is explained by Mr H.G. Bennett who witnessed this unsavoury incident:

> I was working as a gardener at Eastry House, and used to start work at 7.00 a.m., worked until 8.00 a.m. and then returned home for my breakfast, and resumed working at 8.30 a.m. It was as I returned to work that morning that I saw a parachute coming down over the Hammill Brickworks. As most of the dog-fights took place at some altitude, I didn't hear or see the aircraft, but as the parachute came drifting down, I saw quite a number of enemy aircraft circling. Suddenly one of the Messerschmitts dived towards the pilot on the parachute, and then the rest also piled in – I could hear the sound of machine-gunning.

The ARP logbook continues:

11.35hrs: Several HEs dropped between Aylesham and Snowdown.

12.20hrs: Three HEs dropped at Aylesham.

12.40hrs: One HE north of Wingham village.

13.00hrs: Six HEs on Marine Road; Mill Road; Park Lane and Blenheim Road (2 demolished; 55 seriously damaged; 88 slightly damaged; 6 killed; 1 seriously injured; 2 slightly injured). One HE fell south east of Staple village; and one HE at Hammill Brickworks failed to explode.

13.40hrs: Do17Z-3 2669 5K+LM of 4/KG3 after attacking RAF Hornchurch was engaged by RAF fighters off the north Kent coast; and severely damaged by ack-ack fire. Landed off Sandwich Flats, and the crew set the aircraft alight, before being taken into captivity through the grounds of Princes golf club. Obfw W. Lange; Fws H. Berndt, H. Wunsch and Uffz Krostopotsch all wounded; POWs.

13.45hrs: Do17Z-3 3414 5K+GN of 5/KG3, with both engines disabled after an attack by a Hurricane of No. 310 Sqn, ditched in the sea near the South Goodwins. Fw Nickel missing, believed drowned; Fw E. Gudat and Uffz W. Sonntag captured unhurt, Uffz Blasche captured injured, all POWs.

17.50hrs: Shells bursting over St Margaret's; more balloons shot down; one balloon set straw alight at Bere Wood; the fire brigade attended.

Vera Dadd's diary for this day reported that:

No. 1 party sent to Park Lane, Nurse Bashford. When one bomb dropped, a warden (Mr Shotbolt) had a narrow escape – his bicycle, gas-mask, etc. were perforated with holes from debris, but he escaped unhurt.

CHAPTER THREE

September–December 1940

From August onwards, during the shelling the East Kent buses were evacuated from South Street to the south side of Park Avenue, and were parked between the Park ARP post and Gilford Road railway bridge.

Sunday 1 September
09.00hrs: Fire at Bere Wood in farmyard, four stacks were destroyed – burned all night. (ARP logbook)

Monday 2 September
Plenty of exciting air battles over here. Saw a bomber shot down by our fighters; it came down in Betteshanger Park, we think.
 08.00hrs: Bf109E-3 4807 of 1/JG1 shot down in combat by P/O G.D. Gribble of No. 54 Sqn (Spitfire); crashed at Nethersole Farm, Womenswold. Lt Gunter Ruettowski killed.
 12.15hrs: IBs at Adisham Court Farm.

Ken Owen recalls:

> I was at school in Canterbury, but during the holidays some of us used to cycle out to Adisham to help with the harvesting. One of these incendiary bombs fell into the hopper of the thrashing machine, which then caught fire and set the straw stacks alight, and they were all burned out before the village fire brigade could get there.

14.15hrs: Me110D-0 A2+KL 3269 of II/ZG2 exploded over Venson's Farm at Eastry during an attack by F/Sgt J. Steere (No. 72 Squadron). Fw L. Beil and Obgfr J. Oehl both killed.
 18.05hrs: Hurricane I R4178 of No. 303 Sqn was damaged in combat and force-landed at Tye Wood, north-west of Elvington; the pilot P/O M. Feric was unhurt, and the aircraft recovered and repaired.

Tuesday 3 September
Hurricane I P3610 of No. 253 Sqn crashed when force-landing at Snowdown Colliery near Woolage Village, cause unknown. P/O Murch was unhurt.
 21.55hrs: HEs dropped in field between Hammill and Selson.

Wednesday 4 September
10.05hrs: Bf109E-1 6290 of 9/JG51 shot down by RAF; possibly by Sgt Frantisek of No. 303 Sqn 'East of Walton, Eastry'. Pilot taken prisoner.

Thursday 5 September
10.30hrs: Three parachutes seen in the sea off St Margaret's, but with nothing attached to them; one recovered by military.

Members of the 70th Battalion of The Buffs, the 'Young Soldiers' Battalion, who were not allowed to serve in the front line because of their youth, were then based at St Margaret's. Brian Cork remembers that he helped man a machine-gun in the cliffs, until the defence of the bay was taken over by the 5th Battalion Royal Marine Commando. After this the 'Young Soldiers' were moved up to the Knole Hotel until November 1940. Their duties included guarding 'Winnie' and 'Pooh', and the radar station at the South Foreland battery.

Saturday 7 September
16.15hrs: Attack by 1,000 German aircraft between Deal and Margate; target London docks. Local NFS firemen were sent to help fight the blaze. Two HEs dropped on Gilham Grove (4 seriously damaged; 16 slightly damaged); another fell in the sea near Deal Castle.
   17.20hrs: Me110C-1 3117 3A+FL of 1/ZG2 broke up over a housing estate at Eythorne after both its engines were damaged by Sgt G.W. Garton of No. 73 Sqn during an escort sortie to London. Haupt F. Oligschlager and Obfw E. Ottersbach both killed.

The Prime Minister himself was responsible for moving one of the rail-mounted gun batteries down to the Eythorne area. According to the recollections of Mr Jesse Kidgell, a veteran of the First World War and then serving with the 5th Super Heavy Battery RA:

> We had been based at Stallingborough in Lincolnshire to cover the Humber estuary and Immingham docks, but after a visit by Winston Churchill and the Duke of Kent in 1940, we moved down to Shepherdswell. Our two 12in how-itzers were named 'Cleo' and 'Sheba'. 'Sheba' was stationed at Eythorne for a short while after we arrived, but when another battery arrived at Eythorne, 'Sheba' rejoined us at Shepherdswell.

Sunday 8 September
12.00hrs: Nine HEs at St Margaret's.
   19.58hrs: One SH dropped at Wallets Court Farm – it passed right through the farmhouse.
   The South Foreland lighthouse, and both North and South Goodwins light-vessels were illuminated to assist the navigation of destroyers on an E-boat sweep along the French coast.
   'Winnie' fired one round at Basin Canot in Calais Harbour.
   Six HEs dropped (24 seriously damaged; 80 slightly damaged; 4 seriously injured; 16 slightly injured). One bomb fell in the garden of an empty house in St Leonard's Road.

'Sheba' at Shepherdswell. 'Sheba' and 'Cleo' were 12in howitzers belonging to the 5th Super Heavy Rail Battery; they were stationed on the sidings at Eythorne and Shepherdswell stations.

Monday 9 September
We watched the bombing of the French coast from here.
  Blockship *Alfred Colebrook* sunk in Richborough Channel.
  'Winnie' fired four rounds at Framzelle gun batteries.

Tuesday 10 September
'Winnie' fired one shot at Calais Harbour.

At St Margaret's work had now started on the construction of firing spurs at Decoy Junction; and a stable siding at Townsend Farm had been completed by mid-September. Ex-Sapper Peter Kalla-Bishop, serving with No. 195 Railway Operation Company RE, recalls that 'block posts' were used for signalling on the Martin Mill Military Railway.

> The block posts at Martin Mill and RDF junction were in tumbledown sleeper and timber huts. The next block post was at Decoy Junction, in a neat little thick-walled reinforced concrete hut. Except that there were no windows (remedied by cutting a light in the door), this hut seemed just the thing for a block post when the line was about to open.
> The first blocksman in it saw Royal Marine (Construction Unit) carpenters adding a peculiar cylindrical extension on to the hut, but he was too close to recognize that it simulated a gun-barrel. Later that morning he was difficult to raise on the telephone, and when he finally answered, he reported indignantly that he had been machine-gunned. He was machine-gunned again in the

afternoon, but later the German airmen recognized the place for the decoy that it was and he was left in peace.

Wednesday 11 September
Shelling from Cap Gris Nez; we replied. Bombs dropped in the sea just off Wellington Parade. Car and nurse went to the Royal Hotel to attend a woman suffering from shock.

15.45hrs: Six HEs dropped at Worth (2 seriously damaged; 10 slightly damaged; 2 slightly injured).

17.05hrs: Two HEs dropped at Worth. HEs and IBs dropped at St Margaret's.

'Winnie' bombards Calais Harbour and battery.

Albacore L7098 of No. 826 Sqn crashed at Staple after a flight of six aircraft was 'bounced' by Bf109s over the Channel.

So desperate was the state of our air defences at this time, that flights of Royal Navy aircraft, including biplane torpedo-bombers were used for patrolling the coast. They were also engaged in night-bombing targets at Calais and Boulogne, so this crash could have been the result of anti-aircraft gun damage while over France.

Saturday 14 September
RAF night-raided shipping and Channel ports. Hurricane I L1981 TP-E of No. 73 Sqn force-landed at Ringwould after damaged by 109s over Thames estuary. Sgt A.E. Marshall was unhurt, and his aircraft recovered and repaired.

20.35hrs: Two HEs dropped at Elvington (1 slightly injured).

Sunday 15 September
We saw some big air battles; the Nazis came over in two waves.

12.09hrs: Bf109E-1 5197 of 1/JG53 crashed at Adisham Court after its petrol tank was set alight over Canterbury in an attack by F/O D.J. Lovell of No. 73 Sqn (although it was claimed by P/O J.S. Smith of No. 73 Sqn). Fw H. Tschoppe baled out and was captured severely burned.

14.30hrs: Bf109E-4 3266 of 7/JG51 crashed and burnt out at Nelson Park, St Margaret's, after its engine caught fire after a fighter attack by P/O W. Cunningham of No. 19 Squadron. Lt Kurt Bildau baled out; POW.

Monday 16 September
RAF carried out raid on invasion ports. Shelling from both sides of the Channel this morning.

Tuesday 17 September
Enemy made daylight raids over here.

15.20hrs: Big attack by enemy bombers on the East Kent area, crossing the coast at Deal.

Wednesday 18 September
'Winnie' fired four rounds at Calais.

13.10hrs: Bf109E-1 2674 1+ of 9/JG27 force-landed with petrol feed pipe severely damaged after combat with a No. 603 Sqn Spitfire over Canterbury (probably F/O W.A.A. Read). It landed at Willow Farm, on Royal St George's golf course at Sandwich; Gfr W. Glockner set fire to his aircraft, but was captured; POW.

17.05hrs: Bf109E-1 4842 10 + – of 4/JG53 crashed in flames at Guilton, Ash, after being attacked over Canterbury by No. 66 Sqn Spitfire (possibly F/O R.W. Oxspring). Lt Erich Bodendiek baled out severely wounded; POW.

Lieutenant Bodendiek was the Gruppe Engineering Officer, and was actually air-testing this aircraft himself, which seems rather a foolish thing to do over East Kent. 'Pop' Crier saw this fighter crash into a hop garden at Ash:

> I watched it coming down when we were working out in the fields, so we rushed over to where it had landed and when we got there we found it had gone straight into the ground and blown up. But there wasn't a big crater and not enough bits of wreckage lying on the ground around the place to fill a wheelbarrow!
>
> Quite a few hop-poles had been snapped off, but the explosion had sent the soil straight up, so when it came down again it filled in the crater; so the wreckage was just left there.

John Wilson was the messenger boy with the Ash Home Guard. He recalls that the local platoon were detailed off to guard the site of this crash:

> My father was the Corporal and kept the keys to the Headquarters and the ammunition store (containing ammunition, Mills bombs, a Bren gun and some hand-grenades) which were a couple of Nissen huts built on the sandpit next to the village hall in Queens Road, where we lived. I had to rush about on my bicycle to call out the other Home Guard posts around the village. The first post was at Cop Street, and all they had to defend the village with was a 12-bore shotgun. The Home Guard was also sent out to guard crashed aircraft, including the Bf109 which came down in Mr Marchant's hop garden.

Bf109E-1 2669 of 1/JG77 shot down off Deal by RAF, when returning from raid over Thames Estuary; Gefr Still killed. Spitfire I R6925 of No. 66 Sqn crashed at Coldred after suffering damage in combat over the Thames Estuary; P/O J. Mather baled out unhurt. Spitfire P9368 of No. 72 Sqn force-landed near Martin Mill; the aircraft was recovered and repaired, but pilot P/O J. Lloyd was seriously wounded.

At Martin Mill the local Ripple Home Guard appreciated one 'bonus' provided by these crashed Spitfires, as Ron Read recalls:

> I was serving in the local Home Guard at the time, and when the Spitfire land-ed near here only a couple of men were guarding it. Normally you couldn't get near a crash, because as soon as they landed the Army moved in to protect it. However, this aircraft had scattered some of its ammunition, so we were all right for ammo as its .303 Browning machine-gun bullets fitted our Lee-Enfield

rifles. So we picked it up and then used it for rifle practice on a target we had set up along the railway bank.

18.30hrs: Junkers Ju88A-1 3137 3Z+ED of 7/KG2 crashed and burnt out at Millbank Cottages, Eastry, after attacks by Red Section of No. 19 Sqn during an attack on Tilbury Docks. Major M. Kless (Gruppen Kommandant) and Obfr F. Lauth (Gruppe I.A.) killed; Fw F. Himsel and Fw F. Probst both baled out wounded; POWs.

21.00hrs: Fourteen HEs dropped in the marshes north of Fleet Farm, Ash.

This was a little too close for comfort for John Rolfe's family, as it was practically in their back garden, but it presented John with an ideal opportunity to investigate at first hand the human cost of warfare:

We lived at No. 1 Millbank Cottages, one in a row of the three bungalows near Eastry Mill. From about half past two in the afternoon Dad and I had been watching the dog-fights in the direction of Sandwich. We saw one enemy bomber coming from the direction of Statenborough, with its port engine alight, and flying below the level of the tree-tops at the Gun Park. Suddenly it turned to the left, straight towards us, and then Dad grabbed both Mum and me, and pushed us under the table, as the Junkers roared over the top of our roof; then we heard an explosion and the whole bungalow shook.

Dad told me to stay put, then shot out of the back door, up the steps of the bank to our garden. Of course a little while later I went out into the garden to see Dad and some of our neighbours standing on the garden path, looking at the great pall of black smoke and flames rising from the field behind our gardens. Dad spotted me and ordered me back indoors again, so then I went out through our front door, up the road and round through the mill yard. There were bits of wreckage everywhere – one of the wheels had been blown over the top of the houses right opposite Butcher's yard, and had landed between the hedge and a pile of bushel boxes; there was also some debris in Mr Clark's [the miller] garden. Meanwhile, ammunition and Very cartridges were exploding in the wreckage and things were whizzing about everywhere.

The village fire brigade had arrived by now, with their trailer pump towed by a Morris Commercial van, and as Dad and the others were busy watching the blaze, I ventured, keeping out of sight, a bit further along the hedge bordering Mr Prior's field, where the wreckage was still burning away. I spotted some pink 'lumps' in the fire, and thought at first that some of Mr Kemp's pigs must have got out into the field and had been killed – suddenly I realized that they were the limbless torsos of the crew. Later on, Mr Kemp found part of a hand and an arm by his greenhouse, and our other neighbours were asked to look round their gardens to see if there were any more human remains.

When the fire was completely out, a farmworker from Mr Izzard's farm came with some sacks and covered up the remains, and that evening Mr Bob Revell, the local fire chief, came up with his father the local undertaker. Accompanying them was Mr Harry Bugsden from the garage at Eastry Cross in his van, and they went to the wreckage and placed those crew remains in some big bags that they had brought with them, and took them away. Later, as I was walking up our garden path, I came across more bits of wreckage, a machine-gun, some maps, cine-film and hundreds of rimless bullets of the type used in German machine-guns.

Thursday 19 September
Ju 88A-1 of I/KG51 shot down by RAF 3 miles off Deal; fate of aircraft and crew not known.
   20.32hrs: Five HEs dropped around Eastry village, from Farthingate to Woodnesborough.

Friday 20 September
RAF again raided the invasion ports. RN Monitor *Erebus* en route for a planned bombardment of the German batteries was escorted to the South Goodwin light-vessel by the tugs *Muria* and *Lady Brassey*; shoot was abandoned due to heavy weather.

Saturday 21 September
RAF bombed invasion ports, and Coastal Command bombed a convoy of twelve merchant ships near Boulogne. Builders Messrs Collingwood were still working on Stockdale Gardens for Ministry of Works (possibly for Royal Marine Housing) until 28/9/40.

Sunday 22 September
RAF raided invasion ports.
   15.55hrs: Four HEs dropped at Hodling Wood, Eastry, east of the Dover–Sandwich Road.

The East Kent Light Railway, which meandered around the villages of Eythorne, Eastry and Ash, terminating at Wingham, also played a part in the anti-invasion defence plans. It also served the brickworks at Hammill outside Eastry, where there was a spur line into the work's yard. Les Poupard recalls that the siding was in constant use:

> We had a contract to supply dried and ground clay for use by our sister firm at Higham, British Cellacite, for the production of insulating bricks for furnaces. Their supply of diatomaceous earth had been cut off by enemy action. We must have sent some 7,000 tons during the war. We also screened sawdust from Sussex for the same product.
>
> We recruited any labour available, even some military personnel when they were in the area. The clay drying plant was used for reclaiming war-damaged nuts, cereals, etc. This came mostly by rail and one load of water-damaged haricot beans was forced to wait overnight outside Eastry station; the stench nearly evacuated the village. Drying foodstuffs in the rotary dryer had its problems as items such as groundnuts sometimes caught fire.

Monday 23 September
RAF raided Channel invasion ports. Large formations of enemy planes over here all day, with a lot of dog-fights overhead.

From the St Margaret's ARP logbooks:

10.00hrs: Dog-fight over St Margaret's; three aircraft seen shot down, one a Spitfire; a parachute was seen descending towards Ripple.

10.22hrs: Bf109E-4 6304 3+1 of 7/JG53 attacked during a freelance sortie over Deal, probably by P/O Bennions of No. 41 Sqn (or possibly by Boulter of No. 603 Sqn), and crashed into the Channel off Kingsdown. Uffz Karl Elbing baled out and was captured unhurt; POW.

'Winnie' fired four rounds at Calais – there was one large explosion.

14.30hrs: Avro Anson I N4914 of I CACU belly-landed at East Langdon after interception by over twenty 109s while acting as gun spotter for 'Winnie'. It dived to sea level and headed for home; Sgt J.H. Dowley was killed, and F/Sgt McConnell, Sgt McCallister and LAC John were injured. The fate of three Spitfires of No. 41 Sqn which were acting as escort not known (although one aborted with engine trouble).

According to the ARP logbook, the wreck of the Anson was guarded by No. 2 troop 5th Commando from St Margaret's, but it was damaged beyond repair.

From the fields around Ripple and Martin Mill, Ron Read and his brother would watch the enemy bombers crossing the coast:

> We worked between fourteen and sixteen hours a day, starting at 6.00 a.m. and finishing at 8.00 p.m. or even 10.00 p.m. at night during the summer, when double summer time was in operation. During the day fleets of bombers escorted by fighters would come in from over the Channel. As they got over here, their escort would wheel round and turn back across the coast while in the distance a section of RAF fighters would appear, and start to wade into the bombers; I saw that happen several times.

Tuesday 24 September

RAF again raided invasion ports, and minesweepers were busy in the Channel. Two formations of enemy planes came over here this morning; our fighters attacked them. 'Winnie' attempted to engage some E-boats in the Channel.

Blenheim IV T1794 of No. 139 Sqn went missing without trace 7 miles east of South Foreland after attacking E-boats. S/L M.F. Hendry; Sgts Arrowsmith and Davidson all missing.

Bf109E shot down by gunner of Blenheim R3698 from No. 139 Sqn while it was acting as top cover for the E-boats. Pilot's fate unknown.

Wednesday 25 September

03.00hrs: Three HEs and IBs fell between Guston and Tilmanstone.

Thursday 26 September

RAF again attacked invasion ports.

02.00hrs: Three HEs dropped at Betteshanger/Little Betteshanger.

Friday 27 September

RAF night-raided the invasion ports. British and German guns were shelling across the Dover Straits.

15.50hrs: Bf109E-1 3442 12+ – of 4/JG52 severely damaged, and pilot wounded by S/L G.L. Denholm (or P/O R. Barry) of No. 603 Sqn over Thanet. It crashed through high-tension cables and force-landed in Northbourne Park. Gefr Ernst Bosch wounded.

Spitfire X4352 of No. 19 Sqn shot down by 109s over Canterbury and crashed at Coldred; P/O E. Burgoyne killed.

Hurricane 1 V6576 of No. 242 Sqn force-landed near Sandwich with engine trouble; it caught fire after combat over Dover. F/Lt G. Ball unhurt.

Saturday 28 September

RAF raided Channel ports again.

Hurricane 1 V7497 of No. 501 Sqn shot down and burned out at Parsonage Farm, East Sutton, after attack by 109s over Deal; P/O Rogers baled out wounded.

Ju88A-1 3067 4D+BZ of IV/KG30 shot down while on bombing attack over the south east; Oblt Richter; Fw Laege and Uffz Fuchs plus another crew member missing, somewhere near Deal.

19.30hrs: Two HEs fell in fields at Bob Dere's Farm, St Margaret's.

19.40hrs: Four HEs dropped at Holt Street, Nonington, south of the mill; also IBs dropped at Ash.

Sunday 29 September

Daylight raids over here, as well as bombs dropped during the night at Ringwould.

Monday 30 September

We had six large daylight raids over this way; our fighters broke them up as they crossed the coast here, some of them involved in extensive dog-fights. There was shelling from both sides of the Channel. B. Bourner joined the depot as a driver.

02.10hrs: Second *Erebus* sortie to bombard the invasion fleet in Calais. 'Winnie' supported with a single round.

The threat of immediate invasion had diminished somewhat with the victory of the RAF in the Battle of Britain, but on the ground, an organized defence was still somewhat at a premium, according to the memories of Royal Artillery officer Lieutenant R.S. Shelford-Bidwell, who arrived in East Kent at this time:

> I myself, although young and inexperienced, was horrified at the vagueness of my task, viz to dig in my guns, establish an OP and shoot at anybody who seemed to resemble a German! Who was holding the beach in my zone of observation, or who might be invading it by night or day was never made known to me. Those half-witted 'dug-out brigadiers' would flit through Kent, tell us to move, dig new gun-pits and then start all over again in another area.
>
> Maurice Ley, a cynical old boy, on returning from an official visit to London, said to me at the time, 'Ginger' (my nickname), 'there is absolutely nothing to

stop the Germans reaching London within twenty-four hours after they land,
unless they try to get there by train!'

In late September the War Department allocated some ex-GWR 0–6–0 'Dean
Goods' steam locomotives, and three ex-LMS 0–6–0 diesel locomotives to various
railway-gun batteries based in the East Kent area. October saw the 8th Super Heavy
Battery arrive at Eythorne, and the 12in howitzers of the 12th Super Heavy Battery
moved to the Poulton Farm agricultural siding at Ash, and also Staple Halt. The arrival
of these railway-guns, together with their War Department locomotives, initiated major
track overhauls on the East Kent line, the old colliery sidings being extended at
Wingham. When the railway-guns were being calibrated at Eythorne they caused
disruption to train services, with trains being detained at Shepherdswell until the
practice had been completed, thus delaying passengers returning home in the evening.
Damage caused to the line resulting from the military operations was compensated by
the War Department, initially at an agreed figure of £400 per annum but later at £600.
The timber bridge over the Dambridge Stream, between Wingham Colliery Halt and
Wingham Town station was then removed, and replaced with an embankment of coal
dust and shale slate (probably from the old Wingham Colliery sidings).

David Downes recounts one story that sums up the whole ambience of life on the
East Kent Railway during wartime:

> The Super Heavies only fired once, in practice. Next day, a man from the War
> Office went round Ash village paying for the broken windows. The soldiers built
> a dug-out beside the line from lengths of rail torn up from the siding. When a vis-
> iting director of the Railway Company expressed disapproval, he was invited to

The little mixed freight/passenger train of the East Kent Railways was known to the locals as the
'Paddy' and was a familiar sight en route between Shepherdswell and Wingham. It is pictured here on
the Knowlton Bank outside Eastry South station.

To transport the rail-mounted artillery, several ex-GWR 0–6–0 23XX Dean Goods steam locomotives were drafted into the area. This example, No. 177, served with the 17th Super Heavy Battery, and was fitted with steam condensing gear to prevent its presence being betrayed to the enemy when moving the guns.

return the next day; and was surprised to find the siding had been reinstated overnight. The soldiers had driven an engine down the line during the night, taken up rails from another siding, and with them restored the one at Ash.

It was their custom to take the engine to Shepherdswell for their evening pint of beer. On every journey the most important item of equipment was the 'jack' with which to lift the engine back on to the track whenever it fell off – which, owing to lack of maintenance on the line, it frequently did.

There were also other Super Heavy batteries based along local main lines, such as the Dover–Canterbury line at Adisham, where Signaller 'Jim' Woodward was posted:

The 16th Super Heavy Battery didn't come to Adisham straight away, they had first been based at Grove Ferry, but they were not there for very long. Originally their HQ had been in a big house named 'The Lindens', but that burned down – I don't know what happened, it just went up in smoke, so they finished up at the station.

Our perimeter fence was all round the station, which was rather peculiar, because the trains would come puffing through, stop, and people would get off, as the station was still occupied by railway staff. It was also the only battery with a pub within its defensive perimeter!

Tuesday 1 October
RAF bombed invasion ports. Day-raids over here.
  At night *Erebus*, escorted by tug *Muria*, was shelled off the South Goodwins.

The 74th Medium Regt RA gunners at Ash managed to find some musical talent in their ranks, which they put to good use, according to Gunner Roy Baker:

> With Christmas approaching, it was decided to organize a concert. There was considerable talent among the lads so we organized a dance-band. This became very active, playing at various dances and parties; and even had a regular Saturday night booking at the Sandwich drill hall. Some of the lads started 'cribbing' about the band boys manoeuvring their guard duties to leave them free for band work, especially at weekends, so we decided to appease them by spending our next band earnings on buying a baby pig to be fattened up for Christmas. The pig had plenty of swill from the cookhouse and quickly grew big and fat, being duly killed in time for Christmas. Its throat was cut, and it was hung up by the rear feet in the cookhouse to bleed. I was on guard duty in that area that night, when suddenly in the middle of the night, there was an awful moan – it frightened the life out of me. Investigation proved that it was the pig that had made this noise. I didn't know a dead pig could do such a thing!

Thursday 3 October
HM Yacht *Sappho* sunk by an enemy mine in The Downs.

At this time, R.S Senior was serving with the 5th Medium Regt RA. His reminiscences were first published in the Tilmanstone parish magazine:

> At the back of Dane Court, running north towards Eastry, was a low bank, topped by a line of trees, overlooking grassy fields that ran as far as Dover Road. Here on this bank our guns were sited, their muzzles pointing in the direction of St Margaret's Bay, ready to fire on any attempt by the Germans to invade.
>
> Our social life, when off duty, revolved round three places: the local dance halls, the village pubs and the café at Dove's Corner. During the day, the café was the place to be. Tea and wads [cakes] disappeared like magic into hungry soldiers, but there was more to the café than just eats. Pinned or stuck on the wall were the names of various units that had passed that way, with messages from soldier to soldier and regimental signs and badges. Soldiers moving by on the main road would stop for a cuppa and add their contribution.
>
> In the evening it was in the local pubs that friends would meet. A game of darts or dominos, a pint of beer, or two if your finances stretched that far, followed by a bit of a singsong. Both the local pubs were popular: The Rice Arms (now The Ravens) would be the first port of call, then on to the Plough and Harrow on the Dover Road. Without doubt dancing was our favourite pastime; there were dances everywhere – in any place that had a hall. At Tilmanstone they were held in the old Oast House that once stood on the corner of School Road.

Friday 4 October
13.20hrs: Bombs fell in Middle Street and Union Street; also one on Deal Castle. One flotilla sent to Union Street (Nurse Harvey); and one flotilla to Middle Street (Nurse Dadd). I

attended to several cases of shock and minor injuries, and two bodies were recovered from the debris; although we were there until 7 p.m. we could not find the other two. 9 HEs (20 demolished; 51 seriously damaged; 127 slightly damaged; 8 killed; 4 seriously injured; 1 slightly injured).

These bombs were dropped over an area stretching from Upper Deal to Union Street, hitting properties in Short Street, including The Olde Victory pub and St George's Mission Hall, both destroyed. Shops and business premises in Canada Road and on The Strand were damaged, and houses in Union Road and the Wesleyan Hall (used as the Forces Canteen), also suffered damage. The water main in Upper Gladstone Road was cut, but the glass in a nearby greenhouse remained unbroken. Bombs also damaged one block of houses in Stockdale Gardens and properties in Dover Road and York Road. In Church Street, Walmer, near old St Mary's Church, the Walmer Baptist, Deal Congregational and Methodist churches were also damaged. One bonus was that the ugly Governor's Quarters at Deal Castle suffered irreparable damage, and so had to be demolished; there was also some damage to the Castle's dry moat.

When this raid took place, Mary Osbourn was in Messrs Pilcher and Chittenden's greengrocers in the High Street, buying extra tomatoes for the salads at the Old Beach Café, as it was half-day closing. While she was being served, she heard the droning of aircraft engines overhead, and when she glanced up she could see bombs falling from their open bomb-bays. Mary decided she had better get back to the café as quickly as possible:

Bomb damage in Middle Street, 4 October 1995. Sadly one family suffered several fatalities and injuries when bombs were dropped in Middle Street, and on Short Street. The Olde Victory inn also suffered damage. Later other property in the area was demolished to permit the installation of PWD beach-barrage oil tanks.

I went straight across the road and up by Simmonds jewellers and when I reached the corner of Middle Street, I decided to turn left through 'Boatman's Alley'. I had just got to the top, and had turned the corner when the bombs fell in Middle Street. There was a terrible noise as they came raining down, with bricks flying everywhere, and I was blown off my feet.

Mr 'Flint' Roberts come running along, and he stopped and asked if I was all right. I wasn't hurt, as the blast had gone over my head, but I was worried at losing the lettuce and tomatoes, and had lost my coat. Mr Roberts helped me to my feet and he then glanced down the little alleyway where one of the bombs had fallen. I wanted to have a look too but he would not let me.

I eventually found my new coat, draped round a lamp-post on the pier, with all the buttons pulled off it and big holes left in the cloth because I had had them all done up as it was getting cold. Several members of the Harris family were killed but the body of their son-in-law wasn't discovered until the following spring – by some men working up on the roof of the Clarendon Hotel.

Bomb damage to the Governor's Quarters, Deal Castle. The Luftwaffe did Deal a favour by dropping a bomb which damaged this monstrosity on the seaward side of Deal Castle. The Governor's Quarters were totally demolished, and the castle was rebuilt to the original design.

Sunday 6 October

Daylight raids by RAF on the invasion ports. This was our quietest night since the attacks began on 7 September.

00.15hrs: Four oil-bombs dropped in a field south of the Eythorne–Barfreston road.

12.00hrs: Twelve HEs dropped (1 demolished; 4 seriously damaged; 51 slightly damaged; 1 killed; 1 slightly injured).

Three of the bombs fell in the field west of Salisbury Road, one on 'Cobra Cottage' in Gladstone Road, and another on Drum Hill. Mrs Emily Burgess remembered that at Walmer Baptist Church, some of their Sunday school children had a narrow escape:

> My eldest son Leslie and his wife restarted the Sunday school when some local children started to return from evacuation, but they had to ask Police permission. The youngsters had to be sent home if the air raid warning went, but on this Sunday morning five bombs were dropped on Walmer and when the first one exploded, Leslie called 'Lie down' to the children. The church was damaged and the new house in Dover Road was hit.

Monday 7 October

10.20hrs: Six HEs and one oil-bomb were dropped at Stoneheap Farm, near Northbourne. The destroyer *Hambledon* was mined off South Foreland when *Vesper* was towing her to Sheerness. Also shells came over from the Framzelle battery, but only hit the South Goodwin light-vessel – perhaps it was mistaken for other ships on the enemy's radar.

This was the aftermath of an abortive attempt to repeat Drake's famous exploit of setting fire to the Armada ships and was code-named 'Operation Lucid'. Jack Neale was among the crew of HMS *Speedwell* of the 6th Minesweeping Flotilla, escorting these 'fire-ships':

> Our job was to sweep ahead of the force and only turn away when we were within yards of the Boulogne Harbour entrance. Following us were at least one old tanker and some decrepit merchant ships. These ships were filled with inflammable cargoes, including a large amount of Thermite (whatever that was).
>
> When we got into The Downs, we were ordered to sweep ahead with double Orepesa sweeps. This was a hopeless job in strong tides and a narrow channel, and with so little room of course we fouled a Channel buoy with our sweeps and dragged it about a mile out of its station until eventually we parted our sweep. The old fire-ships were underpowered and unmanageable, but we steamed on, giving little for our chances of getting back . . . but then the *Hambledon* struck a mine and the whole thing was called off.

Wednesday 9 October

07.45hrs: Bf109E-4 0966 10+ of 1/JG77 crash-landed at Venson Farm near Eastry when the pilot's dinghy accidentally inflated in the cockpit and he lost control; the aircraft was burnt by Lt Heinz Escherhaus before he was captured unhurt; POW.

With such large numbers of servicemen stationed in the Eastry area, a private enterprise canteen was set up in the village, as Mrs Finnis (formerly Miss N. Clark) remembers:

> The Clarks had a grocers shop in the village High Street, while my uncle owned the local mill and the bakers. Over the shop we opened a canteen for the troops, just like a NAAFI, and I remember seeing them queuing up the stairs in the evening. Dad found an old upright piano and a wind-up gramophone to provide some music for them. My mother, my aunts and cousins all had to help serve, making tea and sandwiches and doing the washing up, while I helped by clearing the tables. Aunt Edie, my grandmother's maid, who used to serve in our shop, also helped at the canteen.
>
> The Clarks were also responsible for delivering supplies to the local villages by van; and also kept an emergency food supply in the Caves. On one occasion I recall being taken into the Caves entrance off the Woodnesborough Road by my father, and seeing the tins of biscuits all stacked up.

Thursday 10 October

RAF bombed gun positions across the Straits of Dover and Calais. We watched guns on both side of the Straits firing.

Bf109E 6267 of 5/JG27 shot down (possibly by No. 41 Squadron) off Deal. Uffz Wiemann was wounded, and picked up by Seenotflugkommando.

Ron Read remembers this event:

> There were no tractors at our farm, so we had to plough with horses in those days. I remember hearing the 'clack-clack-clack' of cannon-fire one day, and round the end of the line of tall trees at the end of the drive to our cottage, came a British aircraft, with a German on his tail. Before they had gone very far, the British pilot half-looped his Spitfire and got on his pursuer's tail, and shot him down off Deal.

Friday 11 October

RAF bombed invasion bases again, and dive-bomb attacks were made by the Nazis over here. More shelling tonight, from both sides of the Straits of Dover.

10.30hrs: Four HE bombs dropped in High Street; one shop was in ruins, and from Queen Street to just beyond Park Street numerous shops were badly damaged, but casualties suffered only cuts and shock. One flotilla went from here to help. (1 demolished; 16 seriously damaged; 39 slightly damaged; 4 slightly injured.)

One bomb struck Faulkner's ironmongers shop, damaging both it, the Westminster Bank and Messrs Golden and Winds music shop, and rupturing both gas and water mains in the High Street. Marjorie Kemp was at work in Clarabut's on the opposite side of the road, when:

> I heard our 'roof spotter' Jimmy Annall running to sound the alarm bell as this bomb was falling, which I thought was a very brave thing to do. From an

upstairs window in Clarabut's I photographed the bomb damage to the Westminster Bank across the road, after it had been hit . . . which at the time was easy to do as we had no glass in the first-floor front windows.

13.50hrs: Bombs dropped again but no casualties and not much damage as they fell on the outskirts and around the level crossing.
   One HE bomb. (2 demolished; 2 slightly damaged; 62 slightly injured.)
   Spitfire K9870 of No. 72 Sqn shot down by 109s near Deal.

Monday 14 October

One HE fell on the Sandhills Road sewage works (8 seriously damaged; 24 slightly damaged).
   09.17hrs: Bf109E-4 1294 7+1 of 8/JG3 force-landed, its radiator damaged by aircraft from No. 229 Sqn (possibly Brown) while on a freelance fighter sortie. It landed near Princes golf course at Sandwich Bay; Oberfw Bauer unhurt; POW.
   Bf109E 0720 '12' of III/JG2 fell into the sea at Sandwich Bay, but could not be located. Its pilot, Oberfr Lux, was picked up; POW.

Tuesday 15 October

15.50hrs: Bombs dropped near Elliot's farm at Sholden. One flotilla went from here, but there was no damage and no casualties because the bomb fell in soft ground.
   Five HEs dropped on Belgrave Villas, Mongeham and Belmont Terrace, St Richard's Road.

Bomb damage in Deal High Street, 11 October 1940. Burying itself in Faulkner's ironmongery shop the bomb badly damaged an adjacent shop and bank, as well as properties from Queen Street to Park Street corner. Fortunately, it only caused four minor injuries, but severed both the gas and water mains.

Here members of the ARP rescue squad are making safe a badly damaged house in Belgrave Villas, Sholdenbank, Great Mongeham. During this attack District Nurse Miss Ada Perry was injured, and her mother killed when their house was bombed.

(3 demolished; 53 seriously damaged; 93 slightly damaged; 1 killed; 3 seriously injured; 3 slightly injured).

17.54hrs: Two HEs dropped near Betteshanger Colliery.

Wednesday 16 October

War Savings in Deal had reached £200,000.

Destroyers *Walpole* and *Garth* rendezvoused at North Goodwins light-vessel before the second bombardment of Calais.

Thursday 17 October

British long-range guns shelled E-boats in the Dover Straits.

13.20hrs: Two HEs fell in fields at Venson Farm and at Knowlton Court, Eastry.

21.30hrs: Gas alert in force (possibly a practice one).

Mr R.L.J. Eames was now working on the Gas Decontamination Centre at the Cemetery Road ARP depot. From now on Vera Dadd's diary contains entries about 'gas alerts' when weather conditions were favourable.

There was also another 'secret weapon' to deter any enemy invaders from landing on our local beaches. Installation of the Petroleum Warfare Department (PWD) 'beach barrage' had started and Mr Bernard Kimpton had been closely involved with its development from the earliest days:

One item which we had plenty of in Great Britain was fuel oil as we had stopped exporting it when war broke out, so the first thing that was done was to lay the pipelines. We had put short lengths of beach barrage in other places, including Thanet, but our main installation was between Kingsdown and Sandwich Bay. We placed the nozzles for the fuel behind the scaffolding, as the flames shot out about 40ft – and after about five minutes the temperature had reached about 500°C, and the pebbles would be 'dancing' – you couldn't go near the beach for well over an hour afterwards. The beach mine fields had to be cleared before we could start work, but we still had to be careful as we had to know our way in through the defences. Even so, we lost three men on Walmer beach.

There were separate fuel tanks for each length of pipeline, and we could manage to pump almost a mile from each pumping station. These 30ft x 9ft diameter cylindrical tanks were delivered by rail to Deal or Walmer station and we used to collect them and take them to where they were going to be installed. Galvanized corrugated iron sheeting was used when we were sinking them into the beach.

We started the installation up by the Royal Marines' rifle-range near the old holiday camp at Kingsdown, but left gaps in front of Walmer lifeboat house and the gun batteries at Walmer, Deal and Sandown castles. We also left a gap by the pier and the strong point at the end. The pumps for this section were in the cellar under the floor of the bar at the Clarendon Hotel. The pipes went under the road and across the Parade, and were laid from the old public toilets near the top of King Street as far as the 'Port Arms'.

All our fuel was delivered by camouflaged road tankers, so each installation had its filling point at the rear, near to a road.

At the back of the Clarendon Hotel we had to demolish two houses to get into the site in Short Street (damaged in the raid of 4 October) because there was a maze of narrow roads and alleyways at the back. To try and turn a 30ft x 9ft tank was impossible, so they just pulled down the two houses, one of which had been a bookmakers, and we used to have fun reading all the old betting slips. These two tanks were then covered with tons of shingle, with sandbags placed on top, then a brick wall was built across the front, between the Clarendon Hotel and Guilford House.

Our pipeline continued right down to Sandown Castle, where it met up with the pipeline from Sandwich Bay, which continued right down past Princes golf club to the River Stour.

Another of the PWD's schemes was the 'defile flame trap' where a narrow stretch of road was provided with perforated pipes along each side, through which petrol would have been hand-pumped. The petrol would then be set alight by some brave 'volunteer' firing a Very pistol cartridge as it flowed down the road. The instruction given was to wait until an enemy vehicle was at the narrowest point, and then set off the trap, hopefully both destroying the vehicle or tank and also blocking the roadway. The main roads into Deal were equipped with this form of defence, with pipes at London Road, by Sholden Church (along the cemetery wall), on the walls of the St Richard's Road railway bridge, and at the Thompson & Son's Walmer Brewery on Dover Road, Upper Walmer. Stuart Harlow remembers that when this installation was tested, the local Walmer Fire Brigade had to stand by in case of any accidents:

I did see it tested once. The pipes ran along the brewery wall and there were tanks of petrol and a hand pump, so that petrol could be sprayed on to the roadway. To witness the test we had a brigadier, a colonel and a major present. When the petrol ran down the road, one of the Army chaps set it alight by throwing a 'Molotov cocktail' [bottle of petrol with a lighted wick] into the road. Although the flames didn't damage the roadway too much, they did set fire to a nearby garden hedge, which we managed to extinguish quite quickly. After this had been done, the brigadier came up and congratulated us on our good work, and even gave the leading fireman a £1 note for the lads to have a drink.

Similar installations were positioned in Lower Street, Eastry, on Bay Hill at St Margaret's, and at the narrow entrances to the town of Sandwich, including along the Ropewalk in New Street and on the Sandown Road bridge.

Friday 18 October
Guns in action on both sides of the Straits of Dover.
  13.15hrs: Three SHs at St Margaret's. 'Winnie' fired one unobserved shot at Cap Gris Nez.

Mrs Pam Andrews was an ATS girl based at St Margaret's:

I was working for the garrison engineer of the DCRE, and my office was in a bungalow along the cliff top, where I answered the telephone switch-board and typed. I used to check all the requisitioned buildings for damage after the service people had

'B' Watch at Denne's Yard AFS fire station, photographed in August 1940. The tanks and pumps at Bert Evans' garage in the background would have been rendered useless by these men should an invasion have occurred. Stuart Harlow is on the left of the front row.

vacated them. The clerk of the works, an elderly civilian gentleman, used to be my partner for this job. There was no glass left in the windows of our bungalow, just cardboard as we were constantly shelled from Calais and Boulogne, and on a clear day we could see, with the naked eye, the railway-gun at Calais across the Channel.

Very often I was taken through a gap in the beach defences on to the beach at Deal or Walmer, to take notes on the progress of the building of the coastal gun emplacements. The Pioneer Corps were the builders, and the Royal Marines were in charge. I did feel quite important doing this duty as I was then still very young, as indeed were all eight of us girls who were billeted at Eastry. After we were bombed out, we were moved to Sandwich.

Sunday 20 October
Heavy shelling from both sides of the Straits of Dover.
   10.05hrs: Two SHs west of St Margaret's. 'Winnie' undertook three unobserved shoots on three enemy batteries.

Monday 21 October
Shelling by enemy guns across the Straits of Dover. Purchase Tax comes into operation.
   17.00hrs: One SH at Newsole Farm, Coldred.
   20.41hrs: Gas alert in force.

Tuesday 22 October
Plenty of dog-fights over this part of the coast. Shelling from both sides of the Straits of Dover.
   07.40hrs: Bombs dropped along Blenheim Road causing severe damage and minor casualties; 18 HEs (19 demolished; 146 seriously damaged; 196 slightly damaged; 1 killed; 3 seriously injured; 10 slightly injured).

These bombs fell in a line from 95 Blenheim Road to 1 Wellington Road; among the properties damaged were the Oak & Ivy pub and St Thomas' Roman Catholic Church. Lew Hilson, who was on his way to work, remembers the raid:

> One morning we had got down to Deal station when the siren went and we could hear the bombers coming over and we could also hear the bombs coming down. So Vic Weston and another bricklayer and I all rushed over the open big fireplace in the waiting room and finished up squeezing into the chimney opening. We sheltered there while listening to the explosion of the bombs in Blenheim Road – Boom! Boom! Boom!

08.15hrs: Eleven HEs dropped in open country near Eastry.

Thursday 24 October
14.10hrs: Three HEs fell at Martin Farm (2 killed; 1 seriously injured).
   20.40hrs: Gas alert in force.
   21.59hrs: Five HEs dropped south of Walmestone (in Staple Parish).

The second bombing raid on Blenheim Road on 21 October 1940 resulted in damage to properties from Gilford Road corner (seen here) to Wellington Road, and included the Oak & Ivy pub and St Thomas' RC Church and presbytery. Father Measures took to sleeping in his garden shelter after this raid!

Friday 25 October
Daylight raids. Many dog-fights over here as our fighters turned them back. A convoy was also shelled from the French coast; our guns replied, and no ships were damaged.
   17.50hrs: Raid on a convoy out here. Heavy ack-ack fire from ships. Mr Clark of Walter Street was injured by shrapnel, and was taken to Park ARP centre.
   21.20hrs: Gas alert in force.

Saturday 26 October
02.30hrs: One HE dropped at Marshborough, and one at Beacon Lane, Eastry.
   21.30hrs: Gas alert in force.

Even getting to and from work could be a hazardous operation, and relief fireman Alan Onions was less fortunate than most working on the East Kent line as he worked 'split shifts'. This involved travelling to and from home twice a day. But it was the darker winter days, and the night blitz on London, which Alan found most hazardous:

> One of the things you had to be careful about was firing at night, as there would be a great flare of light which came up when you opened the firebox door to fire the engine. We tried putting tarpaulin sheets over the back of the cab to cut down the light. It was a bit scary when there were aircraft about overhead, but we had enough sense not to fire the engine when that happened. There were some sharpish inclines, such as that coming over the rise at

Knowlton, or at Coldharbour, and I can remember being a bit nervous in case we should have to fire there when there were aircraft about.

From the ARP logbook:

Sunday 27 October
12.08hrs: Enemy aircraft reported descending into the sea in flames, 2 or 3 miles off South Foreland lighthouse; enemy rescue boat came out to search.

Monday 28 October
17.15hrs: Bf109E-4 5153 5+1 of 9/JG3 force-landed near Wotton crossroads, West Court Farm, Shepherdswell after damage by No. 74 Sqn Spitfires. Oblt Egon Troha (Staffel Kapitan) was captured unhurt; POW.

Tuesday 29 October
Italian bombers, protected by German fighters, took part in raids; many dog-fights over here.
   20.40hrs: Six HEs dropped (22 seriously damaged; 27 slightly damaged; 1 military killed; 5 slightly injured). Four HEs dropped in pasture and woodland at Nonington.

The bombs fell in Cornwall Road, Cemetery Road, and near the railway bridge in Telegraph Road. My uncle Leslie can remember seeing an Italian aircraft flying by after dropping a bomb in front of the Officers' Mess at the RM depot, and on the railway line south of Cornwall Road. There was some damage to the railway bridge,

The wreckage of Oblt Troha's Bf190E at Wooton is here being raised on to its wheels after his crash-landing near Wooton crossroads on the West Court Downs, Shepherdswell. On the cowling (foreground, right) can be seen the unit crest of JG53 and the name 'Erika'.

and houses in Telegraph Road were badly damaged. The officer killed at the RM depot was Temporary 2nd Lieutenant R.P. Nelson.

During this month, work on the installation of the second 14in gun, sited to the north in the valley behind St Margaret's-at-Cliffe, was well under way, the mounting being delivered by road to the village. During the following month Mr Eames was busy erecting air raid shelters in Silver Street and reinforcing one at the ARP depot in Western Road.

From the St Margaret's ARP logbooks:

Friday 1 November
'Winnie' fired two rounds at Sangatte and Wissant.
   12.00hrs: Minesweeping trawlers making for Dover were shelled off St Margaret's Bay.
   14.37hrs: Coastguards reported shells still landing in the sea 2 or 3 miles off Leathercote Point.
   Hurricane V6879 of No. 605 Sqn shot up over Canterbury and crashed into woods at Adisham. Sqn/Ldr McKellar was killed.

Saturday 2 November
'Winnie' again engaged a target at Sangatte.
   13.10hrs: Bombs dropped in Beaconsfield Road, behind Deal Castle in Victoria Road, and in Deal Castle moat; one flotilla sent out; 1 killed, 1 badly shocked and 1 with minor cuts, and some dead fowls.
   Two HEs (3 demolished; 2 seriously damaged; 286 slightly damaged; 1 killed; 1 seriously injured).

One bomb fell beside the Deal Castle moat while the other scored a direct hit on a row of cottages in Beaconsfield Road; 6, 6a and 8 Beaconsfield Road were demolished, and many more houses were damaged in Beaconsfield, Victoria and also in Castle Road.

17.48hrs–18.55hrs: Fourteen SHs at Reach Court, St Margaret's, near the railway line and along the A258 Deal–Dover Road. One HE fell on Sims garage, Kingsdown Road, Walmer (1 seriously damaged; 4 slightly damaged; 4 slightly injured).

Monday 4 November
RAF carried out raids on Channel ports.
   20.00hrs: One HE dropped 200 yards north-east of Richborough Castle.

Tuesday 5 November
00.45hrs: Four HEs dropped in the marshes at Hacklinge, Worth.
   14.27hrs–16.30hrs: More than forty-two enemy fighters in action over convoy off Deal.
   16.00hrs: Two HEs dropped in St Richard's Road, three houses – nos 252, 257 and 259 – slightly damaged, but only minor casualties.

Four HEs and one IB fell at Kingsdown on open ground; no damage and no injuries.
16.15hrs: Three HEs dropped at Goodnestone.

Ken Patterson and his family had two narrow escapes from the bombs which dropped on houses in Deal and Mongeham:

> We had been living at 2 Belmont Terrace in Mongeham Road but had recently moved to 255 St Richard's Road. Just after our move Belmont Terrace was severely damaged by a bomb, which destroyed a house just up Mongeham Road, and everybody had to be re-housed. Within a few weeks, a bomb dropped in front of 255–259 St Richard's Road, blowing a row of poplar trees out of the ground.
>
> Because this bomb had dropped in soft earth, there was only very minor damage to the houses, but the Council's repair gang worked all through the night restoring the road and services. At this time our Anderson shelter had not been erected at our new house, and so we were in my grandparents' shelter at No. 215 when this bomb fell.

Wednesday 6 November
04.30hrs: Two HEs dropped in fields at Eastry.
  22.08hrs: Gas alert in force.

Thursday 7 November
14.20hrs: Two HEs dropped in Herschell Road. Direct hits on two houses, but no serious casualties (3 demolished; 6 seriously damaged; 10 slightly damaged).

Friday 8 November
10.30hrs: Slight casualties caused by cannon shells at Nonington. Tug *Muria* sunk by mine off North Foreland.
  17.00hrs: Hurricane V6922 of 419 Flt (attached to No. 46 Squadron) crash-landed at Ripple crossroads, Ringwould; F/Lt Farley OK.

Ron Read remembers this crash well, as it happened just down the road from his home at Ripple Court Cottages:

> The pilot nearly got away with it, he landed wheels-up in the field just down the road and if there hadn't been a bank in the way, he would probably have been all right. As it was the plane hit this bank, cartwheeled over and the engine split off and landed some 80 yards or so away in the field. Mr Griffin, who lived at 'Folleys', the bungalow by the crossroads, went out to help the uninjured pilot out of the wreckage. The following day the pilot returned to the spot and made it his business to seek out Mr Griffin and thank him.

Saturday 9 November
RAF bombers attacked docks at Boulogne and Calais.

Not all the graves in the military section of the municipal cemetery in Deal contain Allied personnel. The bodies of these three aircrew of a Dornier bomber were washed up on the beach in November 1940 and were buried in Deal Cemetery, where they still lie alongside their former foes.

20.40pm: Do17Z 3495 U5+BM of 4/KG2 crashed into the sea off Kingsdown; cause unknown. The bodies of Uffz H. Fischer; H. Reinsch and L. Kaluza were washed up on Walmer beach; the body of Lt G. Mollenhauer was not found.

Sunday 10 November
20.00hrs: Sixteen HEs and two UXBs dropped along a line from Ashley to Studdal.

Monday 11 November
09.15hrs: Three HE bombs dropped near Corporation Yard at Western Road and in St Patrick's Road; but no serious casualties. Mrs Cox removed to hospital. You should have seen us move! We were all having dinner at the depot when we heard the bomb falling! (28 seriously damaged; 60 slightly damaged; 1 slightly injured.)
15.51hrs: Three HEs fell near Granville Road, St Margaret's (1 killed; 3 slightly injured).

One bomb fell at the back of 'Byron Lodge' and caused damage to properties in St Patrick's Road, St Andrew's Road, and also at the entrance to the Corporation Yard in Western Road. Some damage was also done to the greens of North Deal Bowling Club.

Wednesday 13 November
Our long-range guns fired salvoes across the Straits of Dover. Two HE bombs fell near the Royal Hotel and off Central Parade; the only damage was to the beach scaffolding and there were no injuries.
11.30hrs: One HE fell north of Great Knell Farm, Ash, and another near Telegraph Hill, Northbourne.
15.05hrs: Nine SHs in St Margaret's area (2 slightly injured).

Thursday 14 November
Trawler *The Boys* foundered in The Downs during a storm. Spitfire IIA P7386 of No. 74 Sqn crash-landed at Sandwich after being shot up by 109s over Dover; P/O W. Armstrong baled out.

14.19hrs: Junkers Ju87B 0436 J9+ZL of 9/StG1 shot down by No. 74 Sqn off South Foreland. Obgfr Bietmeyer believed taken prisoner; Obgfr Schmitt killed.

14.30hrs: Junkers Ju87B-2 5641 J9+BL of 9/StG1 ditched 2 miles off South Foreland while on sortie over convoy 'Bounty'; it was shot down by P/O Park of No. 74 Squadron; Olbt O. Blumers baled out and was picked up by MTB and taken prisoner; Gefr W. Koch was killed.

Junkers Ju87B of 9/StG1 ditched as above; Uffz Muller rescued; POW. Bf109E-4 4096 of 9/JG51 shot down by S/Ldr Mungo-Park north-east of Dover; Oblt Schnell rescued by Seenotflugkommando.

16.45hrs: Ten SHs fell at Station Road, St Margaret's, damaging four houses.

On this day, yet another Stuka was claimed by 160th Railway Construction Coy RE at St Margaret's Bay, as H.F. Flak remembers:

> At one time a Sergeant Steele and myself were standing by with a Lewis gun, when our company was attacked by some Stukas. Sergeant Steel managed to hit one and it crashed in the Channel. In front of us on the heights were several black boxes about 16in square, and we were told that, in the event of enemy parachutists being dropped, these would be fired up at them.

Friday 15 November
09.01hrs: Shells fell in Kingsdown Road, at St Margaret's. The tug *Guardsman* sunk by mine off North Foreland; mine-laying carried out off Deal.

Hurricane I P2560 of No. 605 Sqn shot down at Eythorne during Bf109 hit and run raid over Dover; P/O R.E. Jones baled out.

Saturday 16 November
16.15hrs–08.51hrs: Shelling at St Margaret's.

20.50hrs: Heinkel He111H-3 6897 V4+JH of 1/KG1 shot down by LAA and crashed south-west of the Palm Tree crossroads, Woodnesborough. Lt H. Pranesburger; Fw E. Mileska; Uffzs H. Wendtland and L. Muege were all killed.

Sunday 17 November
Gun duel across the Straits of Dover.

'Winnie' fired three rounds at Framzelle battery, and after this shoot it was noticed that its performance was falling off; the barrel was changed the following month.

Monday 18 November
12.51hrs–13.47hrs: Shelling at St Margaret's.

Tuesday 19 November
10.30hrs: Shelling at St Margaret's.

Wednesday 20 November
One HE fell at Adisham Court Farm.

Thursday 21 November
09.02hrs–11.12hrs: Shelling at St Margaret's. One cottage was damaged and one person slightly injured.

Friday 22 November
11.30hrs: Two HEs dropped in field half a mile west of East Langdon Church.
   14.15hrs–15.04hrs: Six SHs at St Margaret's.
   23.15hrs: Parachute mine fell on Johnson's Cottages adjoining Snowdown Colliery (2 demolished; 10 seriously damaged; 3 killed; 7 seriously injured; 3 slightly injured).

Saturday 23 November
09.32hrs–10.19hrs: Ten shells fell on St Margaret's.

Sunday 24 November
15.45hrs: Six SHs at St Margaret's (five fell in the sea). Two HEs, one dropped near RM swimming pool, Walmer Green; shops and houses on The Strand were damaged (2 seriously damaged; 30 slightly damaged; 2 slightly injured).

Monday 25 November
08.50hrs–10.54hrs: Ten SHs fell about 2 miles inland from St Margaret's.
   18.37hrs–22.25hrs: Shelling at St Margaret's.

Tuesday 26 November
09.30hrs–11.38hrs: Ten SHs at St Margaret's.

Wednesday 27 November
RAF raided invasion ports. Daylight raids over here.
   08.30hrs: Spitfire IIA P7499 LZ-S of 421 Flt crashed at Cottington Court Farm, Finglesham, after attack by Bf109; P/O Keith A. Lawrence was blown out of the cockpit, but was picked up by RN vessel and taken to Ramsgate.

John Annall witnessed part of P/Off Lawrence's Spitfire crashing on the outskirts of North Deal:

> I was working for Mr Bill Oatridge, who ran a smallholding in Northwall Road, near the railway line to Sandwich. This morning I had just arrived at work and was out in the farmyard, when I heard the sound of cannon-fire above the overcast. Then there was a second report I'm quite sure about that.
> I looked up towards the north-east, where the sounds had come from, and saw a parachutist coming down out of the cloud. But I thought he must be a

German, as all parachutists were supposed to be Germans at that time! For some unknown reason, I went round the back of the shelter belt of willow trees alongside the footpath, and there on the ground was a Spitfire's wing. It was the right wing but was upside down, and was split from root to wingtip, with the two Browning machine-guns exposed and all the belts of ammunition showing.

I called Mr Oatridge to show him and he then went and telephoned the police station. Later that day a van came to collect it.

Thursday 28 November
RAF bombed invasion ports.
   11.50hrs–15.15hrs: Thirty SHs at St Margaret's; one person slightly injured.
   19.20hrs: One HE dropped on the Oxney estate, St Margaret's.
   During the night about a hundred IBs fell on the open ground between Ringwould and Kingsdown; and two HEs in open country at Ripple Court.

The German batteries were now getting into their stride, and as Lt Col Fellowes noted, constant shelling took place daily, 'the worst day being 28 November when three hostile batteries engaged us and about fifty shells were fired'. One of the Royal Marine officers, Captain Peter Hellings, DSC MC, was reported to have volunteered on one occasion to be hoisted up in a basket under one of the balloons, armed with a Lewis machine-gun in order to engage these attacking Messerschmitt fighters – an offer which was declined! Marine Stan Wyatt recalls this period and the precautions which were taken on 'Winnie's site:

> Bang! Crash! Oh, that's Jerry firing from Cap Gris Nez. So we all move to the other gun site ['Pooh']. Jerry was dropping his shells on the Dover area in an arc to Kingsdown and Deal. But he didn't worry us all that much because if he dropped his elevation, he hit the cliffs, and if he raised it the shells landed about 3 or 4 miles to our rear. But the fun started when we opened up. We could hit Calais harbour, or go about 19 miles inland by using an extra charge of cordite.

Friday 29 November
HRH The Duke of Kent visited the local gun-sites.
   10.20hrs–12.02hrs: Eight SHs 1 mile north of Leathercote Point at St Margaret's.
   16.20hrs–17.10hrs: Eight SHs at St Margaret's.

The narrow streets leading off the sea-front and the High Street in the northern end of Deal caused some problems when it came to the design of surface shelters for the local population. They could not be constructed in the small backyards, some of which were even too small for Anderson-type shelters, so they were built on the roads. Mr Eames recalled that in the months of November and December he had built three air raid shelters in New Street with 'mutual protection' – or in other words, in a row. These were followed by further communal shelters, one in Coppin Street and two in Exchange Street, while others were built in Albert Road, and another pair in the High Street near Union Street.

Even in parts of the North End of Deal where back gardens had enough room to construct an Anderson shelter, there could still be other problems, as Vic Skinner recalls happened in Sandown Road:

> We had our own little shelter in the back garden for which I dug down 6ft, but it is all beach shingle here so I had stones piled up right round the back door to about 6ft. Then I put it all back again on top of the Anderson shelter, building in sandbags all round, and made a very good job. Unfortunately, we used to get quite a lot of water in the bottom of it, but we had to spend a good many hours down there during the bombing and shelling.

Saturday 30 November
14.05hrs–15.57hrs: Ten SHs at St Margaret's.

In December 1940 two farm workers, Reg Blunt and William Harris, were each awarded the George Medal, for continuing to gather in the harvest along the cliffs despite being shelled and machine-gunned during the summer months.

The Stanhope Hall (now the Astor Hall) opened as a YMCA welfare club, while at St George's Hall Monday evening dances were organized by Fred Crump and Mr Bush. The parish hall at Walmer was also run as a canteen, affiliated to Toc H, and both provided some social life for off-duty troops stationed in the Deal area. Miss Peggy Oatridge was one volunteer who helped out at the YMCA canteen at the Stanhope Hall:

Many families were glad of their Anderson garden shelters when the air raids started in earnest. Lew Hilson and his brother shared the work of digging the shelter while their mother took the photograph.

> There always seemed to be plenty of ladies who helped with the canteen, and there was a wonderful spirit there. The ladies included Mrs Ken Crouch, the butcher's wife; Mrs Wakeham from the farm in Golf Road; a wonderful Yorkshire miner's wife, Mrs Wells, who came in every evening to cook the sausages and Miss Tann, matron at the Caxton Home in Alfred Square. There were the two Miss Matthews from Clarabut's, who always came on Sunday evening.
>
> We served the soldiers sausage and chips or sausage and mash, which I think cost 1s 9d, and tea at 2d or 3d a

mug, and apart from the sausages (which were mostly bread anyway) we had bread and butter of course. I was only on duty in the evenings, but the canteen was open all day long, and I think they probably did sandwiches during the day – filled with lettuce or something which was easy to obtain; but the boys were very appreciative.

Thursday 5 December

Enemy bombers and fighter-bombers flew over East Kent. There were gun-duels across the Straits of Dover.

03.20hrs: One HE dropped at Potts Farm, Guilton, Ash, seriously damaging the farmhouse.

One HE and one IB at Elliot's Farm, Sholden (nil damage or injuries).

18.11hrs–19.44hrs: About fifty shells fired at British convoy; seven landed near Oxney Wood at St Margaret's.

Saturday 7 December

Blenheim IV T2395 of No. 53 Sqn crashed at Deal on its return from a reconnaissance mission over the Hook of Holland. P/O Steel and Sgt Hemsley were killed, and Sgt Robson injured.

Monday 9 December

16.15hrs: Ten IBs fell on the road and in a field at Northbourne.

Tuesday 10 December

14.50hrs: One HE dropped at Shepherdswell/Sibotswold.

19.19hrs–19.55hrs: Six SHs at St Margaret's (1 killed; 1 slightly injured).

> One fell two yards over 'Peacemaker' which was parked with 'Scene Shifter' in the siding near Martin Mill Station. These two 13.5in mountings had been moved out of Guston Tunnel under cover of darkness in order that 'Pooh's gun could be sent to Dover to be turned round. The damage was comparatively light, some axle boxes being stripped, but one casualty occurred: Marine Mumford was killed by a shell splinter, which went through a railway block post made of sleepers 250 yards away, and hit him on the head. (Extract from Lt Col Fellowes' *War Dispatches*.)

Friday 13 December

19.25hrs: Two PMs and IBs near Guilford Hotel, at Sandwich Bay; there was some damage, and one person seriously injured and two others slightly injured.

Saturday 14 December

Day and night raids over here. Five HEs at Coldblow Farm, Ripple (nil damage; nil injuries).

18.20hrs: Five HEs near Kings Farm, Ripple (in Upper Walmer).

Mrs Burgess remembers this bombing, as she was living at Kings Farm, on the Dover Road:

The 13.5in gun 'Peacemaker' with its ammunition wagon. The larger mobile railway artillery, including the 13.5in guns 'Peacemaker' and 'Scene Shifter', were housed in the Guston tunnel, only venturing out, complete with ammunition wagon, to fire from the rail spurs on the cliffs at St Margaret's.

Winston Churchill and other VIPs visiting 'Pooh'. By December 1940 the second 14in naval gun 'Pooh' was ready to assist 'Winnie' in countering the German heavy artillery bombardments of the area. Prime Minister Winston Churchill, whose brainchild the idea had been, was proud to show visiting VIPs around the well camouflaged guns.

The operation of the Martin Mill Military Railway was not without difficulty, as this derailment at the catch points near Martin Mill station shows. The SR 0–6–0 diesel engines which collided were used to move the heavy rail-mounted guns from Guston Tunnel.

We dug our shelter in the back garden, but we preferred to use the big chimney arch between the ground floor rooms in our farmhouse. We were only attacked once, and one of our farmhands, who was on top of a ladder at the time, was always convinced that the wing of the German fighter had touched him. However, the bullets had cut the ladder he was standing on in two, and he fell head-over-heels into the hayrick. The fighter then flew inland as far as Whitfield and machine-gunned the water tower on St Richard's Road on his way back.

Sunday 15 December
20.30hrs: Seven HEs dropped at Friths Wood and Appleton Farm, Adisham.

Thursday 19 December
Little enemy air activity during the day.

Sunday 22 December
We boiled two Christmas puddings at the depot. 'Winnie's gun barrel was removed, ready for changing.

Towards the end of 1940 the various individual railway-gun batteries were grouped into Super Heavy Regts. Norman Chandler, who served as a driver with the 15th Super Heavy Battery describes the role of the mobile rail-mounted artillery thus:

The range of the guns covered the area between Rye and Hastings round to Deal and Dover, with various regiments overlapping each other. There were quite a lot of enemy ships going through the Channel, but we were not allowed

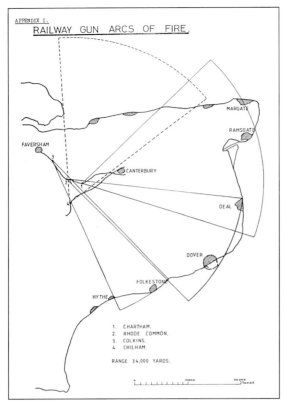

APPENDIX I.

RAILWAY GUN ARCS OF FIRE.

MARGATE

RAMSGATE

FAVERSHAM

CANTERBURY

DEAL

DOVER

FOLKESTONE

HYTHE

1. CHARTHAM.
2. RHODE COMMON.
3. COLKINS.
4. CHILHAM.

RANGE 34,000 YARDS.

Railway gun arcs of fire after redeployment. (John Guy)

to shoot as we were told that we were there for defence. The gunners had their own 'fighting train' made up of ammunition wagons, workshops, stores and gun spares – the guns themselves were camouflaged as goods wagons, with iron hoops placed over them and these in turn being covered with canvas. The remainder of the battery travelled in the 'living train', which consisted of sixteen or eighteen continental-type goods wagons. Each had been converted to take eight men, with bunk beds, a coal stove, folding tables and clothes lockers. The officers used old Southern Railway camping coaches; the train was completed when the cookhouse was attached with the food wagon.

All the personnel at Nelson Hall depot, 1940. They were C. Curling, C. Rowe, H. Neeve, A.C. Jordan, J. Dawson, S. Jordan, A. Baker, G. Clennant, F. Knight, S. Harris, P. Flynn, J. Howard, T. Chandler, A. Cave, Bob Foster and Fred Friend; the drivers were Pat Harris, F. Harrison, T. Twyman, S. Giles, P. Cave, F. Howland, C. Smith, F. Franklin and B. Bourner.

Railway cranes changing a 14in gun barrel. The intricate manoeuvring required to thread the barrels of 'Winnie' and 'Pooh' through their gun mountings may be gauged from this photograph. The Southern Railway's three largest railway lifting cranes were employed whenever piece exchanges had to be made.

Wednesday 25 December

We all had an enjoyable time at the depot in the morning.

Thursday 26 December

We had a bit of a celebration at the depot. I went up to the (miners') welfare club with nurses from the centre.

Sunday 29 December

Despite the bad weather, enemy aerodromes and invasion ports were attacked. The replacement barrel for 'Winnie' mounted in position by railway cranes.

In St Margaret's Bay the Wrens, whose job it was to monitor German radio broadcasts, worked in a very exposed position near the old lighthouse and they found the winter weather very cold. At least one, Betty Salter, suffered from frostbite:

> I was a Wren (Quarters) at St Margaret's Bay for six months from September of 1940. Strangely it was a happy time for me as a Steward. Seeing planes just 'collapse' into the Channel is not a happy memory, but missing a bomb was different from frostbite. I was the stoker for our outside boiler, and it was a very snowy winter. A treatment of soaking my feet in buckets of hot and cold water alternately was prescribed for my frostbite by the Royal Marine doctor – much to everyone's amusement.

CHAPTER FOUR

January–December 1941

The constant air raid alerts, some of which lasted for up to three hours, were caused by the Luftwaffe's continuing 'nuisance raids' which had started the previous November. These raids involved single, high-flying Bf109 fighters or fighter-bombers being sent over the Channel at regular intervals, thus keeping the defences on constant alert. By night the blitz on London continued, and the passage of bombers across East Kent en route to and from the capital made for sleepless nights when the alerts continued until dawn. To combat the threat of fires after the incendiaries had dropped, parties of 'fire-watchers' were recruited at business premises, while local borough fire brigades were taken under the wing of the new National Fire Service to increase their efficiency in dealing with major conflagrations.

Mrs Helen Ward had been working at the Marks & Spencer's store in Ramsgate and had already had a taste of fire-watching before she moved to Deal after her marriage:

> Night watchmen were employed by the firm, but they did not work seven nights a week so the older members of the staff did 'fire-watching' on relief nights. As soon as the girls reached eighteen they were either conscripted into a branch of one of the services or into munitions factories. So Mrs Cluer, the manageress at the High Street shop, her husband Len (porter and part-time fireman), and myself (cashier and wages clerk) were the only people over the age of eighteen. Len was on duty at the fire station during the night, so twice a week the fire-watching duties fell to Frances and myself – we twice saw the sky lit up as Canterbury burned!

The RM Siege Regt were now settling in at St Margaret's and as well as their military duties, they were involving themselves in sporting activities and village life, such as it was. Lt Col Fellowes recalls:

> Throughout the winter we managed to fit in a number of football matches, also some hockey and rugger, cinema shows and a few ENSA concerts being held in the local parish hall, where we had several dances, the music being supplied by our own dance band. Just before Christmas a concert party was formed by Lt Nurse RM, co-opting some WRNS and the village police sergeant, performing most successfully both here and elsewhere.

As well as undertaking their cable-laying work, the Royal Corps of Signals based at Eastry also took part in some Army Co-operation work. John Rolfe remembers:

> When they were at the old Eastry Isolation Hospital we would see a camou-flaged Westland Lysander [Army Co-operation] aircraft flying about, both land-ing and taking off from there. Later on, two poles were erected in the grounds, with a wire stretched between them, and a little Auster AOP spotter plane, with

a hook under the fuselage, would fly between them to pick up the message-bag attached to the wire. There were two more poles erected out at Thornton Farm, for the same purpose.

At night in still weather, the raucous noise of Motor-Torpedo or Motor-Gun boats based at Dover and Ramsgate could be heard, and their operations to engage enemy shipping led to some losses. They would undertake raids on the enemy coast to glean intelligence information, and perhaps capture some prisoners. The new RM Commando units were prominent in these operations, while Army ack-ack gunners volunteered to serve aboard the naval craft to protect them against attacks from the air. Royal Navy operations in The Downs were confined to the passage of convoys, and regular minesweeping.

In January 1941 a Variety Concert was held at the Regent Cinema, supported by film and radio stars, and managed to raise some £150 towards the formation of a Deal Red Cross depot, while Mr Eames was building pairs of communal shelters in Exchange Street, King Street, and in the romantically named Primrose Hill. The prolonged north-easterly gales during the winter months destroyed large sections of the beach scaffolding defences and the installations of the PWD's beach barrage.

Thursday 2 January
Inspection of anti-gas clothing by Mr Hubbard. Very good report.

Saturday 4 January
Meat shortage – tinned steak for dinner.

Monday 6 January
Mr Dawson [depot superintendent] interviewed the food controller regarding the lost butter ration; given ¼oz more tea (2¾oz); 27s worth of meat; 4 lbs sugar (1lb too much); 1lb cooking fat.

During the winter months, those on guard at lonely outposts found it difficult to keep themselves warm, but despite this there were some compensations when returning to base, as Marine E.H. Johnson recalls:

It was a very bad winter, and very cold. I remember guarding a crossroads at Ringwould with a corporal and four others, armed with a 1914-vintage Lewis machine-gun. None of us knew how to fire it.

Perhaps best of all I remember the girls of the NAAFI in the RM Barracks. They always had a smile, and would give us a cup of tea and a bun for free when our funds were low.

Tuesday 7 January
Air raid alert 10.46hrs–16.53hrs.
  Some severe frost, making walking dangerous.
  13.45hrs: Two HEs and UXB fell at each end of East Street Farm, Eastry.

Thursday 9 January

Frost very hard this morning, but it thawed a little on the way to work. Who scoffed our bread? This was the first time we had been short!

Friday 10 January

RAF deliver our first daylight raid on Hitler's invasion ports. It was a sight worth seeing, those young men en masse like that, and a mass of bombers, escorted by fighters. The raid was successful, and all our planes returned safely.

From the St Margaret's ARP logbook:

13.00hrs: L.E. Chapman on duty. Spitfire came down in flames between Bockell and Hope Farms, pilot baled out. Mr Curling of Hope Farm rang the ARP post to request an ambulance, and a fire engine was also sent. The ambulance was not needed as the casualty had already been taken to Portal House by the military.

During the year the St Margaret's ARP staff were responsible for the head-count of the persons in their area, as the annual census was to be waived that year. For January 1941 the total was 329, but this figure was amended the following month to 321 as one person had died and seven had moved from the area.

Sunday 12 January

Air raid alert 18.12hrs–22.50hrs.
  22.20hrs: One HE fell in field at Ash.

Wednesday 15 January

'Fight Fire' Order issued to everyone aged between 16 and 60.

Thursday 16 January

Air raid alert 09.10hrs–09.40hrs.
  From 20 January Wardens to blow whistles to indicate falling incendiaries.
  09.18hrs: One HE and one UXB dropped near railway line at Eastry.

Saturday 18 January

Today it was officially announced that all men and women between 16 and 60 are liable to be called up for compulsory ARP work in additional fire-watching. Heavy fall of snow. Quiet day.

Sunday 19 January

Air raid alerts 18.30hrs onwards.
  A heavy explosion was heard, and nearly all personnel reported to the depot.
  20.20hrs: Two Parachute Mines fell near the Sandwich–Woodnesborough Road, Eastry.
  20.36hrs: Control rang through and reported that the explosions were in the Sandwich area.
  22.15hrs: Two Parachute Mines fell at Wingleton Farm, Sutton.

Lt Col Fellowes noted that on Friday 24 January the Prime Minister, accompanied by Mr Harry Hopkins, visited the RM Siege Regt.

Tuesday 28 January
Air raid alert 12.15hrs–16.21hrs.
  13.50hrs: Seven HEs fell on Goldstone Marshes, north of Ash.

A public meeting was held in the Town Hall with reference to fire-watchers for business premises; three centres were allocated, these being at Mr Allen's hairdresser's shop in Broad Street; the Carter Institute in Middle Street and at St Andrew's Rectory, then on the corner of Union Street. Many people, both men and women volunteered for this duty, usually at their places of employment. Two of the local fire-watchers were rather over-enthusiastic when it was decided to hold a practice to test the time taken to respond to alerts, as Mr Percy Ponting recalls:

> The chief fire-watcher was Mr Allen, the hairdresser, and our headquarters were St Andrew's Rectory. One day we were informed that there was to be an exercise for all the different fire-watching crews, when an incendiary bomb would be set alight on some waste ground. A message would be sent to all the posts to see how quickly they could get there and deal with it.
>
> My pal and I were determined our post would win, so we both hid behind the wall with our ladder, a bucket of sand and a shovel until the messenger rode through the gate of St Andrew's Rectory on his bike. We then set off after him and arrived so fast that the chap who was going to set the incendiary bomb alight hadn't had time to set it going properly!

Wednesday 29 January
There was a proclamation calling up youths aged eighteen to twenty, and men aged between thirty-seven and forty.

Thursday 30 January
Air raid alert 10.49hrs–12.16hrs.
  10.55hrs: Nine HEs fell in line on the marshes at New Downs Farm, near Sandwich.

Friday 31 January
22.30hrs: Received a call from Control to send an ambulance to the Black Horse Hotel, as a man had injured himself and required some treatment. Sent FAP car, and also an ambulance. Party Leader reported on returning to depot that the casualty had only slight injuries; he was taken to Park Centre, and after treatment, was taken in FAP car to his own home, 'Dulverton' in Sutherland Road.

Also on this day, as Lt Col Fellowes noted, Mr Wendle Wilkie [President Roosevelt's Special Ambassador to the UK] visited the RM Siege Regt.
  A party of Royal Marine officers, including Lt Col Fellowes and some Royal

Engineer officers from the 160th Railway Construction Company, reconnoitred the site at Coldblow Farm, Ripple for a 13.5in railway-gun firing spur.

After the experiences of the London blitz, Deal was declared to be one of the special areas which required a fire-watching and stirrup-pump party to be formed in each street. Furthermore, static water tanks were built to provide emergency water supplies and seven were built around Deal. Mr Eames continued to work on the paired communal shelters in Alfred Square, Farrier Street, and Middle Street during February.

Tuesday 4 February
Air raid alerts 14.25hrs–15.09hrs.

14.30hrs: Bombs dropped, one HE in West Street, behind the Working Men's Club, blasting out windows round about, and another, which did not explode, on the High Street, between Clarabut's and Marks & Spencer's. One casualty with bruised back and shock. It was a good job that it did not explode or it would have wrecked a good part of that district. The UXB was rendered harmless next day. (2 seriously damaged, 1 slightly injured.)

Marjorie Kemp was at work in Clarabut's, next door to Marks & Spencer's, when this bomb fell:

> I well remember 'my' bomb which zig-zagged through the roof and down the wall, ending up in Marks & Spencer's window – without exploding. The dust and rubble were unbelievable. We have heard that conscripted workers in Germany sometimes managed to sabotage the bombs, making up the weight by filling them with sand or soil.

Stirrup pump practise at Cemetery Road ARP depot. Vera and her Nelson Hall colleagues are learning how to operate the stirrup pump to extinguish incendiary bomb fires.

Wednesday 5 February
13.07hrs: Two Hurricanes of No. 615 Sqn collided near the 'Roundhouse' at St Margaret's/Martin Mill crossroads; one landed at Appleton Farm near Martin Mill. P/O Wydrowsky (V6618) baled out but died later in the RM Infirmary; P/O Czernastek (V7598) was killed instantly.

According to the St Margaret's ARP logbook:

The village fire engine rushed to the scene, but collided with a military ambulance speeding on the similar errand. Both of the vehicles were damaged, one being put out of action. Both pilots baled out; one was killed when his parachute failed to open, while the other was only slightly injured and was taken to the military hospital at Deal.

Sunday 9 February
Air raid alerts 14.46hrs–18.05hrs.
   Bombs dropped in Sholden, and fire-bombs dropped in Archery Square, Balfour Road and Liverpool Road. F. Howland and A. Cave started delivering handbills about fire-watching.
   One IB fell on 17 Balfour Road; two HEs and ten IBs dropped on Sholden (1 seriously damaged).

This German 250kg unexploded bomb was put on display in Clarabut's, guarded by a Royal Marine. It had fallen between the side walls of Clarabut's and Marks & Spencer's, but fortunately did not explode.

Monday 10 February
12.45hrs: Saw a crowd of our bombers returning over here after a raid on the other side. Gee, a sight for sore eyes!

Tuesday 11 February
17.05hrs: Two SHs landed at Little Fredville Cottage, Elvington, 20 yards south of Terrace Road (1 slightly injured); plus another 200 yards from the first.

Wednesday 12 February
13.30hrs: One SH fell on Holt Street Meadow, Nonington (1 seriously injured).

Friday 14 February
Mr H. Cavell came in to have his hand dressed; he had been badly cut by some glass, and had to have five stitches put in at hospital.

Sunday 16 February
16.05hrs: One SH between Eythorne and Barfreston.

Wednesday 19 February
Removed a patient, Mr Griggs of 'Sunnyside', to hospital with stretcher and ambulance.

Thursday 20 February
Finished delivery of circulars. Fire broke out at 'Seagirt'.
  15.30hrs: Saw two parachutes coming down; two of our pilots had baled out after a fight over the sea. One plane came down in flames, and one parachute was on fire. Its pilot was picked up dead, the other was injured!

From the St Margaret's ARP logbook:

16.00hrs: Spitfire P7302 crashed in flames at East Langdon, pilot had baled out. ARP reported a parachutist in the sea east of St Margaret's – he was seen falling towards the sea off Hope Point; his parachute was in flames and he was seen to drop from it.

Saturday 22 February
Gave the remainder of the circulars to the cinemas on Mr Ford's instructions. Watched a big air battle over the Channel. Weather conditions favourable for gas alert.

Tuesday 25 February
Gas-masks are to be worn after 10.00 a.m. on sounding of first air raid warning.

Wednesday 26 February
Royal Marine Adjutant General visited the Siege Regt. (Lt Col Fellowes' *War Despatches*)

During February and March type C shelters were being built in Western Road and Albert Road, while Mr Eames was also working on some six-person domestic shelters in Middle Deal Road. At Martin Mill, the three ex-LMS diesel locomotives which had arrived during September 1940 were now replaced by three Southern railway C-type 350hp diesel-electric locos, Nos 1, 2 and 3. Peter Kalla-Bishop recalls an alternative form of transport for personnel on the Martin Mill Military railway:

An additional motive power unit was the Wickham petrol-engined platelayer's trolley. Our trolley was simply an open platform with a low handrail at one end. It bore no number and carried eight men in the normal way. Nevertheless, by dint of everyone hanging on to each other we carried twenty-two men on occasion. Exhilarating rides we had too, when we went for meals, for the driver of the trolley always went as fast as he could. Eventually, the trolley was put out of action when a mere twelve men were riding on it – it derailed at a pair of points and a Pioneer Corps man broke his thigh. After this we had to make do with an engine instead.

Saturday 1 March
£2.00 paid into Spitfire Fund by personnel of the depot.

Tuesday 4 March
Lady Clarke's car broke down at Margate. 'Minnie' Howland was the driver. The Ford V8 ambulance had trouble at College Farm – a child patient had to be taken up to hospital.

General Montgomery was inspecting the RM Siege Regt at St Margaret's, and other elements of the 43rd Division based in East Kent on this day. Ron Sommers also recalls a mass parade 'somewhere a little way outside Ash, and people waving from upstairs windows as we marched back past the 'First and Last' public house'.

Wednesday 5 March
The Ford V8 ambulance has gone to Gooche's Garage.
  00.11hrs: Weather conditions favourable for gas alert.

Thursday 6 March
Air raid alerts 11.40hrs–12.28hrs.
  Saw a Spitfire land over the Sandhills.
  11.40hrs: Four HEs at Little Napchester Farm, Sutton.
  20.29hrs: Weather favourable for gas alert.

Saturday 8 March
Removed Mr Turner from Bulwark Row in ambulance to the hospital.

Sunday 9 March
Air raid alerts 07.27hrs–07.43hrs.
  07.25hrs: Saw a huge formation of enemy planes split up by ack-ack fire, and Spitfires over the Sandhills. Bombs dropped at Ringwould.

Sunday 16 March
All girls aged twenty and twenty-one must register for war work by 19 April.
  20.07hrs: Weather conditions favourable for gas attack.

Soon after her bomb experience,

The RM Adjutant-General on a plate-layer's Wickham trolley on the Martin Mill Military Railway. He was paying an inspection visit to the RM Siege Regt at St Margaret's.

Marjorie Kemp became due for her call up, as she was single, not in a reserved occupation, nor caring for small children:

> I heard that conductresses were needed by the East Kent Road Car Company, so I applied to the local depot manager, Mr Chapman, and soon found myself in a job that was much more congenial than working in an office. I remember there only being three male conductors, but within a short time it was all females doing the conducting – but all our drivers were men, and a very considerate bunch they were too.
>
> We started on single-decker buses on the town centre routes, with a day to learn from the duty conductor. Within a few days we moved on to the Kingsdown, Dover and Canterbury routes, also the country routes to Betteshanger, Eastry, Staple, Eythorne and Barfreston.

On Tuesday 20 March there was an explosion in Deal, but it was not due to any bombing or shells. It occurred in Grange Road, Deal at the former home of the owner of Lambert's Laundry in Western Road. An object 'about four feet long and oval in shape' had been discovered by one of a group of twelve Canadian engineers who were then laying anti-tank mines along the Deal–Sandwich Road. Curious about the object, they had taken it back to their billets where, later in the day, it exploded, killing four of them and injuring several others. This incident was kept very quiet, and the house was re-built, which was an unusual occurrence at this period of the war. Mrs Mary Steenhouse was walking out with one of the Canadian sergeants, but even he kept the news to himself for three months:

Miss Majorie Kemp in 'clippie' uniform. By the end of the war all the East Kent Road Car Co. buses were crewed by lady 'clippies' as their male colleagues were called up.

> On the evening of that explosion at 'Southlands', my sergeant, who was a driver, was sitting in a jeep outside the house in Grange Road. He later told me that the whole front of the house collapsed when the missile (he thought it was a hand grenade or possibly an Italian 'aerial torpedo') exploded. He told me that he was very worried about it as his colleagues were trying to open it up – something which they should not have attempted.

Monday 31 March

A lady came in to have her hand attended to – the bone was badly bruised; she had caught it in the door in the blackout. We took her to hospital, then to her home.

Early in April supplies of the new light shell (1,250lb) for the 13.5in guns arrived so that their cross-Channel role could be carried out, and both 'Peacemaker' and 'Scene Shifter' returned to Lydden during the second week of the month.

Mr Eames was working on a shelter at Sholden (in Church Lane) and another on Walmer Green, and was also building up blast walls at Deal Water Works in St Richard's Road. Mrs Dobson, Mayoress of Deal, officially opened the United Free Church Club at the Victoria Baptist Church Sunday School Hall in Stanley Road, while Lady Reading, the president of the WVS paid a visit to Deal, where some fourteen ladies were on duty at the civic restaurants every day. There were also eight Rest Centres (for bombed-out families) and also a six-woman 'Flying Squad' ready to visit the site of any incidents during 'hit-and-run' raids. Part of this WVS 'Flying Squad' was the tea-car, which would be sent out after bomb or shell incidents, to provide refreshments for the fire brigade and heavy rescue squad personnel who were digging people out of the bombed buildings. Miss Peggy Oatridge remembers that the first vehicle was rather ancient:

> The car was kept down at Wakeham's Farm at Sandown, and I really think that it must have been used during the First World War. It had a long running board, and it really was antique, rather like those reproduction vehicles which are built nowadays. If we wanted to check if there was water in the radiator, we

Lew Hillson's father with some of the nursing staff of the Victoria Park FAP, 20 April 1941.

had to put a stick down inside it. Bobbie McGhee had this relic to drive every day and sometimes the thing wouldn't go at all, it was dreadfully difficult to drive, no syncromesh, just a 'crash' gearbox. Eventually she put her foot down and we got the Ford V8 station-wagon which the South Africans gave us.

Wednesday 2 April
A man came in with a head injury – we took him to hospital, where he had two stitches, then we took him home. Took Mrs Davidson to hospital with a haemorrhage.
   20.33hrs: Weather conditions favourable for gas attack.

Thursday 3 April
The borough restaurant was opened by the mayoress of Deal this morning at St George's Hall in the High Street.

Friday 4 April
Air raid alert 16.16hrs–17.37hrs.
   16.25hrs: Went over the North Deal playing fields and saw one of our planes shot down by two Nazis; it came down near Ripple. The pilot baled out, and was taken to the RM hospital here with a broken ankle.

Michael Payne provided the details of this incident:

> Two Spitfires were attacked by Major Adolf Galland of JG26 near Deal. Spitfire P7565 from No. 91 Sqn was flown by a Sgt Spears. He baled out near Deal from only about 4,000ft and was taken to a Deal hospital. The other Spitfire, P7783, was Sgt Mann's aircraft.

Saturday 5 April
Men aged between forty-one and forty-three to be registered.
   20.47hrs: Weather conditions favourable for gas attack.

It wasn't only shrapnel from enemy shells which fell in this area, according to Bombardier Signaller Jim Woodward, serving in the 11th Super Heavy Battery at Bishopsbourne. Their rail-mounted 16in howitzer 'Boche Buster' was based on the Elham Valley Railway, and was covering the invasion beaches from St Margaret's to Dungeness. Test firings were a feature of the months after their arrival in February:

> We had already fired 'Boche Buster' a couple of times by now, but one of our shells must have exploded over the Royal Marines depot at Deal, as the following morning a large piece of shell, weighing about 14lb, arrived back at our Battery HQ. Attached to it was a note from the CO at the RM depot which read 'Is this one of yours?' I was in the office when it arrived – and I wouldn't dare repeat what our CO said after he read it!

Tuesday 8 April
Air raid alerts from 21.57hrs onwards.
  20.51hrs: Weather conditions favourable for gas attack.
  23.15hrs: Three HEs dropped near Military Railway Siding at Coldblow (damage to lines and wagons).

Wednesday 9 April
Air raid alerts 20.43hrs–22.20hrs; 22.28hrs onwards.
  21.55hrs: Weather conditions favourable for gas attack.

Heinkel He111H-2 3148 V4+DJ of II/KG1 crashed into Channel off Deal, believed to be the victim of a night-fighter attack. Lt K. Martin; Fw W. Leisegang and Uffz K. Pauly all missing, but the body of Fw W. Such was found on Goodwin Sands on 22 October and buried at sea.

Sunday 13 April
Attended Church Parade at St George's Church; the mayor, councillors, firemen, nurses and all Civil Defence workers were represented.
  Hurricane of No. 71 'Eagle' Sqn force-landed between Each End and Goss Hall, near Ash. P/O J. Flynn uninjured.

Thursday 17 April
Air raid alerts until 04.59hrs.
  01.30hrs: Four HEs fell south-west of Ham, near Northbourne.
  04.06hrs: Two HEs on Princes golf course, Sandwich Bay.
  21.15hrs: Weather conditions favourable for gas attack.

Saturday 19 April
Air raid alerts from 20.51hrs onwards.
  A very noisy evening altogether, with planes, guns, etc.
  A landmine was dropped at Upper Deal, with terrific blast effect. The church and houses were wrecked, and windows were blown out in the High Street, but there were no serious casualties. 2 LMs (5 demolished; 11 seriously damaged; 24 slightly damaged; 3 seriously injured; 4 slightly injured). Damage was caused to 'Fiveways', 'Sholden Hall', several cottages and St Nicholas Church in London Road at Sholden.

My uncle, Leslie Collyer, and his wife Doris, were walking up Church Path this particular evening:

> We had been to the pictures and we had just reached the row of old cottages at the top of Church Path opposite the burial ground, when there was a terrific 'wallop', and suddenly the air was full of soot and dust. We had been walking up Church Path, but when we came to, we found ourselves walking down the path! A couple of hands reached out from the door of one of the old cottages,

pulled us in and a voice said 'You had better come in here quick!' We found ourselves in a passageway full of other people, and we stayed there for a little while until things had quietened down.

Monday 21 April
Air raid alerts 20.30hrs–22.37hrs; 22.48hrs–00.05hrs.
    Loud explosions were heard; a landmine dropped near Eastry – no serious casualties, but another very noisy evening.
    22.05hrs: Two LMs dropped adjacent to Nonington and Tilmanstone, slight damage.

The new triangular firing spur near Coldblow Farm had now been completed, apart from turfing and clearing up, and it was inspected two days later. Mrs Emily Burgess recalls:

> The Army put in a railway line just behind the line of trees known as Devil's Firs, at the back of Coldblow Farm, and on one occasion I crept over there and just lifted up the corner of a tarpaulin covering over a truck, and was surprised to find that it was full of great big shells.

Thursday 24 April
Air raid alerts 06.35hrs–07.41hrs; 08.12hrs–08.28hrs.
    08.23hrs: One HE at Snowdown Colliery, village machine-gunned; Tilmanstone Colliery machine-gunned, slight damage.

Wednesday 30 April
Tear gas was released this morning (practice gas attack) – no casualties. I was at FAP on the Central Parade.
    20.16hrs: Gas warning, weather favourable.

In May 1941 the first of the annual National Savings promotions was undertaken, and 'War Weapons Week' in Sandwich raised the amazing total of £50,170 17s. Deal War Savings Committee had arranged for a display of artefacts and equipment in the High Street, and as Marjorie Kemp proudly recalls 'My bomb was placed on display in the window of Clarabut's and was guarded by a Royal Marine' for the week.

Mr Eames was now working on a twenty-person communal shelter in Thornbridge Road, and another in Middle Street by Farrier Street, and a third A-type shelter at Walmer parish hall.

One of the ideas which General Montgomery introduced was physical training each morning, much to the chagrin of the RE Railway Operating detachment at Martin Mill. Peter Kalla-Bishop recalls:

> When I arrived at Martin Mill the detachment was well settled in. This easy-going routine was disturbed by a new General being appointed to the area of South-Eastern Command headquarters. He issued orders that got us out of bed

to do physical training in the station yard at 06.30hrs – our pleas that we were attached to the Royal Marines and thus came under the Admiralty notwithstanding.

From the ARP logbooks:

Sunday 4 May
Hurricane Z3087 of No. 601 Sqn shot down by Bf109s; it landed near Eastry; F/Lt H.C. Mayers baled out and was rescued unhurt.

Dog-fight over sea; a Lysander crashed into the sea, and a parachute was seen going in Dover direction.

Tuesday 6 May
Air raid alerts from 22.18hrs onwards.

19.56hrs: Gas warning, weather favourable.

22.20hrs: Three HEs at Aylesham (4 demolis' ed; 60 slightly damaged; 9 killed; 2 seriously injured; 3 slightly injured). One UXB at Ayles am Central School.

This last occurrence was probably caused by a German pilot wishing to dispose of his bomb-load after aborting his mission, and thinking he was safely over the Channel. Another village that received more than its fair share of stray bombing was Adisham, which suggests that the Luftwaffe pilots were still using the same methods as their First World War counterparts by following the railway lines on moonlight nights. The aftermath of the Aylesham tragedy is recalled by Les Poupard:

> There were two large buildings in use on the Hammill Brickworks site. One housed milling machines which we installed for grinding the local farmers' tail-corn, barley, peas, beans, etc. The chickens I kept there were appreciative. The other building was earmarked for use as an emergency mortuary, and I was the honorary mortuary superintendent. I can only remember the building being used once, which was after a bomb was dropped in Aylesham, when nine people were killed, including three children. The most distressing sight was a dead woman still holding her baby in her arms.

Thursday 8 May
Lady Clark's car sent to Ashford. B. Bourner took the Food Controller.

Spitfire P7734 of No. 609 Sqn shot down by Bf109 off St Margaret's; pilot safe.

This Spitfire was lost during a battle against the Bf109s of JG.3 over a dinghy, when a ditched pilot was spotted off-shore. Both sides wanted to rescue the pilot. The Luftwaffe unit involved in combat off Deal lost four of their Messerschmitt Bf109s, two being shot down into the Channel off Deal, while Lt J. Pfeiffer from 4/JG53 was shot down while he was engaged in searching for the other pilot. Enemy machine-gunning was also reported in Hythe and Deal.

Friday 9 May
Air raid alerts 22.55 onwards.

19.15hrs: Spitfire P7305 of No. 609 Sqn crash-landed on the beach at Leathercote point, at St Margaret's, after an attack by Bf109; Sgt Mercer injured.

23.30hrs: One HE fell at Ware Farm, Ash.

The rail spurs at St Margaret's were used for practice firings by the 16in howitzer 'Boche Buster' as well as the smaller rail-mounted artillery pieces. Jim Woodward recalls:

> We were nearly hit at St Margaret's Bay when we were ranging into the Channel; the Germans decided that it was time that they started shooting as well. I remember that there was an elderly couple standing by their cottage near where we were shooting, and every time we fired their roof lost a few more tiles. Then the Germans opened up, and the same thing happened every time their shells exploded and the poor old dears just stood there. They couldn't do anything, but they wouldn't leave the place.
>
> A lump of shrapnel went through our ammo wagon, and another piece went through the gun mounting, and afterwards we picked up some of these pieces and we worked out that they were 15in shells that they had been throwing back at us.

Saturday 10 May
Air raid alert 18.14–20.15hrs.

18.20hrs: Train machine-gunned by enemy aircraft, south of Blue Pigeons Farm, Worth, between Deal and Sandwich. The driver was killed and some passengers injured (1 killed; 1 seriously injured; 1 slightly injured).

Gunner R.J. Hollyer was serving with the 5th Battalion, Wiltshire Regt and recalls that this was not the only occasion that trains on this stretch of line had been attacked:

> We were billeted at 'The Redoubt' in the club house on the golf course at Sandwich Bay. I was nearly killed there by one enemy plane which came over low from the sea. I also remember two occasions when trains on the Deal–Sandwich railway line going across the open space were attacked by a German plane, which riddled them with bullets, and all the steam came billowing out from the holes the bullets made. When this happened, another train had to come and tow them back into the station.

Monday 12 May
Air raid alerts until 05.26hrs.

01.30hrs: Four HEs dropped at Old Downs Farm, Sandwich Bay.

02.30hrs: Six HEs dropped in the sea opposite the Guilford Hotel.

Wednesday 14 May
Austin GC3074 taken down to Pain's Garage, for the springs and carburettor to be seen to. Took over the Dodge from Mill Hill.

Saturday 17 May
Delivered handbills about War Weapons Week to shops in the High Street.

Also on this day Lt Col Fellowes recalled that Brigadier G.H. Seath DSO ADC, accompanied by the Brigade Major, Chatham Division RM, visited the RM Siege Regt.

Saturday 24 May
Deal War Weapons Week commences – Clarabut's shop had sideshows, stalls, etc.

Thursday 29 May
Air raid alerts 00.10hrs–04.56hrs.
  02.05hrs: One UXLM on the foreshore at Worth (Sandhills); and one LM 230 yards south of Princes golf club.

During June 1941 plans were drawn up to revise the road layout at the Sholden Hall corner, the junction of London Road with Sholdenbank. The old tea rooms in the garden of Sholden Hall had been converted to a 'strong point' in 1940, which had done nothing to ease the sightlines at this blind corner.
  The 74th Medium Regt RA moved their RHQ to Rowling House, near Goodnestone, while 'C' Battery was moved to a new position in Tilmanstone Woods.

Wednesday 11 June
Nazis make leaflet raid on Britain.
  00.40hrs–00.55hrs: Ten shells; one landed at Hope Farm, St Margaret's, one at Oldstairs Bay, Kingsdown, and the rest fell in the sea.
  19.41hrs: Gas warning, weather favourable.

Leaflets were dropped by parachutes from aircraft. John Rolfe found one of these devices near Eastry, complete with its launching mechanism:

> One day I went along the top road towards Thornton, in front of the Isolation hospital, and found a parachute with a wooden box attached to it, just lying on the footpath. It had four little sand-filled linen bags attached to the container, which had open sides like a packing crate. There was also a fuse wrapped round inside the box, which contained hundreds of leaflets. I could not read them, so I think they must have been in French.
> I gathered some grass and rubbish to hide the parachute and the box, which was about 2ft high, and 12in square, then I pushed it all into the hedge, and then ran home to tell Dad. He contacted Sgt Hill, the local 'copper', who let me keep the parachute.

Town Hall,
Deal,
April, 1941.

DEAL, WALMER & DISTRICT
WAR WEAPONS WEEK
24th to 31st MAY, 1941.

OUR AIM:- £55,000

Dear Sir or (Madam),

We are making a supreme effort in our War Weapons Week to create a record second to none. You are no doubt aware of the splendid response being made elsewhere, and a highly successful campaign in this area would shew to the Country and to the World that the spirit of our citizens will never be daunted. It would not only render invaluable aid to the Government in winning the war, but would stimulate that local feeling of confidence and security so vital to the life of our community.

An intensive campaign is being conducted to enlist the support of every class of investor, and every sum invested will be welcomed. I appreciate that many patriotic citizens have already invested substantially, but I am addressing this special appeal to you in the confident hope that if you have not already done so you will support our effort to the fullest extent of your available resources.

I shall be pleased to send you, on request, a form of authority addressed to your Banker. If you are in any doubt regarding the most suitable form of investment your Bank Manager will gladly advise you. Instructions may be given at once, but in order to be included in the figures for War Weapons Week, the investments must be completed during the period 24th—31st May.

I shall be grateful if you will kindly forward the authority in question to one of the following Banks in DEAL:—Barclays Bank Limited, Lloyds Bank Limited, Midland Bank Limited, National Provincial Bank Limited, Westminster Bank Limited, or to the Hon. Sec., MR. W. H. CAVELL, 21a, High Street, Deal.

Please accept my grateful thanks in anticipation of your support.

Yours very truly,

E. J. Dobson,

Mayor.

Leaflet advertising Deal's War Weapons Week.

Having given up her war job, Peggy Oatridge had to go before the Employment Board, but her brother-in-law helped her out with an offer of an 'essential' war job:

> John Tapping, my brother-in-law, was very busy during the week baking bread in his bakehouse in South Street, and his shop was still open. He had the contract to supply all the Army bread depots in the area. One of these was at Lydden, and he used to go to Eastry Union three times a week. There wasn't much cake about, so John baked currant loaves, and I can remember being so hungry that I used to pick the currants out of these loaves.
>
> As I wasn't a very experienced driver (the longest trip I had ever done was taking my mother up to Wembley), John said he had better show me how to change a wheel if I was going to drive the bread-van, which he did. Of course, I thought this will never happen to me, I'll never have a puncture! Well, I did!

Deal Gas Works' War Weapons Week scoreboard. There were several National Savings Campaigns, including Salute the Soldier, Warship Week and in May 1941 War Weapons Week. During the latter workers at Deal Gas Works aimed to encourage people to save sufficient money to purchase two machine-guns.

> It was right out at Shepherdswell, so I had to change the wheel and tighten up the wheel-nuts again (so I thought). The next day I was going up Mongeham Hill, with our dog sitting beside me, when suddenly I saw him leaning over against the door and when I looked in the mirror, there was this wheel rolling back down the hill! I thought it was very funny at the time.

Some of the troops who helped Peggy replace her wheel may well have been from the 229th Battery 58th Field Regiment RA, which had been moved from Lydd to Little Mongeham to replace the 94th Field Regiment. Amongst these new arrivals was Sgt C.A. White, who remembers:

> 'A' Troop was sited in a wood along a track through a large farm [Chapman's]. In those days we had very little knowledge of what was going on, and without maps we had no idea of where the shells would land. Our guns were American 75mm guns, made by the Bethlehem Steel Corporation, USA, and dated from the First World War. Thank God we never had to fire them, as I am sure they would have dealt a blow for Jerry, especially since we also had 'long-fuse' ammunition of the same vintage. We stayed there for a few months, and then moved on to Richborough Castle.

Wednesday 25 June
Two Westland Lysanders of No. 239 Sqn collided near Shepherdswell during a tactical reconnaissance exercise; F/Lt Tuppen and Sgt Clapperton in V9377, and P/O Parrish and Sgt H. Taylor in V9429 were all killed.

By July Mr Eames was busy at a Warden's Post, No. 296 St Richard's Road; he was also building some blast walls and constructing basement shelters at the Council Offices in Queen Street. Another redeployment of the 13.5in rail-mounted guns took place, largely because it was such a difficult and lengthy procedure to position them on the firing spurs on the cliffs near St Margaret's to cover any attempted enemy landing. The ex-SR and LMS diesel locomotives, supplemented by several ex-GWR 23XX 'Dean Goods' steam locomotives, which had been modified for steam condensing, were redeployed around the area, including on the East Kent Railway.

Wednesday 9 July
Visit here of the Regional 'big noises'. Depot commended, everything OK.
   20.24hrs: Gas warning, weather favourable.

Saturday 19 July
01.05hrs–01.25hrs: Sixteen shells were fired at a convoy off St Margaret's.

When convoys were escorted through the narrow sea passage between the Goodwins, they were subjected to a continuous bombardment from enemy artillery and aircraft, as ex-RN gun-layer H. Beauchamp recalls:

> I was transferred to Sheerness as a gun-layer and posted to HMS *Roebuck*, which acted as an escort ship for cargo-ships going through the English Channel. We usually took the ships through the Straits at night to dodge the Junkers Ju 88 and Ju 87 dive-bombers.
>   By day we went through the bombardment of the 11in guns fired from Calais and Cap Gris Nez on the French coast. We had four RAF personnel on board to operate the balloons that were flown at a certain height to keep off the dive-bombers by day; these balloons were taken down at night, especially if there was a full moon, as Jerry could locate our position from them on the moonlit nights.

Monday 21 July
07.41: Five hundred empty oil-drums arrived at the depot to be cut open for use with stirrup pumps.
   20.10hrs: Gas warning, weather favourable.

Tuesday 22 July
02.45hrs: Five shells fired at St Margaret's; one landed at Hope Farm, one at East Valley Farm, and the other three fell in the sea.

Thursday 24 July
RM Siege Regt inspected by Brigadier W. Swinton MC, Commander 12th Corps RA. (Lt Col Fellowes)

By the end of July the 5th Medium Regt RA had relieved the 74th Medium Regt, who had handed over their guns to the new arrivals; the 74th Medium Regt then moved to their new base at Hadlow, near Tonbridge. During the first week of August 1941, a detachment from the 604th Railway Construction Company, with men from the Pioneer Corps, was working on an extension to the spur at Ripple Farm, Coldblow, while sappers from the 160th Railway Construction Company erected the buffer stops about a month later.

By August the RAF's new navigation system, code-named 'Gee', had entered service. RAF Hawksdown was the 'Mouse' station and worked in conjunction with the 'Cat' at Trimmingham in Norfolk to provide our bombers with pin-point accuracy over targets in Germany on their nightly raids.

G.C. Salisbury, then serving with the 15th Battalion, Royal Fusiliers in the Walmer area, recalls that 'anti-invasion precautions' were still in force hereabouts. The precautions may well have been to prevent an enemy commando raid on the RAF's experimental radar station on the site of the former First World War Royal Naval Air Service aerodrome on Hawkshill Down:

> Each evening at a given time, a local workman arrived to put in place two steam-rollers across the road running past the side of Walmer Castle [Granville Road], to form a road-block. Each morning the process was reversed. During the day soldiers would man the road-block and if the siren sounded, we were soon down in our slit-trench by the side of the road, and ready for action.

Thursday 7 August
Spitfire Vb W3523 of No. 610 Sqn landed in the minefield on the beach at Deal, after damage by Bf109. Sgt Mason was wounded.

Monday 18 August
Bristol Beaufort I L9959 of No. 22 Sqn ditched off Walmer after suffering flak damage during a shipping strike off French coast; P/O Stevens and Sgt Calvetti were both killed; Sgt Furzey and Sgt Newland were picked up.

Under the reorganization of Auxiliary and Borough Fire Brigades, the Deal and Walmer Brigades became 8/9th Company 'D' Division of the National Fire Service. Mr Lionel Denne became the Divisional Officer of 'D' Division, with responsibility for some 200 square miles around East Kent. The town was split into three sub-divisions, the main fire station at Deal Town Hall having Station Officer Charles Matthews in charge. Mr Matthews was also responsible for No. 2 Station in Mill Road, while No. 3 station at Denne's Yard, Walmer, was under the command of Mr Lionel Denne's brother, Stanley. The reorganization allowed much more flexibility in dealing with major fires; the 'mobilizing officer' was Mrs Olive Harlow:

I had joined the NFS as a telephonist at Walmer sub-division office at Wellington House, Drum Hill. We worked 48 hours on and 24 hours off; the second night we could have off if we were not too busy. I lived locally, but the billeting for the other five girls was at 'Leelands' School in Grams Road. Occasionally we went to the Mill Road or Deal fire stations as 'relief' telephonists.

We had a large wall-mounted board, with hooks. Every time a pump went out, its tag was hung on a hook and its destination written beside it. This was reported to the Sub-Division at the Town Hall, and they reported it to the Divisional HQ at Broadstairs, and then to the Regional HQ at Maidstone, so that during an air raid they knew where they could get the pumps from. When there were heavy raids in other towns such as Canterbury, we provided additional crews to help them, and likewise our men relieved crews in London, to let their fire crews come down here for a break!

From the St Margaret's ARP logbooks:

Wednesday 27 August

08.45hrs: Spitfire reported to have force-landed at Oxney Wood near Nelson Park, St Margaret's, out of fuel; pilot safe.

At this time, Lt Col Fellowes had little to report in his *War Dispatches*, apart from the continuance of their training, and further development of ground defences:

Mrs Olive Harlow in NFS uniform. Olive was appointed mobilizing officer at Denne's Yard NFS sub-station after being trained at the Star and Garter Home, Sandgate.

The number of visitors remained about the same and included HM the King of the Helenes, Mr Mackenzie King (Canadian prime minister), the Russian trade delegation, General Wesson (US Army), Messrs U. Saw and Tin Tan (Chinese delegation), and various British and foreign officers.

In September 1941 Deal businessmen formed a Mutual Aid Salvage Scheme to save business stock in the event of a major blitz. Cecil Prime was in charge and the HQ was at White Fuller's outfitters shop on the corner of High Street and King Street, with five other branch offices sited the town. The early autumn saw work commenced on the construction of the new gun-pit at Bockell Farm, St Margaret's; this would house the 'hypervelocity' gun of new design, which had a calculated range of 84,000 yards (more than 45 miles).

From the St Margaret's ARP logbooks:

Thursday 4 September
16.35hrs: Unidentified aircraft down in the sea off St Margaret's Bay; the pilot was seen to bale out, and was picked up by boat.

Sunday 7 September
Civic Service at St George's Church on the first Anniversary of the 'Battle of Britain'.

Although hit and run raids and shelling continued, time was found for entertainment and sports at the Royal Marine Barracks at Deal when training permitted. The Holding Battalion based there in September 1941 even arranged a sports day and dance, as Emily Callighan, a chargehand at the depot's NAAFI recalls:

> When I joined the RM depot NAAFI I worked in North Barracks, where we had three cooks. We used to cook cheese puffs, egg and bacon flans (using tinned powdered eggs), gingerbread, Parkin and lots more. We also had a 'beer bar' that was served by men. Cigarettes were rationed to forty per man – there were no coupons but we had to take their names to prevent bulk-buying. We also sold toiletries.
>
> One afternoon we had a sports day for the Marines, and it was held on the drill field behind the depot church. It was a fine day, with races, high-jump, tug-of-war, etc., and then in the evening there was a dance, and anyone could attend so long as they had a ticket. There were plenty of Army people there, but not many sailors.
>
> We had monthly dances, which were always good because there were plenty more men than girls, so that meant we had lots of dances.

Tuesday 16 September
Fifteen SHs fired against a sixty-ship convoy, illuminated by a new powerful searchlight from Cap Gris Nez.
  19.30hrs: Gas warning, weather favourable.

Wednesday 17 September
20.15hrs: Two HEs landed near Princes golf course and exploded a number of land mines.

The explosion of these parachute mines (they were actually naval mines which drifted inland when dropped over The Downs) also caused problems for Bernard Kimpton:

> The whole of Sandwich Bay had been barricaded off and was occupied by the Army, and they had put this huge minefield in there. We had a problem down there one night when a German bomber hit this minefield and the explosion destroyed all our pipework, the pumphouses and everything. So we had to send an SOS to round everybody up to get it repaired over the weekend.

Friday 26 September
Exercise in Blenheim Road. S. Jordan went with a car to a lady at Stanford House, Beach Street, who had had a fit. Mr Byng visited the depot.
    19.35hrs: Gas warning.

Saturday 27 September
Mr Byng visited the depot. Received a phone call for an ambulance to be sent to Park Street where a young lady had had a fit. H. Neeve went and they took her home to 5 Golden Street. We supplied four men to act as casualties for the reinforcement exercise.
    19.05hrs: Weather conditions favourable for gas attack.

In the autumn of 1941 some powerful searchlights were installed along the Kent coast to aid the coastal gun batteries in engaging enemy E-boats and other surface craft which ventured too near in-shore. By this time the installation of the emergency gun batteries at Walmer, Deal and Sandown castles had been completed, and the twin 6in CD guns had been installed by the RMBDO unit, and then were handed over to the Royal Artillery. The guns of Sandown Castle battery were located on the corner of Godwyn Road, and by the house nearest to the castle ruins. Captain R.D. Roome MC commanded the 235th Battery there until late 1942, and recalls details of their emplacement:

> The guns were installed on concrete slabs, but without the usual steel shields, while sleeping accommodation for the twelve-man crews was provided below the gun floors. Shells for immediate use (allowing 10 minutes continuous firing) also had to be stored there, and had to be 'humped' up a flight of concrete steps. Each shell weighed about 100 lb. The guns had a 60° traverse, and we were only protected by low concrete walls, so a 'near-miss' would have put us out of action. Their range was 5,000 yards but we never fired 'in anger', but only in practice at a target towed off-shore by a motor-boat.
>
> We had a square, three-storey Battery Observation Post, with a Barr & Stroud rangefinder on the top floor, with the sleeping accommodation for the two 'off-duty' watches. (Crews were split into three watches – A, B and C.) The house on the corner of Harold Road and Sandown Road was used as our mess for meals, and we had one searchlight installed in the left front room of the Sandown Castle Hotel.

Captain Roome spent his time and talents in sketching on the walls above the observation slit a panorama of the view from the BOP, including various wrecks and landmarks, marked with approximate ranges. His work was commended by a visiting officer, so he did the same in their sister battery's BOP at Sandwich Bay. He also recalled the coastal defences in the surrounding area:

> The beach in front of the battery was not mined, but there was tubular scaffolding right along the seashore. Along the ends of the nearby golf course there was a buried minefield, and on one occasion all five hundred of these went up at once by 'sympathetic' detonation, most probably set off by a straying dog. We were dive-bombed from the air on one occasion, but our Bren gunner, who was

Sandown Castle Coastal Defence battery personnel. The two 6in coastal defence guns of 235 Battery at Sandown Castle only ever fired at practice targets towed offshore. The personnel posed for the photograph in front of the Sandown Castle Hotel; in one of the front rooms was sited one of the battery searchlights.

stationed on the roof of one of the nearby houses, got in a burst of fire on the enemy aircraft, and it was seen to dive into the sea.

With the darker evenings drawing in, despite the introduction of double summer time to help farmers harvest their crops in daylight, out on the country routes, the poor 'clippies' on the East Kent buses had difficulty in knowing when to announce the stopping places to their passengers. Marjorie Kempe recalls:

> In the blackout all we had was a hooded cycle lamp, with a metal strip on the back which fitted into a button hole on our uniforms. This gave just enough light to see our ticket machine and to check the cash. On the country routes it was sometimes difficult to know where we were in the blackout, but we soon got used to every turn and bump in the roads. The Sandwich to Woodnesborough, Marshborough and Westmarsh bus routes were covered by driver–conductors in 20-seaters known as 'Pigs'. Those drivers knew everybody on those runs and where they all lived and stopped accordingly. There was a small garage beyond Saunders Lane in Ash where these small buses were kept when not in use and overnight.

October 1941 saw the mayor of Deal, New Jersey, sending a cheque for over £1,000 to the mayor of Deal, to be used for the relief of those in the town who were suffering from bomb and shell attacks. Mr Eames was working on an air raid shelter in Park Street; followed by two others in Station Road, Walmer, and at the end of Victoria Park opposite the Brickmaker's Arms pub. Bernie Kimpton was involved with testing the sections of the PWD beach barrage installation that had now been completed, although there were still accidental losses of life from the beach mines.

By now around a thousand children had returned from South Wales, while others from Sir Roger Manwood's school who lived locally were escorted home for the school holidays. The return of these schoolchildren, either because their parents were unhappy with their living conditions in Wales (one of my cousins developed asthma, another was homesick and was not well treated) or because of an understandable desire to be reunited with their children, became something of a problem for the Education Authorities. Most schools had either closed or been evacuated in June 1940, and many of the buildings had been requisitioned for use by the military. Others in vulnerable parts of the town had suffered bomb and shell damage, as Miss Peggy Oatridge recalls:

> A lot of children were evacuated, but there wasn't any legal safeguard to prevent their return, so they could be brought back whenever their parents liked. They really didn't have to stay away, and so many of them did come back. Of course, the authorities then had to find somewhere to send these children to school, but it was very difficult – the Secondary Modern [now Castle High] was full of soldiers, and the poor old Deal parochial school was hit three times by bombs or shells.

Troops defending the coastline were still being redeployed. Upon their arrival at Richborough Castle the gunners of the 58th Field Regt found the new location was a distinct improvement over their previous accommodation under canvas at Little Mongeham. Sgt C.A. White recalls:

> There were four huts on one side, cookhouse, mess room, stores and the office, as well as billets for the men. We sergeants were billeted in the third house along the road up to the Castle and our guns were in pits of concreted sandbags. Now that we could see the sea we had a little idea of what was what. We had to dig fox-holes all over the place, some for us to get into but others were either covered with sticks as booby-traps for anyone who was not permitted to be in the area to fall into, while others served as basic alarm signals, being covered with corrugated iron sheets which made quite a noise when trodden on. All the soil had to be sifted through to see if any coins came to light – makes you think, doesn't it!

Wednesday 1 October
Air raid alerts 21.35hrs–21.46hrs.
  19.00hrs: Weather favourable for gas attack.
  20.37hrs: Gas works siren blew, and then sounded the 'all clear' at 21.14hrs.
  23.55hrs: Four HEs and two IBs fell in fields at Jossingblock Farm, at East Langdon.

Thursday 2 October
  20.00hrs: Fifteen HEs dropped; five landed at Solton Farm, five near Westcliffe Farm, St Margaret's, and five in fields at East Langdon opposite Swingate RAF camp.
  21.45hrs: Four HEs fell at The Droveway, St Margaret's.

Friday 3 October

Air raid alerts 19.43hrs–21.18hrs.

  20.14hrs: Three HEs fell in open fields, and two others in Ackholt Wood at Nonington (1 slightly injured).

  20.23hrs: Gas warning.

The Civil Defence War Diaries for this day record:

Fifty IBs dropped in open fields at Womenswold. One UXIB – a British-made one marked 'Novova XII 1941' was recovered.

The YMCA canteen van was used to tour the more isolated Army positions, but Peggy Oatridge and her friend Bobbie McGhee had quite a drive from Deal before starting on their run round the balloon-, searchlight- and gun-sites:

> The depot for the YMCA canteen van was at 'St Albans' [later the Physical Training College], Nonington, and we had to drive there to get the tea. There was a lovely man there, 'Horace', who had a 'gammy' leg, but who did all the loading up for us.
>
>   All we had on the van was an urn of tea, and by the time we got to the end of the run it wasn't very drinkable. Biscuits were rationed to two per person, and we also had a tray of pink cakes (they put cochineal in to make them look a bit more palatable) and the soldiers could have one of those each, and one chocolate bar each. Then we had the precious cigarettes, which were rationed to five each. I always remember that when I gave one man his cigarettes he said 'The NAAFI tart always gives us ten!'

With the increasing attacks on Deal and the surrounding area, barrage balloons were stationed all around the town, including this one at the end of Southwall Road, photographed surreptitiously by Bill Fenn around the end house in the road.

Sunday 5 October
18.59hrs: Gas warning.
   19.25hrs: Call came in from the main fire station to send someone to St George's Hall, where a lady had had an accident.

Wednesday 8 October
Mrs Prisgrove injured her hand, so we took her home in the car to 52 Stockdale Gardens as she was suffering from shock.

Sunday 12 October
12.20hrs–14.23hrs: Two shells landed at Langdon; four more fell in the sea off St Margaret's and another fell south-east of the Deal–Dover Road.

Tuesday 14 October
Blenheim IV T1951 of No. 1 CACU hit a tree during a practice attack and crashed at Shepherdswell; Sgts J.W. Treeby; N.J. Wosencroft; S. Yates and P/O V.P. Corbett-Thompson all killed.

Wednesday 22 October
09.00hrs: Convoy of thirty vessels shelled while passing through The Downs.
   18.56hrs: Weather favourable for gas attack. At 21.29hrs we received a local gas warning, but the danger had passed by 21.35hrs (possibly it was only a fog-bank).
   Body of Fw W. Such [from the Heinkel crash on 9 April 1941] found on Goodwin Sands.

Based in the Battery Observation Post at Deal Castle, Fred Newton had recently arrived from his duties on the Admiralty Pier at Dover:

> After Russia entered the war, things in Dover got a little quieter and I was sent to Deal on similar duties, being part of the Barr & Stroud [rangefinder] observation set up, monitoring the Channel convoys and enemy cross-Channel shelling.
>
> As well as my OP duties, I also had to enter a daily log of the enemy routine shelling from Cap Gris Nez, and appearance of the Messerschmitt Bf109 fighter-bombers attacking Deal, and machine-gunning the anti-aircraft positions along the sea-front.

Thursday 23 October
A small child with a small cut on his head was brought in by his mother.
   19.06hrs: Weather conditions favourable for gas attack.

Monday 27 October
From today the 'Yellow' air raid alert is to be abolished.
   Spitfire Vb W3601 of No. 401 Sqn crashed near Deal; Sgt S.L. Thompson (Canadian) baled out.

Thursday 30 October
A young boy, David Hill of Prospect Villas in Western Road, came in to have a small cut on his head attended to.
   Practice with the Control Centre; sending and receiving messages with respirators on.

Tuesday 4 November
Medical Officer of the West Kent Regt and stretcher bearers, paid us a visit here. This visit was part of the programme during the military exercises.

These exercises were a regular feature of life in East Kent and it was during one such 43rd Division event that Bombardier George Cornwell and his 59th Anti-Tank Brigade RA colleagues, based at Ripple, had to survive on 'bully' beef and biscuits for ten tough and wet days:

> So we 'bad lads' celebrated the last night by 'liberating' about three-dozen chickens, a sack of potatoes and some other veg from a farmer and had ourselves a midnight feast. The next thing was that we were all on parade and were told the cost of the farmer's bill, and that the whole battery owed him 2s 6d each on pay day. We were also told we would do all the extra guard duties for HQ RA 43rd Division, plus our own, plus any aeroplane guards needed. Hence the experience of yours truly being taken out in deep snow to a chicken farm in the Sandwich–Wingham area where a Hurricane had been forced down among a field full of chicken huts. One of the huts was raked out, some straw thrown in and that was our billet! I finished up sleeping in the cockpit of the Hurricane – it smelt fresher!

Wednesday 5 November
19.00hrs: Local gas warning.
   Two men were supplied from here to assist Col Goodwin to remove stores from the Forester's Hall to Tormore School.

Friday 7 November
23.05hrs: Local warning; 23.55hrs: danger passed.
   Two men again supplied to assist Col Goodwin to remove the stores to Tormore School.

Sunday 16 November
Attended Church Parade this morning at the Victoria Baptist.

Wednesday 19 November
A young man, Henry Denne of 5 Niton Terrace, Northwall Road, was brought in for treatment after falling down. We suspected a dislocation of the shoulder, so put his arm in sling and sent him to hospital in car.
   · F. Harrison left the depot.

Thursday 20 November
Mr Gentry and a regional building inspector visited the depot, and inspected our shelter.

Sunday 30 November
A small boy, Frank Shaw of 'Cotswolds', Northwall Road, was brought here for treatment; he had a rusty nail through his finger. Sent him to hospital.

During the months of November and December Mr Eames was working on the strengthening of air raid shelters at the West Street ARP depot. By December 1941 the population of Deal had risen again to 12,140 persons, although this figure was to fall later. During December a Flag Day organized in aid of Russia raised £100. With the War Department in charge of parts of the East Kent line it was not at all surprising that accidents occurred, owing to the confusion about their working procedures but one of the accidents unfortunately resulted in the dismissal of two of the East Kent's employees. This event, which occurred at Shepherdswell, was set out in detail in a letter from the General Manager, Mr William H. Austen:

> The wagons were left, contrary to all regulations, on a section of the main line when the driver concerned was not in the possession of the relevant staff [a railway token held by the driver to allow him exclusive use of a length of track]. The instrument for that section of the line was in the possession of the Military authorities to permit a WD engine to enter it. When it did so, in total darkness, the War Department signalman and brakesman could not avoid a collision, resulting in two of the seven loaded chalk wagons being demolished and the main line blocked for five to six hours.

Saturday 6 December
A small child treated for cut on right leg.

Sunday 7 December
Demonstration in Blenheim Road by the Kent County Mobile Reserve.

Wednesday 10 December
H. Neeve finished painting mobile canteen for the WVS. A section of the beach barrage at Deal was tested.

Monday 15 December
15.10hrs–17.31hrs: Four SHs fell at St Margaret's.
  15.30hrs: Two SHs fell near Napchester, Sutton; one person seriously injured.

Tuesday 16 December
Received a call from the police for an ambulance to take an unconscious man, found lying outside 'Worchester House' on Central Parade, to hospital.

Scaffolding defences near Walmer lifeboat station. This network of steel scaffolding, barbed wire and landmines prevented local fishermen from launching their boats until the end of 1941, when arrangements were made for a gap to made through the defences near the Walmer lifeboat house for the limited number of boats still remaining.

Wednesday 24 December
The mayor, deputy mayor and others visited the depot.

Thursday 25 December
Major O'Callaghan, Mr Ford and Mr Taylor paid us a visit. Personnel on duty today were given two hours off.

Sunday 28 December
Attended to a man at the 'Jolly Sailor' who had had a stroke. Dr Hutchinson was sent for.

Tuesday 30 December
Second borough restaurant opened at 'Tormore'.

Wednesday 31 December
Went to 'Fireman's Social and Dance' at the Caxton Home.

At the end of the year the Walmer lifeboat had returned from its repairs in Norfolk, sailing from Lowestoft with Dr Hall, who enjoyed the experience of a longer journey at sea, in contrast to his more usual short trips to vessels in The Downs. The fishing restrictions placed on local longshoremen were lifted, but the Deal boats had to be moved along to the Walmer beach nearer the lifeboat station, and were launched through a gap in the beach defence scaffolding opposite.

CHAPTER FIVE

January–December 1942

The new year did not see any relief for Deal and District from an increasing number of attacks by the Focke-Wulf and Messerschmitt hit and run raiders, leading to some of the most tragic incidents during the whole of the war. These raids were either undertaken early in the morning from the sea, or late in the evening from inland, as were the attacks on the Dover balloon barrage, so that the sun would dazzle the anti-aircraft gunners trying to draw a bead on these low-flying aircraft. Instances of machine-gunning by enemy fighters had increased, and for those working in farm fields this was particularly dangerous. On one occasion Bernard Burgess was ploughing a field known as 'No Man's Land', at Ringwould, along the Deal–Dover road, when an enemy fighter machine-gunned a lorry making towards Deal:

> This lorry was carrying bags of flour for Tapping's bakery in South Street, Deal. The driver was injured in the face by the shattered windscreen, but managed to continue his journey into Deal. However, the baker refused to take delivery of the flour as it had been contaminated by the bullets which had gone through the sides of the lorry and ruptured the flour bags.
>
> The following day I was again ploughing in the same field, when I caught sight of something from the corner of my eye – it was flying towards me from the same direction that the German fighter had arrived the previous day. I jumped off the tractor to take refuge underneath, only to discover my 'attacker' was a rather large seagull!

The New Year saw part-time compulsory education introduced for a growing number of children who had returned from evacuation. This involved a shift system, because of the lack of room at those schools which had been partially requisitioned by the military. Civilians tried to carry on as normal a life as possible and even undertook voluntary work in their off-duty hours, but sometimes damage to their homes would involve a temporary move to another area. Those civilians still living in the area were also encouraged to 'dig for victory' by cropping their gardens and taking on allotments so that they would be self-sufficient in food. Ken Patterson's father tilled a spare piece of ground in St Richard's Road:

> Food was sufficient, as Dad grew many vegetables and he also kept rabbits and chickens. Mum used to bring home the 'windfall' fruit from the London Road houses where she worked as a cleaner. She was also the caretaker of the Isolation Hospital school (opposite St John's Roman Catholic Church in St Richard's Road) which I attended. Concentrated orange juice and milk powder were issued for the younger children. Dad brought our sweet ration home on Tuesdays and Fridays.

Early in the year the Dorset Regt arrived to take over Coastal Defence of the area. The coastal defenders were constantly changing, units being taken out of 'the front line' so to speak, either for rest, re-training for overseas service, or for the 'Second Front'. One of those who arrived with the Carrier Platoon at Drum Hill, Walmer, was Corporal Les 'Timber' Wood, who recalls that not all injuries were a result of enemy action:

> Our platoon officer was fresh from 'battle school' and so had an assault course built in these grounds, which we had to go round before breakfast, while this officer fired his revolver, not always into the air! This continued daily, until the CO stopped it after the platoon had suffered one broken wrist, one broken arm, and a fractured ankle – this assault course caused more casualties than the enemy!

In January 1942 the 74th Medium Regt left Tilmanstone for Sevenoaks, while members of the 5th Battalion of the Wiltshire Regt were based at 'Sandilands' at the southern extremity of Sandwich Bay. It was a very cold month, with lots of snow, and this resulted in one of the bitterest episodes in the turbulent story of the Kent coalfield. The opening up of coal seam '2S' saw miners working in impossible conditions, and they were unable to achieve the 4 tons per man per day production rate which would have earned them a bonus. The refusal by Betteshanger Colliery management to pay any bonus for the lower production rate brought things to a head and a strike was called. Mr Dick Sullivan well remembers the infamous '2S' seam:

> The coal was bad, and very hard to get at. There was muck and water coming at you the whole time, and some of the seams were only two feet high. I was a miner for forty-nine years and they were the worst conditions I ever came across.

Dorset Regt carrier platoon personnel. The carrier platoon of the 5th Dorset Regt was based in several of the larger properties on Dover Road in Upper Walmer. As well as training at 'Otty Bottom', Kingsdown, they found time to relax in the Marke Wood Recreation Ground during their off-duty hours.

Monday 5 January
Air raid alert 18.26hrs–19.54hrs.

A call came in from the control centre for an ambulance to be sent to the High Street, opposite Carthy & Fox, where an elderly man, Mr Walker of the Merry Hall, had had an accident and had received facial injuries. Took him to hospital where he was detained. Mr Byng and Mr Smith visited depot.

Thursday 8 January
Messrs S.A. Harris, H. Neeve, B. Bourner went out in car with Mr Byng on the loudspeaker, telling people about Wastepaper Salvage week.

Sunday 11 January
Air raid alert 18.33hrs–20.00hrs.

18.50hrs: Convoy going through. We heard two planes above our heads machine-gunning; they seemed quite low, so we kept near a shelter in Downs Road, just in case.

Monday 12 January
The start of the Betteshanger Colliery strike, involving up to 1,600 men, after pit management refuse to negotiate.

Wednesday 14 January
Air raid alerts 08.35hrs–08.54hrs.

At dinner-time we saw a big German bomber going over out to sea; two of our fighters intercepted it, and when last seen it was heading out to sea but getting lower and lower, with black smoke coming from it.

Saturday 17 January
Mr Byng visited the depot, asking for three men to be detailed to be in attendance at the mayoress's sale [National Savings shop].

Monday 19 January
Loudspeaker out making announcements about the local alarm system. T. Chandler, F. Knight and F. Neeve on duty at the mayoress's sale.

Wednesday 21 January
Loudspeaker out this morning, with four men on waste paper salvage.

The Betteshanger miners voted to stay out on strike, despite the underground workers being summonsed.

Saturday 24 January
Mr Dewell taken to hospital with dislocated shoulder.

The Betteshanger strike leaders, Joe Methuen, Billy Powell and Tudor Davies, were all sentenced to hard labour at Canterbury Court, with fines or imprisonment for the other strikers.

Sunday 25 January
Planes were practising cannon shelling on the wrecks out here – what a din!

Monday 26 January
A party sent to 3 Stafford Cottages, Western Road, where Mrs Johnson had fallen downstairs and fractured her left tibia; taken to hospital in our ambulance, with Nurse 'Wiggins' [Vera] in attendance.

Betteshanger miners voted again to continue the strike; only nine of the 1,017 underground workers fined had paid up.

Tuesday 27 January
The Betteshanger management agreed to pay full rate for men working on seam '2S' after negotiation by KMA & National Mineworkers Federation of Great Britain, but the miners decreed there should be no return to work while their leaders were still jailed.

Wednesday 28 January
Work re-started at Betteshanger Colliery after the three strike leaders were released from Maidstone Prison following KMA negotiations with the management, who agreed to the pay increase without victimization.

All strikes were illegal in wartime, so any industrial action had to be dealt with very harshly, even though Betteshanger, the nearest colliery to the front line, could so easily have been abandoned in 1940. Joe Burke remembers:

> The boys at Betteshanger did a marvellous job during the war. It was one of the most dangerous pits to work in, as were all the Kent pits, because so many bombs were being dropped in the area. But the boys kept working and kept up production. The men were asked if they wanted to abandon Betteshanger and move to the Midlands, because it was so dangerous here, but they refused, because they knew they could do more good where they were. Coal could get to London, where it was needed, in only 1½ hours by rail from Kent.

Saturday 31 January
On duty at 07.00hrs. Another team practice; I was the patient! Mr Dawson, Dr Kirk and Major O'Callaghan were the judges. We also had a visit from the regional transport officer who inspected all our vehicles.

During February Mr Eames was no doubt grateful for one 'inside' job, as he was painting and decorating the parochial school; he was also at work on strengthening the children's shelter.

As part of Exercise Flotsum, 'A' Troop of the RM Siege Regt supplied the equivalent of three infantry platoons to 'attack and generally harass' the defenders of the coast batteries at Sandown Castle, Deal Castle and Kingsdown.

The delivery of goods to retail shops was rationalized by the setting up of a scheme whereby goods were delivered to a central point, from where they could be fetched by the individual shopkeepers, thus saving petrol.

The KCC ordered some reduction in the numbers of ARP wardens and FAPs, which did not go down too well.

Monday 2 February

Snow about 6in deep and still snowing. A. Baker, A. Fletcher, L. Kirby and E. Terry on snow shovelling.

We had a practice this afternoon, with the practice casualties being sent to Park Centre.

Tuesday 3 February

We had the last team practice for the contest on Thursday; the casualties looked real, and the team did well.

Thursday 5 February

Team for Canterbury: party leader, H. Neeve; deputy leader, J. Lock (Mill Road depot); B. Bradshaw; C. Curling; nurse, D. Harvey; sitting car driver, F. Howland; party driver, F. Hawkin; ambulance driver, A. Parker; and depot superintendent, Mr Dawson. Nine nurses from the Park Centre and S.A. Harris went from here as Reserves. They came second.

Nurses and FAP staff at Park ARP centre. It is all too clear why they needed to reduce staffing after the evacuation; here are members of the St John Ambulance Brigade, Red Cross and Auxiliary Nursing Services surrounding Dr D.W. Kirk, the Chief Casualty Officer and Medical Officer of Health for Deal, soon after the official opening of the Park ARP centre.

FAP personnel at Nelson Hall, photographed in the back yard outside the ambulance garage, 19 April 1942. Back row, left to right: A. Bourner; A. Jordan; A. Baker; S. Jordan; S. Harris. Front row: R. Howland; Nurse Harvey; B. Moore.

Saturday 7 February

Cold and snowing. Dr Kirk, Mr Clark (Mill Road depot) and Mr Dawson in conference here this morning. Note from Dr Kirk that staffs of all depots are to be cut down. From here we lose T. Twyman, T. Terry, F. Chandler, A. Cave, E. Valentine and G. Davis; F. Knight and L. Kirby transferred to Park Centre.

Sunday 8 February

What a to-do about cutting down the personnel! It is now 11.12hrs, and most of the personnel are gathered here to see Dr Kirk, who is coming down to talk to the men if they have any complaints to make.

Tuesday 10 February

Mr Hubbard examined anti-gas clothing at 14.00hrs. There was some shelling from the French coast today.

Wednesday 11 February

Had a good gas practice exam at 2.30 p.m., which I passed OK. Gas clothing needing repair has been sent to Mr Hubbard.

What a din going on, with shelling from both sides of the Channel, and there seem to be hundreds of planes about.

The Regimental HQ of the 5th Medium Regt was moved from Sandwich to Knowle Park, Sevenoaks, while the 74th Medium Regt was back again, this time employed on beach defence duties in the Sandwich area, with their RHQ now at 'Dunearn', Sandwich Bay.

Thursday 12 February
Quite a din going on all day, with planes and shelling from both sides.

   12.33hrs–13.50hrs: Thirteen SHs fell in the St Margaret's area, after the local gun fired at 12.19hrs.

Lt Col Fellowes reported in his *War Dispatches*:

> A certain amount of activity took place when the German convoy with the *Scharnhorst* and *Gneisnau* passed through the Straits. The area was shelled without damage; in reply to our 9.2in coast guns opening fire, the 14in guns fired one round each on a predetermined position supplied by CCRA 12th Corps, but owing to the short notice and the men not being closed up as the Coast Battery men were, but scattered over a wide area carrying out training, no more rounds could be fired, nor was there time to bring up the 13.5in guns.

The Royal Navy had monitoring posts along this stretch of coast, who were also undertaking radar-jamming duties. Former operator Alan Johnson recalls the day he arrived:

Excavations for HMG 'Bruce', 12 February 1942. The extent of the excavations required for heavy artillery may be judged by the relative size of the figures in this photograph of the mounting for the 13.5/8in 'hypervelocity' gun 'Bruce' at Bockell Farm, St Margaret's. However, it was not successful, and was scrapped after firing a few test rounds.

There were five main stations, some of them in private houses, around the coast from Sandgate to Deal, manned by naval ratings. These 'Z' stations were equipped with receivers and transmitters used for jamming the German radar on the French coast.

I was posted to the house with a windmill at St Margaret's Bay where I stayed for 18 months. The day I arrived, those German battleships did their 'runner' through the Channel. You can imagine the noise at the Bay, with the four 9.2-in guns firing over our heads, and the enemy returning fire. I remember thinking, 'I hope it's not like this every day.'

Saturday 14 February

14.32hrs: Local warning; 14.32hrs: danger passed.

07.25hrs: Went to see Mrs Parsons at 14A Water Street. It was a confinement, so we fetched the midwife. Bombs dropped somewhere around here, and there was shelling again during the day.

Thursday 19 February

The medical officer of the Hampshire Regt visited the depot with stretcher-bearers. Shelling again. In the morning a convoy of fifty ships, carrying protective barrage balloons and escorted by planes, passed slowly through The Downs.

Thursday 26 February

Mr Byng visited the depot. The minesweeper, yacht, and motor-boat models at the depot are to be auctioned for Warship Week. [Nelson Hall had formerly been the headquarters of the local Naval Cadet Force.]

Early in 1942 it was decided to restart a St John Ambulance Brigade Girl Cadets Corps under the command of Miss Dyer.

In February and March Mr Eames was working on the erection of shelters at the Deal Methodist School in Union Street.

March saw girls aged sixteen and seventeen required to register for youth service, while the age limit for men joining the Services was raised to forty-five.

The 74th Medium Regt HQ moved to Dane Court at Tilmanstone, while 'B' Battery (now re-designated 'Q' Battery) took up new gun positions slightly north of their original ones in Tilmanstone Woods.

Saturday 7 March

S. Jordan and Nurse Harvey attended to a lady in Middle Street who had injuries to her wrist (fracture). Later an ambulance was sent to Broad Street where a Corporation employee had fallen off a lorry and was badly injured. Attended a small boy with a cut over his eye; sent him to hospital to have stitches.

Saturday 14 March

Warship Week opened with a procession, headed by the RM band, and a detachment of Marines. The Dorset and Hampshire Regts with their bands, WRNS, WVS, WLA, and ARP personnel, St John nurses, the lifeboatmen, and the fire service, complete with engines, paraded through the town. The fun-fair opened, and Will and I won 7s 6d in savings stamps; it was good fun.

During Warship Week the people of Deal raised a total of £91,500, and those in Sandwich some £36,342. One Wren who arrived at Deal Barracks during March 1942 was Eva Turton, who had just avoided a posting to Dover, where life was even more hectic than at Deal:

> We had taken over from the Royal Marine cooks in one of the old hexagonal buildings, and the white tiling all round the walls had been splashed with grease – it took us weeks to get it looking right. We cooked the main meals and puddings in the old steamers, although we did have gas stoves on which we boiled eggs. After the food was cooked it was stored in hot cabinets until it was served. We had a daily delivery from the stores, allocated by the quartermaster, but only had rations for 24 hours, so if anything was spoilt, it was just too bad.

Wednesday 18 March
Warship Week has already raised £62,000 – the price of a trawler or minesweeper.

Monday 23 March
20.58hrs: Local warning; 21.37hrs: danger passed.
  21.00hrs: Four HEs dropped at Sutton; one HE at Ripple Farm.

Ron Read recalls this incident:

> We also had one big bomb drop in the field at the back of Ripple Court. The police and ARP men came and looked at the crater and decided that it had exploded under the ground. We all stood around, gazing into the hole, and then decided to go off for a cup of tea, and we were just sitting down in our cottage when there was a loud explosion nearby. We all said, 'That was a near one!', and so it was – that same bomb we had been gazing down at a few minutes earlier had exploded!

Tuesday 24 March
Spitfire Vb BL963 of No. 121 Sqn crash-landed at Deal returning from escort duty; P/O Skinner (USA) baled out unhurt.

Wednesday 25 March
Air raid alert 23.18hrs–23.59hrs.
  23.15hrs: Ten HEs fell on the cliffs at St Margaret's; another HE fell at Pixhill Farm, Great Mongeham (1 seriously injured; 7 slightly injured).

Sunday 29 March
Went to church this morning as today is a National Day of Prayer.

During March and April Mr Eames was busy building blast walls in front of Wellington House, Walmer (Denne's Yard fire station, later Bowzell's Yard) for the NFS, as well as laying a concrete floor to form an underground shelter in the basement of builders E.B. Cavell in Oak Street. The work he had done on building the air raid shelter at the parochial school was to no avail, and it had to be rebuilt after the Park Lane bombing raid of 5 May.

This month 'P' Battery (the renamed 'A' Battery) of the 74th Medium Regt was amalgamated with 'B' Battery at Tilmanstone as their mobile reserve, while 'Q' Battery constructed and occupied the observation posts near Deal, and carried out defence patrols by night along the local beaches. (By August the 74th Medium Regt was at Sennybridge training camp; there they were ordered to mobilize, and thus did not return to Tilmanstone.)

Friday 3 April
00.23hrs: Local warning; 01.53hrs: danger passed.
  00.20hrs: Three HEs dropped at Crixhall Farm, Staple. Some buildings were damaged and one person slightly injured. Another HE fell at 'Hope House', Kingsdown (2 seriously damaged; 8 slightly damaged).
  01.00hrs: One HE fell at Womenswold.
  01.05hrs: Four HEs dropped east of the Dover Patrol memorial at St Margaret's.
  01.45hrs: Two HEs fell near Hope Farm at St Margaret's.

Sunday 12 April
  13.59hrs: Spitfire Vb BL643 of No. 412 Sqn ditched 1 mile east of Walmer Castle; the body of Sgt C.G. Napier later picked up by HSL.

Thursday 16 April
  Removed Mr Moore of 3 Hood Villas, Golf Road, to hospital by stretcher ambulance.
  Spitfire Vb AD193 of No. 129 Sqn, damaged by FW190s and crash-landed at Studdal; Sgt Barker safe.

Tuesday 21 April
Mr F. Knight was buried today; most of the personnel attended his funeral. Later we assembled civilian gas-masks.

Saturday 25 April
Spitfire Vb BL239 of No. 121 Sqn was abandoned 2 miles south of Ramsgate after its engine cut out; P/O Downs (USA) picked up OK; while AB793 was abandoned '4 miles off Ramsgate'; the fate of its pilot unknown.

From the St Margaret's ARP logbooks:

Sunday 26 April
07.50hrs: Local warning; 07.54hrs: danger passed.

07.40hrs: Four HEs fell on the power-house at Betteshanger Colliery; Nos 1 and 2 boilers were destroyed and Nos 3 and 4 were damaged (only two boilers escaped damage). (2 seriously injured; 9 slightly injured). All trapped men at Betteshanger brought up by midnight.

Vera's diary noted:

When the bombs dropped on the Betteshanger power house, all our lights went out. Among those injured were Mr F. Rundell and Mr Sneller.

Tuesday 28 April
Col Sandilands from regional headquarters visited the depot and inspected the vehicles.

By May 1942 the local ARP organization had been reduced to 160 paid and 418 unpaid personnel, while the Control Centre at Tormore School had been manned by some twenty-six men at its peak.

Mr Eames was still busy; having completed some thirty-two communal shelters around the town, he was now employed on strengthening the warden's posts at 34–36 Dover Road, 4 Canada Road, and 'Cherry Orchard' in London Road; as well as constructing an air raid shelter at the Nelson Hall ARP depot. The basements of the Roman Catholic Church and school in St Richard's Road were also reinforced to provide shelter accommodation.

From this time on, because of a severe drought, all house-holders were obliged to have four gallons of water handy inside their front doors to deal with any outbreak of fire. On Rogation Sunday prayers were said after thirty-three days without rain.

Monday 4 April
We auctioned the late Mr F. Knight's belongings, and the money was given to Mrs Knight. A. Fletcher resumed duties.

Wednesday 5 April
06.27hrs: Local warning; 07.00hrs: danger passed.
  06.30hrs: Bombs dropped in Alfred Square, Mill Road, Park Lane and near The Potteries. Two parties from here worked in Alfred Square, with Dot [Harvey] and I as ambulance nurses. Five casualties to Park Centre, three taken to hospital; three more found dead. Post 2 phoned for someone to go to Middle Street, to deal with a lady suffering from shock. Sent an ambulance to Alfred Square, where a Corporation workman, F. Dadd, was suffering from abrasions to leg and hand. Took him to Park Centre, and after treatment took him home. We lost one upper window at home – the glass was blown out – and the ceiling came down a little. It was hectic while it lasted. 4 HEs (10 demolished; 77 seriously damaged; 113 slightly damaged; 7 killed; 3 seriously injured; 7 slightly injured). One of the bombs fell on 'Myrtle Villa', Mill Road; and property was also damaged in Park Lane, Alfred Square, College Road, Sandown Road and Albert Road.

Vic Skinner was helping with the clearing-up in Alfred Square, but recalls that the bomb had missed its intended target:

When the pilot flew over he was aiming for the gas works, but when he let the bomb go it caught on one of the spikes on the framework of the gasometer and veered towards the Caxton Home. It glanced off the side of the building, bounced on the ground and then shot across the road and exploded outside Smith's fish shop, the butchers, the greengrocers and a house on the corner of Alfred Square.

Peggy Oatridge witnessed the incident at 'Myrtle Villa' as it was just below 'Wellington House' in Mill Road, but she thought at first that the aircraft that dropped the bomb was 'one of ours':

When I came back from Winchester, people had told me about those lovely Spitfires which used to fly over each morning – the Dawn Patrol – and it used to be quite romantic seeing these British fighters up there protecting us.

It was very early on a beautiful May morning, when I heard this aeroplane, and thought 'There's the Dawn Patrol', so I stuck my head out of the window to watch them go by. The next thing that happened was I'd been blown back into the room, as one of those Messerschmitt fighter-bombers which used to come over and drop just one bomb – really nasty of them – had hit 'Myrtle Villa'. I can remember thinking, 'Well, that wasn't a Spitfire!'

After attending the incident in Alfred Square in May 1942, the Deal NFS firemen were glad to see the Salvation Army's tea van arrive. Behind the van is the Lloyd Memorial Caxton Home, used as a billet for those firemen drafted into Deal from outside the district.

After this, Mr Eames noted that he was working on some emergency bomb-damage repairs at the end of College Road, including the warden's post at No. 3, which was being equipped with a new 'hy-rib' reinforced concrete roof, which would afford some protection for its occupants.

Friday 8 May
13.18hrs: Local warning; 13.40hrs: danger passed.
  13.17hrs: Bombs dropped in Park Street and the railway station yard; No. 1 Party went to Park Street, No. 2 Party to Albert Road. No. 1 Party removed four casualties to hospital; No 2 Party took two casualties to hospital and arranged the removal of one killed. No. 2 Party was then sent to Park Street, and took one casualty to Park Centre, and two shock cases to the rest centre. We are now short of blankets after Park Street. I was with No. 2 Party. 4 HEs (1 demolished; 60 seriously damaged; 108 slightly damaged; 3 killed; 10 seriously injured; 15 slightly injured).

One bomb had fallen in the station goods yard, killing one man and injuring another; a second fell in Ravenscourt Road, whilst a third hit the elementary department of the RC convent school in Park Street, where several children were buried, and two were killed. This raid also caused widespread damage in the area. Bernard Kimpton's sister-in-law was working in the old Park Street library at this time, and he recalls how the book shelves fell down into a 'V' and protected her from harm. Emily Callighan rushed home from work to see if her younger brother was safe:

> My small brother was at school at the convent as it was the only school still open in Deal – he had to pay 2s 6d per week. When the bomb dropped in Park Street, behind the Odeon cinema, I was given time off to go and get him. At first the ARP warden wouldn't let me go to him, but in the end he was found safe and sound, although very dirty with brick dust from the explosion.

Another of the buildings damaged by the bombs was the Deal labour exchange in Park Street, which was fortuitous for Mary Osbourn:

> Opposite the library in Park Street was the labour exchange and one bomb blew the top floor off, damaged the building and destroyed all their records. I had been registered for war service not long before, and they lost track of me; I was just a 'nobody' and it wasn't until two years later that they caught up with me! By then I was married and thus was exempt from war service.

Saturday 9 May
Spitfire Vb AA851 of No. 457 Sqn crashed in the sea off Deal while returning from escort; its pilot was Sgt Halliday (Aust) – fate unknown.

Monday 11 May
We had a phone call from Post 1 to go to North Street. Mr A. Jordan and I went. It was dark

and raining hard. A man had gone a bit 'potty' in the head. Dr Milne gave us some tablets to give him, which quietened him, and we reported back to the depot. He was taken away at 2 p.m.

Thursday 14 May
Small boy named Dadd of Landport Cottages, Western Road, was treated for a cut on his forehead, and was to taken to hospital to have a stitch put in.

A Spitfire of No. 124 Sqn dived into the sea off Deal from high altitude; fate of pilot unknown.

Monday 18 May
06.20hrs: Had a hit and run raid this morning. Bombs were dropped in Canada Road; with a UXB at the gas works in Cannon Street. Everyone was evacuated until the UXB had been removed – which was at 2.30 p.m. Two persons killed in Canada Road: one HE/one UXB. (5 demolished; 4 seriously damaged; 30 slightly damaged; 2 killed; 2 slightly injured).

06.25hrs: Two UXBs at Betteshanger Colliery; one in the winding house and one on the railway; both cleared by midday.

Despite the devastation caused to the St Mary's Convent Junior School by bombs in Park Street, this statue of Jesus was untouched.

One bomb bounced from the RM depot parade-ground, through the boundary wall and into 85–91 Canada Road, while another was diverted through a house in Cannon Street and landed on the steps of the Deal Gas Company offices. Vic Skinner believed this bomb was also intended for the Deal Gas Works, but fell somewhat short of its target:

> Unfortunately the pilot missed his aim and the bomb struck a cottage in Cannon Street. It went through the back wall, just missing an elderly lady lying in bed, and back out through the front wall, making a perfectly round hole in each wall. It landed right on the steps of the Gas Company offices, but, thank God, this one didn't explode either, as it was a dud.

Mr P.J. Handley, a Betteshanger miner, was also serving in the Home Guard platoon based at the drill hall (later the Kent Brush Co.) at Mill Hill. This morning he had a nasty surprise after arriving to start work on the day shift:

> On reporting at 6.00 a.m., I and many others, needless to say, were walking up to the iron gantry to gain access to the cage, prior to our descent underground, when there was a terrific explosion and clouds of smoke. There was chaos

everywhere – a complete shambles. We were eventually shepherded out into the pit yard and were all horrified to see a huge bomb embedded in the earth, separating the winding house from the shaft – a direct hit! Fortunately for the hundreds of men there at the time, it had not exploded, and was eventually defused under the normal routine of war. Afterwards no production of coal was possible to help the war effort for some time. All the men were transferred to Snowdown and Tilmanstone for many months, but returned at a later date. The irony for me was that being a member of the Home Guard my duties included going back to Betteshanger to guard the site, and this monstrosity!

Tuesday 19 May
Private Goldfinch, Nelson Street, taken to the hospital to have his wound re-dressed. He was a casualty from the bomb incident at the railway station.

Wednesday 20 May
New messenger boy Thompson started duty. We visited contact points in Kingsdown. ARP office respirators disinfected.

In June 1942 both the Deal borough restaurants had to be extended because they had proved to be very popular, offering a good basic meal at a very reasonable price. Although there were other catering establishments, among those who patronized the 'civic' restaurants was Helen Ward:

> Myself, and one or two girls from the food office in Victoria Road used to meet up and go to the 'community kitchen' in St George's Hall to have our lunch (for 6*d*) or, if we were feeling reckless, we could splash out at Catt's Restaurant, round in Middle Street, where two courses and tea cost us 1*s* 6*d*.

During this month more representations were made to the authorities against reducing the ARP personnel in the town any further, as there was still a need to keep a viable organization to deal with casualties and damage caused by the hit and run raids.

Two new shelters were being erected by Mr Eames, one at the Methodist School (for fifty children) in Union Street, and at the Roman Catholic elementary school which had now moved to 'Beach Court' in Glack Road, Upper Deal.

A proposal by the CO of the 540th Coast Regt RA, that the Royal Marine Siege Regt should take over local beach defence duties was turned down because these guns were to be retained for cross-Channel bombardments.

Monday 1 June
00.47hrs: Local warning; 02.31hrs: danger passed.

Gee! what a din last night and early this morning. I woke Will up when the planes started diving, and made a cup of tea when it was a bit quieter. Canterbury was the target, and was badly damaged by HEs and incendiaries.

02.00hrs: Two HEs fell at Poulton Farm, Ash.

This large conflagration in Canterbury was dealt with by the city fire brigade, supplemented by others in 'D' Division, including those from Deal. The station clerk, Mr Alfred Holmes was left to 'man the fort' alone at Deal Town Hall:

Mr James Hampson of Betteshanger Home Guard in the garden of his home in Circular Road near the colliery.

I was the clerk, working out rosters and paying out the wages, so I didn't pick up a hose 'in anger' all through the war, although on the occasion that Canterbury was blitzed, I was packed up all ready to go. All the spare personnel were collected up and sent off to Canterbury, or London when they were needed, leaving just a skeleton staff to man the appliances in Deal. I had to sleep on a bed in the corner of the garage (under the Town Hall) where the fire engines were kept behind the wooden doors, facing out on to the High Street.

Wednesday 3 June
02.25hrs: Local warning; 03.53hrs: danger passed.

Noisy night and early morning again, some poor devils have caught it. Walked to 'The Chequers' in the sandhills, to watch our planes 'letting them have it' on the other side – it shook the buildings on this side.

03.10hrs: IBs dropped over a wide area at Ash.

04.00hrs: IBs dropped at Langdon Abbey Farm, West Langdon.

Friday 5 June
Plenty of air activity, mostly ours going over to the other side. This afternoon two of our fighters collided over the sea, while practising diving on the wrecks. Both caught fire and sank; one pilot was picked up dead, the other wasn't found.

14.45hrs: Hurricane BL423 of No. 174 Sqn collided with BP754 of the same squadron off Deal, while doing some practice attacks on the Goodwins shipwrecks; F/Lt Hunt and W/O Merryweather were both killed.

Saturday 6 June
A young woman came in to have her foot dressed; something had pierced her foot.

Sunday 7 June
01.30hrs: IBs dropped at Ware, Ash; fire at Downfield Farm; eight IBs dropped at Wingham and four IB containers at Blackley Hill and Brook Farm; IBs at Adisham Court Farm.

Wednesday 10 June
'M' Balloon Unit RAF relocated to Walmer.

Originally deployed in France at the beginning of the war, this balloon unit was evacuated to Manston in May 1940, where they restarted their operations on the night of 16/17 July. Having been bombed out during the 'terror raid' of 24 August 1940, they were redeployed to Birchington, but their activities conflicted with the night-bomber operations from RAF Manston.

Due to the 'secret' nature of their operations, unit members were ordered to refer to themselves only as RAF Walmer. One of those who remembers seeing balloons launched from this site was Mrs Emily Burgess, then living at King's Farm, on Dover Road:

> These balloons were launched from the old tennis courts behind 'General's Meadow' in St Clare Road, Walmer, and also from Kingsdown. During the day they would send up single balloons which were to gauge the wind direction in the upper atmosphere, and if that was right, groups of balloons carrying either leaflets or incendiary devices were launched at dusk by the RAF personnel based at 'Iverson House', Walmer. Sometimes these balloons were not set off properly and exploded over Deal, showering the inhabitants with bundles of leaflets printed in German or other foreign languages. Others would catch fire in flight, and set light to the cornfields when they landed.

Sunday 14 June
There was a big church parade at St George's for United Nations Day.

During the following night the Royal Navy minesweeping trawler *Tranquil* foundered after colliding with the wreckage of Deal Pier, leaving only a single barrage balloon above the water to mark the spot, this later being replaced by a marker buoy.

Wednesday 17 June
First operation by 'M' Balloon Unit from 'General's Meadow'; 350 balloons sent to targets in France.

Friday 19 June
A boy from Western Road was brought in to have his hand dressed; sent him to hospital to have it stitched.

Tuesday 23 June
Guns going off all morning; we could hear the shells whistle over.

Wednesday 24 June
S.A. Harris on duty at mayoress's 'junk-shop'. The band of the Hampshire Regt gave a concert in the grounds of Warden House.

Thursday 25 June

Officers of the Hampshire Regt held a garden party at Warden House.
  06.00hrs: Guns fire from St Margaret's to Sandown.

Friday 26 June

S.A. Harris helped again at the mayoress's junk-shop. A boy came in with a fish-hook embedded in his leg; sent him to hospital.

Saturday 27 June

Hampshire Regt sports day. S.A. Harris helped at mayoress' junk-shop.

During July 1942 a second air raid shelter (for forty children) was under construction by Mr Eames at the Deal Methodist school, while the local ack-ack defences were strengthened by batteries from No. 122 LAA Regt, 71st AA Brigade RA. Around Sandwich the defences were sited at Little Stonar; Stone Cross; at the southern end of 'the Monks Wall'; and near the Ash Road railway crossing. In Deal, the Bofors guns were positioned at Sandown Castle; on the North Deal playing-fields; Walmer Green and in 'The Dip' in Victoria Park. Other batteries were stationed near Tilmanstone and Snowdown Collieries, and out on the coal 'tip' at Betteshanger. Charles Grant remembers that they had an early warning system in operation, the Bofors gun crew being given a bell to ring in the colliery yard if they saw enemy aircraft mounting an attack.

Sunday 5 July

A lady called here from 109 West Street with a burned foot; we dressed it and sent her to hospital, where she was detained.

The 5th Battalion Dorset Regt were undertaking beach guard duties at St Margaret's Bay and Les Wood remembers that it was quite a scary place to be – especially if there was to be an invasion:

> The first time I went on guard I found it quite eerie; as the water receded it took the pebbles with it and the sound could easily have been mistaken for footsteps on the beach. The guardroom was in a house with a garage attached, and in this garage was a switch which the guard commander had to throw if the enemy appeared. This would have blown up a section of the promenade which was heavily mined. The warning of an enemy attack was a combination of different coloured Very lights to be fired into the air, which would have then brought down an artillery barrage on the sea-front – the guards were expendable!

The St Margaret's ARP logbook contained the following reports:

Wednesday 8 July

05.30hrs: Edge Cottage, St Margaret's Bay, hit by shell; greenhouse and west wall demolished; two killed and nine injured.

Thursday 9 July

01.45hrs: Shelling from both sides; some soldiers were killed at St Margaret's.
    02.57hrs–03.30hrs: Eleven SHs fell at St Margaret's; many houses damaged.

Wednesday 15 July

Dr Kirk and Mr Daniels phoned; we are to arrange a dance, a whist-drive or a concert for Salvage Week.

Thursday 16 July

A deputation from the Canterbury Chamber of Commerce visited Deal to advise on the town's Salvage Scheme.

Saturday 18 July

The loudspeaker was out, making announcements about Salvage Week.

Sunday 26 July

Telegram from Kath, to say she was arriving at 2.15 p.m. Met her at the station. The police were there, taking people's names and addresses, and telling them they are only allowed to stay three days.

August 1942 saw the practice of using strengthened cellars as air raid shelters finally abandoned as the town was now equipped with an adequate number of surface shelters. However, the continued hit and run raids and intermittent shelling led to the evacuation of various borough council departments from the town centre. The town clerk's and borough surveyor's departments, together with the fuel office, moved up to Milestone House in London Road. The borough accountants and ARP fire guard moved to 'Kent House'; while the public health department was rehoused at 'Cherry Orchard' in London Road. The council offices in Queen Street then became the fire-watchers' HQ.

During the summer of 1942 Deal's business premises had suffered a succession of air raids, but despite this many shops in Deal were kept open. Some had boarded-up windows, with the sections which had suffered damage partitioned off, as at Marks & Spencer's. Miss Peggy Oatridge recalls that many of the shopkeepers and local residents had taken to 'sleeping out' of the town centre by this time:

> Several businesses kept going throughout the war, including Clarabut's, Pilcher & Chittenden's, and Walter's Dairies, and I was friendly with that family. But very wisely they went up to Mill Hill every night to sleep. So many houses were empty in Mill Hill, so they never stayed in the town at night.
>
> Our home 'Wellington House', was in Mill Road, overlooking Victoria Park. We had wonderful cellars under the house and they had all been shored up and we had one more or less gas-proofed, but my father thought that he would catch pneumonia down there. So he wouldn't go down, so my mother also refused, and therefore I couldn't go either, and so we never used them – we

always stuck it out. But we were all right there as the house was low and very solidly built. We did have glass blown out of the windows several times, and I can remember sweeping it all up; it seemed to be an everyday occurrence.

The elderly Doctor Neil had now returned from the Bristol area, and was made a Medical Officer of Incidents for air raid casualties, but according to Dr James Hall, this work mostly involved sorting out bits of corpses.

Certificates of Merit were presented to Southern Railway staff at Deal, for their fortitude when the station was bombed.

Work was started on four concrete 'hards', equipped with oil pipelines and wooden jetties, along the sea-front.

Monday 3 August: Bank Holiday
St John Ambulance Brigade's garden fête at the old Manor House was a 'washout' in more ways than one!

Saturday 8 August
07.25hrs: Local warning; 07.27hrs: danger passed.
   We had five minutes' excitement – quite a barrage of AA fire.
   21.30hrs: Little girl was brought into the depot with a fractured right arm; we splinted it and sent the child to hospital.

On Sunday 9 August, the St Margaret's ARP logbook contained the following:

St Margaret's ARP reported that a bright light was visible from the Knoll Hotel, The Droveway. The field ambulance station was informed and asked to have it attended to.

Tuesday 11 August
01.05hrs: Local warning; 01.54hrs: danger passed.
   18.07hrs: Bombs dropped without warning; in College Road, the gas works, the station and the East Kent garage, also in Queen Street and Albert Road. There were several people killed, and many other casualties. D. Harvey went out with No. 1 Party to College Road and I was out with No. 2 Party in Church Path. Two of our windows blown out. Deal is now a mess! 8 HEs (18 demolished; 292 seriously damaged; 406 slightly damaged; 8 killed; 6 seriously injured; 55 slightly injured).

One bomb hit the London Road railway bridge, demolishing the station-master's house; another fell at the end of Albert Road, near the level crossing, and damaged the engine shed and surrounding property, with pieces of railway line being blown hundreds of yards. The 'Queen's Hall' in Queen Street, and Curzon Terrace received damage, while the roofing sheets on the Odeon cinema were stripped off. One bomb fell next to the Swaffield's Laundry, also damaging 66–68 College Road and houses in Ark Lane; another fell in Cannon Street and damaged the gas-holders at Deal gas works. Leslie Collyer recalls:

I'd had my tea and had strolled out of the laboratory when the special Cuckoo air raid warning went. [This double-note siren was used for hit and run raiders after 1941.] I'd just reached the gate when the bombs started exploding, so I dived behind a wall at the bottom of the steps to the stores – the only place that I could think of quickly. When I looked out all I could see was No. 3 Holder, over by Wakeham's Field, all alight and coming down fast. One of the Oatridges was with me, so I told him we had better go and turn the valves off, and put the No. 2 Holder on to the town supply before No. 3 Holder ran out.

As we ran towards this holder, the planes were firing behind us and I saw cannon shells piercing our two tar-tanks, and around the rim there were little glowing holes. So as we ran on, looking northwards we could see another half-dozen planes coming in low, and at first glance they looked like Spitfires. But just as that thought crossed my mind, they released their bombs, so I shouted to young Oatridge to get back to some shelter.

We hadn't got anywhere near the valves, so we ran back across to the other side of Cannon Street; he dropped down behind the wall near No. 2 Holder, the oldest one, and I ran on across the road. Just then a bomb went off, and I can recall looking at the weigh-bridge window, which was a huge 10ft by 8ft window made up of little panes. I can remember watching it bending out, looking just like a curved piece of graph paper, and seeing it coming down to the ground. I am still convinced to this day that I actually ran through that window as this happened!

When I reached the air raid shelter, the boilerman, one of the Redsull brothers, was there already, and told me I couldn't use the phone as it was hanging off the

Like Blenheim Road, College Road suffered several bombing raids, mostly directed at the town's gas works in nearby Cannon Street. Helping to remove the rubble after a raid in August 1942 is one of the Deal Corporation dust carts and a couple of lorries, while the ARP rescue squad searches the ruins of nos 66 and 68 for survivors.

In an attack on Deal railway station on 11 August 1942, one of the pilots missed his mark and his bomb fell on houses at the London Road end of Albert Road. Also damaged was the ARP post at 'Beechwood' opposite.

The station-master's house at Deal station after a bomb had scored a direct hit; during the same raid Deal Gas Works and College Road were also hit. Watched by a lone policeman (Sgt Jarrett?), Norman Cavell photographed the wreckage from the station platform on the Down side of the line.

wall. As he turned round, No. 2 Holder split, with the rivets popping open – just like a row of buttons. This bomb had also knocked down part of the bund wall around the oil tank, and taken a piece out of the wall opposite, and had then gone through our old house in College Road – the people living there then were killed.

Wednesday 12 August
Many minor casualties kept coming in this morning. I finished at the depot at 3 p.m. today. Heavy shelling at night.

From the St Margaret's ARP logbooks:

Thursday 13 August
15-in guns at Wanstone Farm, St Margaret's, ready to fire.
　02.30hrs–08.00hrs: Ten SHs reported in the St Margaret's area.

Saturday 15 August
00.40hrs: Nine SHs reported in St Margaret's area, but eight of them fell in the sea.
　04.30hrs: Direct hit by a shell demolished 'Seaton', Granville Road, St Margaret's Bay; luckily the house was unoccupied so no casualties.
　21.18hrs: Thirteen SHs in St Margaret's area: one at 'Salters', Sea Street; one in Bockell Farm meadow and four on Bockell Farm; two each at Townsend Farm and West Cliffe Road; one at Reach Court Farm; one on the Dower House, Oxney Court and one in Oxney Wood.

John Wilson recalls this particular night very well but for a totally different reason:

It was about midnight when there was a terrific knocking at our door, and when we opened it there stood an Army dispatch rider. He informed my father that the 'Invasion' alert had gone off and that there was a general call-out on. Dad rushed over to the Home Guard HQ, while I got dressed and set out on my bicycle to knock up the rest of the platoon. Looking across to the north-east, towards the Stour Estuary, all hell had been let loose. I could see machine-gun fire, flares, and star shells all going up, and even the anti-aircraft guns at Manston aerodrome seemed to be firing almost horizontally across Pegwell Bay.

One clue as to what was going on that night emerged later. At the Reed Barn school in Ash village was a detachment of the Dorset Regt. They were on duty in the pillboxes down at Sandwich Bay for three days a week, and then came back for a three-day rest, then went back on duty again. One of the local girls had become friendly with one of the young Dorset lads, but as her parents did not approve, she used to bring him up to our home.

She had arranged to meet him the evening after all that rumpus down at Sandwich Bay, but he did not turn up, and neither did he appear on the following evening, so she started to get worried. We asked some of the Dorset lads what had happened to him, but we couldn't get anything out of them. Father had dealings with the Dorset detachment about rifle and ammunition supply for the Home

Guard, so he tackled their sergeant about it after a few days, but all he could get out of him was, 'Well, it was their own fault, they were all asleep!'

Nothing more happened until six or seven months later, when the young lady concerned arrived at our house in tears, having just received a Red Cross postcard from her young man – from Germany!

Tuesday 18 August
Heavy shelling at night; bombs fell at East Langdon and at Ringwould.
  00.42hrs: Six SHs reported at St Margaret's.
  01.30hrs: One SH near the East Kent Light Railway at Tilmanstone/Knowlton.

On Wednesday 19 August Mrs A. Bradshaw noted in her diary:

A constant rumble from the other side while our planes have been going over on sweeps. Americans, Free French and Canadians made a landing on the French coast this morning, with tanks and artillery.

The ill-fated raid on Dieppe involved some of the Canadian troops who had trained at Betteshanger Park, and the night before they left local villagers recall them trying to dispose of all of their surplus stores. Mrs Jean Donaghy remembers that they were even burning personal effects such as prayer books. Wren Annie Scragg remembers these Canadians arriving at the Deal RM depot from Scotland. She had been seconded from Dover to assist with their victualling, and remembers that it was hard work for a few days, and that she was very glad to return to the Caves at Dover. Peggy Oatridge, still driving the bread-van on her rounds, recalls:

When I came back from my Lyminge trips, I would have to come through Willow Woods, and there were camps full of Canadian troops. They used to make a cordon across the road and stop the bread-van, not letting me pass, because all they wanted was to have a chat. They were so nice and never any trouble. There were more Canadians based in Ripple at Ripple Down House – they were great lads, and not so 'pushy' as the Americans.

Monday 24 August
04.50hrs–05.32hrs: Six SHs fell on open ground at St Margaret's; slight damage to houses.

Tuesday 25 August
Dawn: Three HEs. Three enemy aircraft bombed the RM Infirmary; one bomb fell on Patchin's Store at the rear of 'Epworth', Park Lane, then into Harris Mayes' garden; debris fell on Deal bowling club pavilion and greens; some damage in Park Lane, London Road and Upper Gladstone Road. (47 seriously damaged; 85 slightly damaged; 5 slightly injured).

Thursday 27 August
Spitfire Vb BM248 of No. 154 Sqn damaged by FW190 and crash-landed near Sandwich; F/O A.S. Turnbull (RCAF) unhurt.

Friday 28 August
An unknown aircraft [possibly an American P-47 Thunderbolt fighter] crashed on the Deal–Sandwich railway line near the Betteshanger Colliery signal box.

During September 1942 the Deal Borough Entertainments Committee lodged their claim with the Admiralty about the damage that the *Nora* had caused to Deal Pier. After long and protracted negotiations, skilfully conducted by the town clerk, Albert Daniels, officialdom admitted their liability and a war damage payment was agreed.

Thursday 3 September
Spitfire Vb W3312 of No. 65 Sqn abandoned 10 miles east of Deal; P/O N.R. MacQueen killed.

The St Margaret's ARP logbooks record:

Friday 4 September
21.10hrs–22.30hrs: Ten SHs fell on open land at St Margaret's.
   22.20hrs: Direct hit by shell on 'Crossways', St Margaret's; casualties nil (all five safe in shelter).

Saturday 5 September
Gas leak reported from 'Crossways'.

Sunday 6 September
The Odeon Cinema reopened after having temporary roof repairs.

Saturday 26 September
11.25hrs: Spitfire Vb EM771 'DL-U' crashed in field near the St Margaret's/Martin Mill crossroads; pilot safe.

Tuesday 29 September
09.22hrs: Bombs on Betteshanger Fan House, with extensive damage to the two winding houses, the power-house and the buildings over the winding gear. Likely to be six weeks before full production is resumed. 2 HEs (2 killed; 3 seriously injured; 26 slightly injured). Houses in Kingsdown machine-gunned (4 slightly damaged).

Charles Grant recalls that with the winding gear out of action the emergency service cage had to be used, and it took seventeen hours to get all the men up. The two casualties caused at Betteshanger were both workers from the Ramsgate builders, Grummant Brothers: a lorry driver and his mate were killed while they were delivering cement. The mine was shut, and most of the miners were moved to the other collieries. Stuart Spears recalls the attack:

   I was crouching under the table in the wages office as there was no way we could have got out in time if the bombs had exploded. As the fan house was hit, there was no possibility of getting ventilation down to the coal faces, so a number of miners were transferred to Snowdown Colliery, leaving only a skeleton staff to run the pit. I think we worked on the open shaft system and relied on natural ventilation. All the air doors had to be wedged open to allow air to circulate, but it was still very hot down below.

Monday 5 October
19.00hrs: Shelling on both sides; one landed on the RM depot football-pitch in Canada Road. Houses damaged; 4 SHs (5 seriously damaged; 19 slightly damaged; 1 seriously injured; 1 slightly injured).

Friday 9 October
Spitfire IX BS443 of No. 306 Sqn crashed at Sholden, returning from bomber escort; Sgt M. Kordastewicz (Polish) killed.

Sunday 11 October
Spitfires AB792 and AD298 of No. 453 Sqn collided off Deal (Sgt A.R. Menzies and Sgt B.T. Rossiter both missing).

Ron Read recalls these Spitfires and the reason why they crashed:

Female office staff at Betteshanger Colliery. The colliery became a target for the hit and run raiders during 1942, the power house, fan house and winding gear all being damaged. Fortunately, not all the bombs exploded, as these office girls would have had no chance of escaping from their boiler-room shelter, as Mrs Doris Speares (seated, third from right) recalls.

Two Spitfires came down over towards Martin Mill, they had had a good fight over the Channel and were doing a victory roll when their wing-tips touched and they both crashed; one of them came down just up the field behind Ripple Court Cottages.

Friday 16 October

07.00hrs: Two enemy aircraft at sea level; dropped one bomb each, one on Deal station goods depot, the other on railway lines beyond the level crossing; Deal goods department was transferred to Walmer station for the remainder of the war. 2 HEs (I demolished; 45 seriously damaged; 79 slightly damaged; I slightly injured). Damage in Southwall Road, Middle Deal Road and West Street.

Serving with the 122nd LAA Regt RA local ack-ack defences was gunner John Lythgoe, who recalls that he had only just been posted to Deal with his battery, the 402nd:

We moved to Deal on 28 September, specifically in my case to No. 4 gun-site. It was in a field just on the left of the road north of the level crossing, but our stay was only until 18 October. A hit and run engagement during this time lasted no more than a few seconds, though we had advance warning, and were waiting. It so happened that a lone Typhoon, which was similar in outline to the FW190, happened to be overhead at the same time, so the pilot was not at all pleased. Fortunately he was beyond our range.

Thursday 22 October

09.00hrs: Early morning attack; bombs on College Road, High Street and Stanley Road. 3 HEs (15 demolished; 68 seriously damaged; 96 slightly damaged; 15 killed; 7 seriously injured; 15 slightly injured).

Percy Comfort's ironmongers shop, the 'King's Bazaar' toy shop, Martin's bakers, Cox's chemist and St George's Hall were all demolished or badly damaged. The young lad who had lived next door to Mary Osbourn at Circular Road, Betteshanger, was killed in this raid when Gordon Blain's greengrocers suffered a direct hit. Charles Grant recalled the search for the boy:

Young Raymond Files was only fourteen years old and he was thought to have been down in the basement of Gordon Blain's. His father came into the Betteshanger Club on Saturday night to tell us he was going to try to find his son, and asked if any of us would like to help him. We were all dressed in our best clothes, so we went home and changed, then came into Deal in an old lorry without any seats in the back. We dug down into the debris as far as the basements steps, but could find nothing. What made things worse was that bits of meat from the butchers shop at the back were scattered amongst the debris. We worked on until 2 a.m. on Sunday morning, when the 'Sally Army' canteen van arrived with some tea and sandwiches for us.

During this bombing, the east window of St George's Church, and the window at the end of Deal Corporation pew were both shattered. Bernard Kimpton recalls that only a portion of the east window was saved – a piece with the word 'Hope' on it, so this was incorporated into the lower portion of a new window depicting Walmer's lifeboat *Charles Dibden*.

Saturday 24 October
Some of the air raid victims were buried today; two more have died, and the damage is appalling.

Friday 30 October
Mrs Roosevelt, wife of the president of the USA was on a visit to East Kent. She slept overnight in a coach belonging to the 16th Super Heavy Rail Battery at Adisham – very well guarded!

Saturday 31 October
17.00hrs: Four waves of FW190s came over at roof-top height, machine-gunning; AA engaged while they were en route for Canterbury. MG (18 seriously damaged; 38 slightly damaged).

17.05hrs: Focke-Wulf FW190 5250 2+ of 5/JG2 shot down by LAA at low level, and crashed at Little Stonar, near Sandwich. Fw A. Hell baled out and was taken prisoner.

Bomb damage in Deal High Street, 22 October 1942. Three shops were obliterated when a German pilot dropped his bomb on Gordon Blain's greengrocery shop early one Friday morning. There were no strategic targets nearby, so perhaps he had mistaken the lantern light on the roof and the St George's clock tower for similar features on Deal Castle and the Royal Marines East Barracks.

17.10hrs: Ash, Nonington, Eastry, Mongeham, Woodnesborough, Worth and Staple – whole area machine-gunned during the daylight attack on Canterbury. Two HEs dropped at Ash.

17.15hrs: Four HEs dropped at Worth; fifty fire-pots over the sea (possibly as markers).

Bernie Kimpton remembers seeing one group of fighter-bombers come in over Deal, with another group from the direction of Whitstable. Two of the first batch attacked Betteshanger Colliery as he watched from Ripple Down. Working out in the fields at Ripple Court Farm, Ron Read and his brother had a grandstand view of these attackers:

> On the day of the big raid on Canterbury, we saw the German aircraft 'hedge-hopping' so low that they disappeared from our view as they went down in the dip in the field towards Sutton. They had obviously been expected, and I didn't know that we had so many anti-aircraft guns around here, until they all opened up on these aircraft: Bofors, cannons and machine-guns – a lot more guns than normal.

Three of these enemy fighter-bombers were shot down near Sandwich, one falling near Felton's timber yard, another in Sandwich Bay and the third in Pegwell Bay. During the attack, country roads were machine-gunned, and bombs fell at Richborough, in Ash and along Sandown Road, at Sandwich. Another eye-witness was 'clippie' Marjorie Kemp, who was on her way to Canterbury with a bus full of passengers, when these raiders swept in over Sandwich:

> On the Saturday afternoon that Canterbury was badly bombed, we were near-ing the Richborough railway crossing on the Ash road out of Sandwich, when my driver spotted the German aircraft. He stopped the bus and yelled 'Get Out!' to everybody. Amid a great deal of machine-gunning, we fell out on to the road and into a dry ditch. The money in my cash bag went flying in the long grass, but I suppose I must have found it all later. It sounded as if the enemy was machine-gunning the windmill, but it could have been Sandwich radar station nearby. After all that, we were turned back at the top of St Martin's Hill when we finally reached Canterbury.

20.00hrs–21.00hrs: Another raid; big fires in Canterbury. HEs and incendiaries fell in surrounding fields and it was very noisy.

20.30hrs: Two HEs at Sutton; two HEs and one container of IBs dropped at Nonington.

20.40hrs: Seven IB containers dropped at Ripple; three UXBs in Nonington Woods; eight HEs and IBs at Adisham, causing a fire in the straw and wheat stacks.

21.00hrs: One HE at Ash.

Another fund-raising week in November saw the townspeople raise £681 19s 3d for Anglo-Soviet Friendship Week, but due to the damage to St George's Church, the mayor regretfully had to announce that no Civic Service would be held that year.

The need for more accurate bombing of enemy targets required a better system of marking by the Pathfinder aircraft, which dropped flares or target markers before the main bomber stream arrived. One of the first stations involved in these operations was at Walmer, where a device code-named 'Oboe' came into its own this month.

One WAAF posted there was Mrs Irene Davis:

> We were getting our kitbags from the train when a hooter started blasting out, and on turning round to ask the RAF corporal sent to escort us to our billets what it was, we realized we were the only two people on the platform – everybody else had disappeared. We soon found out why, as a shell landed, and the noise was horrifying. We both dashed into the ladies' waiting-room – which incidentally was a good choice at that particular time. When the 'All Clear' went, we returned to the platform and the corporal turned up, and asked why we hadn't followed him, to which we replied that 'it would have been polite to tell us where you were going'. What a creep he was, and the Army lads let him know it, as he watched us struggling with our kitbags, steel helmets and gas-masks, etc, and didn't offer to help us.

Mr Eames was now involved in constructing some underground shelters at the Canada Road junior school, and the new group warden's post, at 3 College Road. Another job was bricking up a window in South Street. A static water tank in Marke Wood recreation ground was being worked on, as well as a surface water basin built at the Victoria Park First Aid Post. These were in addition to the small circular water tanks which could be used for relay pumping by the fire brigade if water mains had been damaged, as explained by Mr Stuart Harlow:

> We drew up a Relay Plan, which involved pumping water from the static tanks to the basins, and from there to the fires. The plan involved a system of cards with an area map showing the hydrants, basins and tanks, matching the large map we kept at Denne's Yard at Walmer. When a crew was sent out, the leading fireman was handed the card for the appropriate area so he knew immediately where everything was located. I also went round the town with a 100ft tape and a pot of yellow paint, and marked on the wall/road where our pumps were to be positioned between tanks or basins for relay pumping. On any wall nearby we also marked details of the size of main, pressure and flow at that particular point. My tasks produced some very sarcastic comments from the locals such as 'Haven't you got anything better to do?'

Sunday 1 November
01.20hrs: Six HEs at Cooting Farm, Adisham. Fire-pot IBs and two HEs in the same area.

Thursday 5 November
Deal was bombed again this morning. One bomb on Cannon Street demolished three houses; there was also damage in Golf Road. 4 HEs (7 demolished; 25 seriously damaged; 33 slightly damaged; 3 killed; 1 seriously injured; 6 slightly injured).

Sunday 8 November
Spitfire Vb EP381 of No. 165 Sqn dived into the sea 7 miles east of South Foreland; P/O G.C. Griffin missing.

The St Margaret's ARP logbook for Monday 9 November records:

Germans bombarded the sites of 'Winnie' and 'Pooh'; the latter's ready-use magazines were hit, and the power-house for the former. Ack-ack site also targeted and eleven men killed.

At the end of 1942 Winston Churchill briefly visited Walmer to inspect progress on the new beach 'hards', and the Sandwich Home Guard Battalion took over the 338th CD Battery RA's guns at Sandwich Bay. By December the resident population of Deal had fallen again to 11,187, probably as a result of the constant hit and run raids on the town. However, the borough council formed a 'Post-War Reconstruction Committee', and the mayor was present at the 'passing-out' ceremony for four squads of recruits after their six-week course at the RM depot.

Wednesday 2 December
10.05hrs: Four Focke-Wulfe 190s machine-gunned the area, en route to Manston aerodrome. One aircraft was shot down by F/Sgt Haddon of No. 609 Sqn. MG/Cannon (2 seriously damaged; 25 slightly damaged; 4 slightly injured). There was some damage to property in Cross Road, Cemetery Road, Campbell Road, York Road and Mill Hill; and some houses were slightly damaged in both Ripple and Upper Walmer. Two people were injured.

Another obvious target was the Royal Marine depot. Jack Pickup, who stayed for only a short time in Deal, nevertheless recalls the constant attacks:

> My main memories of the life in barracks are of the dive-bombers on their hit and run raids from France. They happened frequently and without warning; the most dangerous time was when they machine-gunned across the parade-ground – it happened so quickly, we only had time to think of the underground shelters, and get there as quickly as possible.
> After completing the training, my detachment was drafted to the Orkneys. When we left the depot for the last time to march to the railway station, as the band led us through the streets of Deal, we were touched to see people standing on each side of the road waving us off.

Thursday 3 December
Wellington 1c DV819 of 1474 Flt damaged by Ju88 while on radar 'spy' mission; ditched off Kingsdown. Crew rescued: they were all injured and taken to Deal hospital for treatment.

The navigator on board this Wellington was Canadian 'Bill' Barry who, some forty years later, still vividly recalled the events which led up to their unscheduled arrival off Kingsdown beach that morning:

> We had the special radio operator, Bigory, on board, who had been tracking the German night-fighter's signals (that was the reason for our mission); he had been badly wounded and we felt that he would not survive in the cold water if we ditched with him still on board. Consequently we did one quick circuit over Deal,

took him to the escape hatch, secured the ripcord on his parachute to the aircraft, and pushed him out of the hole in the back of the aircraft. I understand that he landed on the side of a church in Deal, and slid down a tree to the ground.

Then we flew the aircraft out to sea, for five or six miles – and ditched it. As soon as it was ditched successfully we all struggled out and endeavoured to inflate the dinghy, but it was full of bullet holes and absolutely useless to us. So we were all in the water with just our Mae Wests [inflatable life-jackets] keeping us up. It was between 6 and 7 a.m. and it was just getting light.

Fishing for sprats nearby was Frank Arnold, a Kingsdown fisherman, who quickly up-anchored and made for the wreckage, lifting the five injured crew members out of the water, and making for shore. Bill Barry continues his account thus:

He brought us in at Deal, but we were so stiff with the cold that before we were taken to Deal hospital, we had to be lifted out of the boat. However, once at Deal hospital we were each given a warm water bath and that revived our circulation – and that was about it!

Fatigue and cold may well have caused Bill to believe they were over Deal when the radio operator was ejected from their aircraft – but it actually happened over Ramsgate. The pilot, P/O Edwin Paulton RCAF, was awarded a DFC; Special Radio Operator P/O Harold Jordan RAFVR, the DSO; and F/Sgt William Bigory RCAF, the other radio operator, the DFM. Their mission had provided the clue to the night-fighter radar system code-named 'Lichtenstein', and thus ensured that a successful jamming system could be devised.

Thursday 10 December
23.56hrs–01.44hrs: Eleven SHs fell in St Margaret's area; slight damage. 2 SHs in Deal (14 seriously damaged; 15 slightly damaged; 1 slightly injured). Damage to Southwall Road, Gladstone Road and London Road; windows broken and roofs damaged over a wide area.

Tuesday 15 December
15.44hrs: Worth and Ash machine-gunned; one person slightly injured.

Friday 18 December
14.12hrs: FW190A 0712 of 10/JABO/JG26, hit by LAA fire and attacked by No. 609 Sqn Typhoon (F/O R.A. Lallement); it crashed in the sea 1 mile east-north-east of Deal coastguard station. Staffel Kaptain Oblt K. Muller's body recovered from sea off Deal.

Four Focke-Wulf FW190As had bombed and machine-gunned Sandwich. One house in Fisher Street was demolished; and damage was caused to the toll bridge, Upper Strand Street vicarage, and to both the parish halls. Windows were broken in Manwood Court, the Masonic Hall, and at the Bell Hotel. Two enemy aircraft were brought down, one of them falling near St Bart's Hall – according to Mr Rolfe.

The extensive damage caused during a raid on Sandwich on 18 December 1942 included the Barbican toll house on the bridge over the River Stour. During the attack two Focke-Wulfs were shot down; one pilot's body was later recovered from the sea off Deal coastguard station.

Saturday 19 December
Two enemy planes brought down in the sea, the gunners in the Caxton Home got one, and were awarded seven days leave.

Monday 21 December
00.45hrs–03.10hrs: Twenty-one SHs fell in the St Margaret's area.
   First operational trials of 'Oboe' undertaken during an attack by No. 109 Sqn Mosquitos on Lutterade, in Holland.

The newly arrived WAAFs, including Irene Davis, soon settled in at Hawkshill Down, but found their first Christmas in their lodgings at Walmer somewhat traumatic when it came to Christmas Dinner:

> Our first Christmas away from home was the pits, as the couple we were billet-ed on had had a domestic quarrel on Christmas morning, and the poor rabbit that was supposed to be our dinner, was used as a weapon. The poor, sad crea-ture was so battered and bruised that we didn't have the heart to eat it, so we went back to camp and begged something from the nearby Army cookhouse.

Thursday 31 December
Second operational trial of 'Oboe' during a raid on Florennes in Belgium.

CHAPTER SIX

January–December 1943

By 1943, rumours were circulating that the Germans were developing a 'secret weapon'; in fact they had two: the V1 flying bomb and the V2 rocket. Precautions and countermeasures were undertaken, and an attempt was made to locate the launching sites of these weapons. Sergeant (RA) Surveyor John Whitehouse belonged to the No. 2 Sound-Ranging Unit RA recruited to perform this task:

> I was finally posted to Canterbury, under Major Jessop, and dug a forward observation post on the cliffs at St Margaret's Bay. We had thirty-six microphones stretching from Colchester to Eastbourne in order to locate V2 rockets, which we did successfully.
>
> In 1943 my party had to equip one microphone, situated about a mile up the coast road from Deal, and on the west side of the River Stour. That was too much of a cross-country trek from Richborough Castle, so we managed to borrow a boat (with no rowlocks!) from the Royal Marines at Deal, and managed to sling a line across the river and ferry our stuff over.

The 12in howitzers of the 8th Super Heavy Regt RA at Eythorne were still in position at this time, and took part in the usual defence exercises which were mounted to test their readiness. On one occasion the results caused some embarrassment, as Bombardier W.H. Bourne recalls:

> During my stay with the battery I remember a Regimental 'Defence and Attack' scheme which was not particularly exciting or conclusive. However, it was conclusive to the effect that we still had a lot to learn. Our adjutant, Captain Pepper, sporting three days' growth of beard, and wearing scruffy civilian clothes, tested our security level by walking straight through the lines – he wasn't challenged by anyone. He could have been a very successful fifth columnist – that took a long time to live down.
>
> Our guns were not static; we had several shoots at St Margaret's Bay, and on one occasion I had a very comfortable observation post, in beautiful weather, atop the water tower at Walmer.

Although some guns in the area were certainly dummies, there was one top secret gun which existed for a short while behind Bockell Farm at St Margaret's. This experimental gun, code-named 'Bruce', was a combination of an 8in barrel wedded to a 13.5in gun chamber and mounting; this meant that the charge for the heavier shell could propel a smaller shell much further. However, the drawback to this was severe wear in the rifling of the barrel, which wore out after only a few firings. Stan Wyatt remembers:

> There was also an experimental gun which was under our Corps in the Royal

Marine Siege Regt. We did a couple of test-firings, at a range of approximately 60 miles, but then we closed our site, and I did not know what happened to it. I think it was sent back to Shoeburyness testing ranges.

On 1 January Mr Eames was building a surface water basin at the ARP shelter in Cemetery Road; he was also continuing the modifications to street shelters in Victoria Park (opposite the Dames' Homes), and on The Strand (by East Barracks). He recalled:

> If the main entrance of a street shelter became blocked there was no escape for the occupants until it had been cleared, so I was sent round to cut a 2ft hole in the 9in thick end wall at the opposite end. This hole was then rebuilt with single skin brickwork, set in lime mortar, which could easily be knocked out to provide an emergency escape route.

Monday 18 January

19.00hrs: Enemy aircraft fly in from the sea, en route for Dover; engaged by HAA and LAA; almost full moon.
19.45hrs–20.00hrs: Nine HEs and fire-pot IBs at St Margaret's. Two HEs at Napchester, IBs and eight fire-pots in the Preston/Ash area.

Tuesday 19 January

A bomber crashed at Overland Farm, Ash; three of the crew were thrown out during the landing, but the pilot was trapped and had to be rescued by the Eastry Fire Brigade.

Wednesday 3 February

Lockheed Ventura I AE744 YH-V of No. 21 Sqn damaged by fighters and force-landed at 'Poor Start', Thornton Downs, Eastry. Sgt D.H. Lear injured; P/O J.R. Hutchinson and Sgts J. Childs and J.T. Price all unhurt.

It was not surprising to find that John Rolfe and his chums took a great interest in this aircraft:

> On my way home from school the RAF crash-tender came up Mill Lane and the driver stopped to ask his way to the crash site. Mr Stokes, an attendant at Eastry Union, in his police-like uniform, was trying to direct the driver. He advised him to take me with him as I knew the way. So up in the cab I climbed and sat between the driver and his mate and away we went; scraping along hedges, and going partly up banks, we came across the Ventura.
>
> It was sitting in a field near the road, without wings or tail-planes; another RAF truck and a crane were already there and the men were stripping out the guns from the turret, with other gear from inside the fuselage. I walked down through the gap in a belt of fir trees which was strewn with wreckage of the wings, engines and tail-planes and broken down trees.

The wreckage was later moved down to the bottom end of the village, into a field near

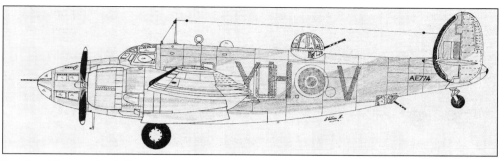

Sketch of the Lockheed Ventura 1 AE774 YH–V that crash-landed near Eastry, leaving a permanent reminder of the event by removing a number of trees from the row of larches along Thornton Downs – the 'Bomber Gap'.

Buttsole Pond, just off the Dover Road, where it was to remain for several days. John and his friends took full advantage of this to have some 'fantasy flights' in the aircraft:

> I think it was 5 February when I heard that a plane was down at Buttsole Pond, just on the edge of the village. Along with our gang of lads, we went to find it. On reaching the fields behind Eastry Hospital I could see it was my Ventura left there on the trailer. It was sitting in a cradle, quite high up and looked a lot larger than it had in the field.
>
> We climbed up on to the side of the trailer, and by lifting one of us up to the door handle, we opened it up and got inside. We all wanted to be the pilot, and being 'over crewed', took turns as different crew members. As I remember, by pushing a foot pedal down on the side of the turret we could turn it round. On our many 'bombing runs', the navigator in the Astro-dome and the gunner had to watch out for our worst enemy, the little black Hillman truck with the local 'copper' [Sergeant Hill] in it; he was responsible for patrolling the area, but as luck had it, he never came into sight, otherwise we would have had to bale out quickly, or he would have clipped us all round our ears.

Wednesday 10 February
20.40hrs–22.33hrs: Twenty SHs landed in the Langdon/St Margaret's area.

Sunday 14 February
06.06hrs: Six SHs at West Langdon; thirteen SHs landed in the sea off St Margaret's.

Monday 15 February
Convair Liberator 41-23800 of 68th Bomb Sqn; 44th Heavy Bomb Group USAAF, damaged by flak and enemy aircraft attack, crash-landed on Sandwich Flats.

With the build-up of the 8th United States Army Air Force in the UK, many bombing attacks and their aftermath were watched with great interest by lads of Eastry. John Rolfe:

The other types of aircraft flying over here were the American bombers, flying out in formation very high up to bomb Germany; then on their return all coming back flying low down and trailing smoke, with holes in their wings and tails and with bits missing from the rudders. We would count the number of engines that were still working, sometimes there were one, two or even three out of action.

Tuesday 2 March
09.30hrs: Two SHs (2 demolished; 6 seriously damaged; 37 slightly damaged; 1 slightly injured). Shells landed on The Strand, damaging Snow's bookshop, Hinds estate agents and Boothby's butchers; another fell on 'Hova Villas' in Golf Road and also damaged houses in Cannon Street.
   21.26hrs: Eleven SHs landed in St Margaret's area in reply to our bombardment.

Thursday 4 March
04.30hrs: Eight HEs fell on St George's golf course, at the back of Worth village.

Tuesday 9 March
Hawker Typhoon DN481 of No. 609 Sqn broke up in the air during aerobatics; it crashed on the road near Little Knell Farm, Ash. Sgt Booth was killed.

Kathleen Upton, then working with the Women's Land Army at Westmarsh, remembers that some Army lads based at Poulton Farm, Ash, were sent out to guard the site until the wreckage could be taken away.

> In those days Little Knell Farm was just known as Knell Farm and next door was Great Knell Farm, where the Stickles family, two brothers and two sisters, lived. We were on market gardening, but they did have some cattle, we also hoed swedes and riddled potatoes. When there was double summer time, I can remember we were stacking corn at 10 o'clock at night. The produce which we harvested was taken up to Covent Garden market on a truck marked 'G. Stickles and Son, Great Knell, Ash'.

Friday 12 March
02.27hrs–04.50hrs: Ten SHs fell in open ground all around St Margaret's area.
   03.30hrs: One shell landed in a field at Winkland crossroads, Ripple.

Responsibility for the 13.5in rail-guns was transferred from the RM Siege Regt to the 3rd Super Heavy Regt RA on 17 March; the rail-gun 'Peacemaker' was taken over by the 7th Super Heavy Battery RA. Roy Catherick recalls that at least one test-firing was undertaken at the new railway spur:

> On one occasion I was working on top of a straw-stack at Ripple, and was quite high up. On looking over towards Coldblow I saw one of the railway guns with a large number of soldiers standing by it. Suddenly the gun moved

backwards and flame and smoke belched out of the barrel, then I heard the noise and felt the shock wave as I felt the straw-stack move some two feet or so!

By the spring of 1943 the new 'hards' on Deal and Walmer sea-front had been completed, so the Ministry of Works office in South Street was removed. A brick-built look-out appeared at the Deal Pier entrance and more surface shelters and static water tanks were being constructed. Short timber jetties were built at each hard, which would act as emergency loading points for tankers. A system of pipes was laid through the town to connect the jetties with three large oil storage tanks built at Coldblow. Fortunately, they were never needed, as the PLUTO (PipeLine Under The Ocean) system introduced after the D-Day landings was a great success, but the construction of hards and jetties also aided the Allies' 'Fortitude South' deception scheme to hide our real invasion plans. Stuart Harlow was involved with testing the water-tightness of the first of three large oil storage tanks at Coldblow:

> I was called out to test the first tank to be completed, but it had to be cleared with the Deal Water Company, as we require large amounts of water to fill it, when testing for leaks. When I rang them I was told that this would be satisfactory, providing that the NFS paid for the water (at 1s 6d per gallon). At the top of Dover Road, on the boundary between Deal Borough and Ripple parish, were two hydrants which could be interconnected, so that if the Deal main was damaged, we could switch to the Wingham Water Company supply. I briefed the men who were to fill the tank, and told them to be sure that they connected up to the right hydrant – the Deal main.
>
> It was three or four weeks later that the paperwork started coming through from Divisional HQ, with claims from the Wingham Water Company for gallons of water! Furthermore, when the supply was turned on to fill the storage tank, many of the houses at the top end of Dover Road had their supplies cut off! The occupants informed the water company and we were able to correct the error, but I never heard whether we paid up or not.

Major K. O'Callaghan, the ARP Training and Civil Defence Liaison Officer resigned in April 1943. Meanwhile Mr Eames was busy building another surface water basin at the local gas decontamination centre, Swaffield's Laundry in College Road; a new 100,000 gallon static water tank was also under construction at the end of Walmer Green near the RM swimming baths.

Sunday 4 April
Westland Whirlwind P7002 of No. 137 Sqn ditched off Deal after being hit by ack-ack fire.

Monday 5 April
00.30hrs–01.00hrs: Five SHs (2 demolished; 12 seriously damaged; 49 slightly damaged; 1 seriously injured; 2 slightly injured). The shells fell in the sea off South Street; near the RM baths; in Granville Road; in Stanhope Road and in Harold Road, where 'Aspao' and 'Glynde' were hit. One shell landed at Ripple Farm, Ripple.

05.05hrs–16.25hrs: Five SHs fell at East Langdon; and in the Oxney, Solton, Westcliffe and Swingate areas of St Margaret's district.

Night shelling was followed by an intermittent five-hour cross-Channel gun duel; at 1.30 p.m. one shell fell at the rear of 'Broad Oak' in Stanhope Road; and during the evening another one fell in Harold Road. Peggy Oatridge remembers the Stanhope Road bungalow being shelled, as one of the REME lads based there would visit the Stanhope Hall WVS canteen in the mornings and help peel all the potatoes.

> Just before the invasion, in 1943, the town started to fill up with troops, and you really couldn't move for them. On Saturday nights in the canteen, I have seen them queuing right out to the door and outside waiting to get served. But they had nowhere else to go. I felt so sorry for them as they found Deal so dull.
>
> We saw a lot of the REME lads from the bungalow in Stanhope Road because their workshop was at the Deal Motors Garage in West Street. They really had a good billet, being so near to their workshop and to the canteen, but when they were shelled out they were moved up to one of the empty houses in London Road, near the police station.

A new air raid alert was sounded in Deal for the first time on this occasion. So serious had the constant bombardment of the area become that the authorities had introduced a special 'shell warning'. So now the residents took particular note of what type of siren was being sounded before deciding what precautions to take. Martin Hall remembers the 'shell warning':

Shell damage on The Strand, Walmer, 2 March 1943. Amongst the properties damaged in the first shelling incident of March were Boothby's butchers shop, Messrs Hinds estate agents and Snow's bookshop. The latter had a first-floor front room that was used by nurses from the Forester's Hall FAP.

Once air superiority had been regained by the RAF over the Channel, the 'shell warning' was a much more serious threat, which originated on 'our side'. Attempts by British gunners at the St Margaret's batteries to attack enemy shipping off the French coast were preceded by the 'shell warning'; each attack brought a terrible retribution from the German 14in cross-Channel weapons based in the Pas de Calais area opposite.

For that reason, people in Deal and Walmer could be seen counting the seconds before that 'second warning' when the alerts sounded. 'Thank God it's only an air raid!', my mother would say in a rather blasé manner, and go on doing whatever it was she had been beforehand.

On a fine day, the turbulence of a passing shell could actually be seen, perhaps a thousand feet up in the air, presumably because the missile was now more than 25 miles from its firing point, and would have slowed appreciably. This was accompanied by a terrifying roar like an express train, which was particularly frightening at night as we cowered in our puny shelters.

Mrs Helen Ward also remembers the shell warnings, and the difficulty she had with shopping when the enemy bombardment was at its height:

The most inconvenient thing I found with the 'shell warnings' was that shops used to close when it was sounded. The 'All Clear' went an hour after the last shell had dropped and then the shops reopened. You could only buy your food at shops where you were registered, and I was registered with Vye's grocers and Thorp's butchers in Queen Street. Sometimes I left my home in Stockdale Gardens on the 'All Clear' and pushed the pram as far as the junction of Queen Street and Blenheim Road, when the warning sounded again, so it was back home again to wait for the 'All Clear', or if it was too late in the afternoon, I had to wait and try again on the morrow.

One new item which appeared in the streets of Deal was the 'pig bin' where all food scraps, kitchen waste and the like could be deposited. Once a week the driver of a small van, towing a two-wheel trailer, would arrive to collect a now bulging pig bin, and leave an empty one for the next week's contributions. Stan Blacker recalls that at Townsend Farm the collection was somewhat rapid:

One of our biggest laughs, although it wasn't funny for the two people concerned, was that each time we were on 'fatigues' at the galley we had to help with the waste food collection. All the left-over food from many meals was placed in metal dustbins. This was known as 'the swill collection'. Each morning at 8.00 a.m. a lorry used to leave from somewhere near Martin Mill with a civilian driver and his mate, and trundle up the road to clear all the 'swill' from us, and all the other units in the St Margaret's-at-Cliffe area.

This lorry used to swing into the yard at Townsend Farm flat out and screech to a halt by where we were waiting to load. Both men used to jump out, sweating with fear, and load up the swill in double quick time, and drive away again at break-neck speed. They told us that if they lived to be a thousand, they would never get over their fear of approaching the two static machine-guns guarding the road into the village. They were always nervous and on edge when they were in St Margaret's, and were never happy or relaxed until they were back at Martin Mill, at a safer distance from the coast.

Tuesday 13 April
Republic P-47C of 78th Fighter Group ditched in the sea near the Goodwin Sands; Lt Col J.E. Dickman USAAF was rescued.

During the evening, another familiarization operation – 'Rodeo 202' – was flown by the 4th Fighter Group USAAF to Dunkerque. The 63rd Fighter Sqn, 56th Fighter Group, were also undertaking their first operational flight at this time. Capt Dyar suffered an engine failure, and turned out of the formation to glide his P-47 Thunderbolt back across the Channel. As he crossed the coast he was fired at by the local ack-ack units and after deciding he could not reach RAF Manston, he managed to land to the west of Ripple village. Roy Catherick also recalls another USAAF fighter which crashed opposite the old school house in Northbourne Road, Great Mongeham.

> Most of the big air raids were over, but there were still the tip and run raids and we still had poles in the larger fields to stop gliders landing, so we had to work round them. I was working for Mr W.F. Solley as a farm lad at one guinea a week for about fifty hours work, but after a while my main job was with the 'horseman', and in the dairy.
>
> The Army occupied most of the big houses, including the Rectory which was the Officers' Mess, and the school on Northbourne Road which was used as the stores for the Royal Artillery gun battery which occupied 'Crayford Meadows'.
>
> In the field next to the school was a double row of Nissen huts, while another by the school served partly as the cookhouse and partly as a messroom.
>
> I had a cushy job at times watching that the heifers grazing in the meadows did not stray, as the Army 'Quads' [gun-towing tractors] were constantly in and out of the field, and gunners always left the gate open; there was a bonus though, in getting round their cook for a tin of corned beef or herrings in tomato sauce. But sometimes one of our heifers would fall in their slit trenches.

Monday 19 April
00.40hrs: One HE landed in a field at Aylesham, one person slightly injured.

Friday 30 April
Typhoon R8883 of No. 609 Sqn dived into the sea off South Foreland; P/O M.L. van Neste (Dutch) was killed.

In the spring of 1943 Mary Evans joined the Womens' Land Army at Gilbert Mitchell's Reach Court Farm, St Margaret's. He was the area manager for the Kent War Agricultural Executive Committee (KWAEC), which had been set up

WLA girls photographed amongst the apple blossom in an orchard at Uphousden Farm, Westmarsh, in May 1943. Kath Hilson has identified them as follows. Back row, left to right: Nancy, Kath, Connie, Joan; front row: Olive, Joyce, Emily, 'Bubbles'.

to run those farms in 'Hellfire Corner' that had been vacated when their owners were evacuated in 1940. The farm was also the local HQ for the KWAEC:

> At first there were only three of us girls, but gradually more came until there were about fourteen of us. We worked 5½ days a week and our wages were between £3 10s and £4.00 a week, with plenty of overtime at harvest time. Bicycles were supplied by the KWAEC for us to ride to and from work, and they had a distinctive yellow 'flash' painted on them. If the weather was bad, we would travel in to work by bus, but during the cross-Channel shelling, the buses did not run. When this happened, sometimes the soldiers would be kind enough to run us home (as I was then living at Walmer) in lorries, and once I was taken home in a Bren-gun carrier! Our tea and lunch breaks were spent at Mr and Mrs Crannis' lovely café in St Margaret's.

May 1943 saw Colonel W. Sinclair resign from the Deal ARP Committee, but the town's Wings for Victory Week raised £94,873, and Sandwich raised a very creditable £41,668 15s. Mr Eames was working on another surface water basin which was being built at the Warden's Post at Jones' Stores in Park Road, Upper Deal. Local Home Guard units were now allocated guard duties on the Coastal Defence guns, and Ronald Read recalls how the Ripple and Mongeham platoons were 'taken for a ride' after taking part in a training 'scheme' at Wingham:

> We had been told that if we passed, it would mean an end to our turns of night

duties, drilling, etc. – so we all passed this test. At the end of the parade we were told 'Fall out all those units – apart from Ripple and Mongeham'. We were detailed off to stand guard on the twin 6in RA guns installed at Deal Castle. We of the Ripple platoon were to take charge of one gun, while the Mongeham lads had the other. Still this released some of the regular troops to be sent away for training, ready to go over the other side.

I would just get to bed after working all day, when our dispatch rider would come up to our cottage on his motor-cycle, with the message that we were to report to Deal Castle. So off I would go on my bicycle, with pack, uniform and rifle, to be greeted on arrival by an officer with a stop-watch. When all the lads from Ripple and Mongeham had arrived, this officer would say, 'Very good, 20 minutes' – it had only been a practice call-out! Still we were told that the canteen in the castle was open, but I didn't usually bother to go in as I had to be up at dawn for another day's farmwork.

Saturday 1 May
Leading Fireman Percy Farmer of Dover Road, Upper Walmer was killed at Sandwich when the turntable ladder collapsed during the Wings for Victory Week demonstration in the Market Square.
22.15hrs: One shell landed on grassland at Sholden.
22.48hrs: Two SHs at East Langdon; and one each at Solton and St Margaret's village.

Sunday 2 May
Three SHs fell on the Potteries, Albert Road; in Middle Deal Road and in Church Path, Deal. (1 demolished; 4 seriously damaged; 26 slightly damaged; 1 seriously injured; 1 slightly injured.)

Many members of Mongeham and Ripple Home Guard put in a full twelve-hour day of farmwork before marching out to guard the Coastal Defence guns at Deal Castle at night. Notice that some LDV armbands were still being worn when this photograph was taken in 1940.

Saturday 22 May
One HE fell in open ground at Coldred.

Sunday 23 May
One HE fell in Granville Road, Walmer (10 slightly damaged); one HE fell in Otty Bottom, Kingsdown.

During the summer of 1943 the anti-aircraft batteries in the area were strengthened. The reinforcements included a few of the first HAA (Mixed) batteries in which ATS girls manned predictors, height-finders and range-finders. Mongeham-born youngster Ken Patterson lived next door to one ack-ack site in St Richard's Road:

> There was an anti-aircraft gun-site behind 275–277 St Richard's Road, which was manned at different times by British, Canadian and American troops. The tented areas for these troops were situated next to No 255 and around 259–279, and there was a large call-out bell next to our house (No 255) that was often used, as were the guns. The old chalkpit between St Richard's Road and Redsull Avenue was used for the storage of equipment and vehicles.
>
> I remember soldiers on summer evenings, standing alongside our fence drinking tea and listening to the news on our radio, which could be clearly heard through an open window. The camp's cobbler even corrected my father in the mending of our shoes.

Having completed their training on 'Winnie', the experimental gun 'Bruce' and the multiple pom-poms, so that they could be placed in any of these gun's crews, Stan Blacker and his colleagues took turns on village patrols and clifftop guard duties.

> The whole of the gun-sites and our main camp were surrounded by minefields as all of St Margaret's village, and several miles inland, had been evacuated of civilians. The only road from Martin Mill was closed to all but authorized traffic and was manned day and night by Royal Marines. It was also covered by two machine-guns on fixed lines (this meant that you only had to pull the trigger and gunfire covered the whole width of the roadway).
>
> We were informed by our colleagues in 'A' battery that one night a member of the Guinness family, taking a wrong road from Martin Mill, was driving his car at high speed towards our camp. For some reason he ignored the warning signs, and seemed to have no intention of stopping. The Royal Marine manning the machine-gun covering the road opened fire, killing him instantly.

While the Mulberry Harbour units were under construction at Port Richborough, security measures along the Sandwich–Ramsgate Road were increased. The existing concrete wall was raised and topped with barbed wire. Top-deck passengers on the East Kent's double-decker buses were in for a surprise, according to Don Gill:

> On the double-decker buses between Ramsgate and Sandwich, all the windows

on the top floor were blacked out, and a soldier with a rifle and fixed bayonet would board the bus during its journey past the old Richborough Port complex. He sat on the back seat on the top deck to ensure nobody tried to peep out; I can still recall how the tip of his bayonet used to bump on the bus roof whenever he reached the top of the stairs.

Some twelve months before D-Day the Fortitude South deception operation started in earnest. Around Deal and Sandwich troops could be seen on route marches, and Mr W.H. Cole, then serving with the 9th Battalion, Royal Warwickshire Regt, recalls driving small tanks and Bren-gun carriers around Deal. Some Churchill heavy tanks on wheeled transporters, complete with their crews and partially camouflaged with branches of trees, rumbled over Deal's recently repaired Queen Street railway bridge. Roy Catherick recalls that some inflatable 'dummy tanks' were placed in the fields off Northbourne Road, and the Army set up a checkpoint near the old schoolhouse. Signaller Jim Woodward took part in yet another part of the Fortitude South deception at Adisham:

> Another thing which we signallers did, when the invasion scare was on . . . we had a lot of wireless traffic, and then wireless silence! This was just to kid the Germans that we were going across, then the activity could also mean that we were going in. We had to fill the airwaves with all sorts of nonsense just to keep the German troops guessing, because their telegraphists were picking up everything. This sort of thing went on for some months. We sent all sorts of daft messages, and my job was to write them out and hand them over to the Signallers. But when we got the order for wireless silence, whatever happened, nobody could switch on.

On Sunday 13 June the new ground control interceptor (GCI) radar station at Ash Road, Sandwich, entered service. It was to play an important role in tracking the 'night intruders', which by 1943 had become something of a nuisance. Sqn/Ldr John Bond was given the task of seeing this new station into commission. Alice Bond, his sister, recalls:

> Like most Second World War radar stations, no doubt, the Sandwich GCI was a four or five vehicle mobile unit to begin with, and was probably updated to Intermediate at the end of 1940. After serving at various other radar stations, I finished up at Sandwich and the 'Happidrome' was commissioned, as I remember, after a round-the-clock effort. This station had already helped make its mark on the Focke-Wulf FW190 fighter-bombers and the odd Junkers Ju 88 night-bomber.

Sunday 20 June
Mobile canteen from South Africa presented to Deal WVS.
  02.05hrs: One HE each landed at Coldred and St Margaret's village.

One of the helpers for this WVS mobile canteen was Miss Peggy Oatridge, who recalls why there was an urgent need for the new vehicle in the Deal area:

I had a friend, 'Bobbie' McGhee, who was driving the canteen van delivering tea to the gun-sites on the cliffs. She was the regular driver, but she had a different WVS helper every day, and I helped one day a week, so I saw quite a bit of the local area during the war. When I first started we had an ancient Ford and it was very difficult to drive, so nobody wanted to volunteer to go out on it, but as soon as we received the new one, the ladies were queuing up to go out on it.

Tuesday 22 June
Whirlwind P6993 SF-A of No. 137 Sqn crash-landed 1 mile north of Sandwich with flak damage; Sgt J.M. Barclay unhurt.
   03.00hrs: One HE landed in a field at Soles Farm, Nonington.

Friday 25 June
01.10hrs: One HE landed at Hacklinge Farm, Worth.

Sunday 27 June
16.27hrs: Four SHs at St Margaret's.

Monday 28 June
20.30hrs: Six SHs at St Margaret's.
   23.00 hrs: Two SHs; one landed in the road near 'Quinton', Ranelagh Road, rupturing the gas and water mains; also an airburst above 14 Railway Terrace, Albert Road (3 demolished; 8 seriously damaged; 31 slightly damaged; no injuries).

Tuesday 29 June
00.30hrs: Two SHs at Worth.

Monday 5 July
02.00hrs: Two SHs: airbursts over the town, Gladstone Road, Granville Road and seawards between Deal Castle and the RM swimming baths (8 seriously damaged; 41 slightly damaged).
   04.45hrs: All Clear.
   02.16–02.44hrs: Three SHs at Worth.

Saturday 17 July
Winston Churchill and VIPs visited the railway and static guns in the area.

Saturday 24 July
The South Street hard was tested by two invasion barges, but as predicted by local boatmen, each high tide covered the hard with beach pebbles and so bulldozers were required to keep the hards clear of shingle.

With the plans for the Second Front now well advanced, three weeks later three bulldozers started to remove the anti-tank girders on the promenade. Concrete anti-tank blocks at the top of King Street were demolished and concrete tank 'corners' were substituted. A Royal Electrical and Mechanical Engineers unit also removed pillboxes at St Leonards Road and Sholden Church corners; hurricane lamps appeared on footpaths to guide Army convoys by night; additional Army cooks and NFS firemen were drafted into this area; new hydrants were installed, and static water tanks were connected to the mains.

Wednesday 28 July
Typhoon DN591 of No. 245 Sqn crashed after engine failure 1 mile south-west of Eythorne; F/Sgt T.H. Gray unhurt.

Friday/Saturday 30/31 July
'Ground Grocer' radar jamming system started at Walmer.

A bumper harvest in 1943 needed gathering in, so extra men and women from all areas were organized to help, including some troops from the 70th Royal Sussex Regt, who were stationed at Deal for a period. Len Thorogood was one of these trainee soldiers who enjoyed the break from Army routine of standing guard along the coastline. In the autumn of 1943 the Wrens serving at the depot were also invited to volunteer for harvest work. One of those who enjoyed a break from the sweltering heat of the galley was Thelma Mansell:

> Produce was localized to save petrol and man power. Kent being the 'Garden of England' meant that civilians and Service people were fortunate enough to enjoy the most delicious fruit and vegetables. Farmers were desperate for help, and notices would appear on the board appealing for off-duty Wrens to assist. We would climb into the ancient vehicles provided as transport and be driven out into the countryside to delightful old farmhouses.
>
> I remember picking huge nets of peas, runner beans, and once, tomatoes. The pay was very little, but these afternoons out in the lovely country made a great change from the galleys, as did an hour or two at St Margaret's, near the famous steps, where regular dances were held at some of the more palatial houses.

August 1943 saw the armoured cars of No. 2728 Squadron RAF Regt, previously based at Deal, redeployed to Eastry with ground-mounted Hispano aircraft cannon. At Deal they were replaced by No. 2752 Sqn RAFR, based at Hawkshill, Kingsdown and St Margaret's; they were followed by No. 2844 Sqn with their Armadillo armoured cars which were based at Walmer, according to Mr C.P. Smith. Mr Ken Patterson recalls that there was not much aerial activity for these RAFR gunners to deal with:

> The Betteshanger Sports Ground opposite St John's Church in St Richard's Road was our playground, and for a period an armoured car with a gun

mounted on it was stationed there. One day when we were out playing, there was a sudden burst of machine-gun fire – the RAF chap in the armoured car had got so bored that he had accidentally touched the gun trigger. A Spitfire flew over shortly afterwards, possibly responding to a report of gunfire in the area.

Sunday 8 August
Typhoon JP390 PR-J of No. 609 Sqn was hit by flak and ditched off 'Wendover', The Marina, Deal; F/Lt L.E. Smith was picked up suffering from 'slight burns'.

Rumours of people being snatched from the cliffs and beaches apparently persisted late into 1943. James Nice has studied these reports and in one case seems to have found confirmation that at least one person was 'lifted' from this area:

Although most historians dismiss the idea as folkloric, it just is too silly to think that Germany occupied the opposite coast for five years and never once came over to take a look round, either at the time of 'Sealion' or as 'Overlord' drew near. Indeed, much of the information I have gathered actually suggests there were such incidents in 1943 and 1944.

My best lead concerns a Home Guard seen in Stalags [prison camp] by two former POWs. I have interviewed them both and received corroborative evidence from elsewhere. Apparently well into his sixties, the man claimed to have been snatched from St Margaret's Bay (that nest of intrigue!) and brought back to the Continent late in 1943. He was repatriated before the end of the war by the Red Cross, but their records are confidential.

Wednesday 11 August
10.20hrs: One SH at St Margaret's.

Thursday 19 August
Mr Eames working on brickwork at the front of Auxiliary Control Centre at the Mill Road Infant's School.

Monday 23 August
01.01hrs: One UXB near West Street House, Finglesham.

Tuesday 31 August
Spitfire IX MH385 of No. 129 Sqn crash-landed on South Foreland after its engine cut out; F/Sgt Roggekamp slightly wounded.

September 1943 saw Mr Eames rebuilding shelter exits and blast walls at houses in College Road, Cannon Street, Godwyn Road, Harold Road, Northwall Road, at 'The Jolly Sailor' in Western Road, Cornwall Road, St Andrew's Walk and in St Patrick's Road. Blast walls were built at St Andrews Road and Gordon Terrace, while at Deal central schools in Mill Road trench shelters were excavated alongside the buildings, while the walls alongside the Mill Road entrance were reinforced with concrete.

Marjorie Kemp, soon to become Mrs Fenn, recalls that some alterations were made to the bus routes through Deal at this time. Deception schemes for the planned invasion were also still in operation, causing some inconvenience to visitors, and a sudden travel restriction almost ruined Marjorie's wedding ceremony itself:

> By the time we married in September a one-way system was in operation in the town. We went from Southwall Road to St Leonard's Church via London Road, but returned down Middle Deal Road. Relatives who attended our wedding had to obtain One Day permits to enter Deal, and there were soldiers on the station platforms checking everyone in and out. A sudden ban on servicemen's leave was imposed a few days before our wedding, but Bill was granted 48 hours leave – at the very last minute.
>
> I wore a borrowed wedding dress and my two bridesmaids also wore borrowed dresses – at least my veil was my own! In turn, this veil was loaned to five other war-brides – word would go around that so and so had a dress, a veil, or whatever to lend.

The security measures mentioned above were probably in connection with an air, sea and land exercise which took place in Deal between 5 and 11 September. A one-way traffic scheme in the town had to be introduced as tanks, lorries and guns were parked in many roads, while under a fighter umbrella, amphibious operations were undertaken from the beach hards. Meanwhile, heavy air attacks on airfields and coastal defences in France were carried out. Training at Deal RM barracks at this time was Marine Charles Lumsden, who was on a night exercise near Wingham, when these raids on the French ports took place:

> We had to dig trenches and make them as comfortable as possible as all we had for cover were our gas capes, and of course our ground sheets. We were to be the defenders and await the arrival of the attackers in the dark; to be successful, they had to get into our trench and claim our rifles. This 'enemy' was a crack Assault Party of Royal Marines, but when they came at us they threw apples instead of bombs, as they had been entrenched near an orchard.
>
> The next move was on the following day when we had to defend a wheatfield – an imaginary airfield. While we were on this site we had a great view of our bombers going over to France with their loads and we could also hear the noise of the explosions, so they must have been near Calais, because they had not been gone long before they appeared on their way back – but not all returned, and some were damaged as we could see as they came in very low, some with flames coming from them; they were such brave men!
>
> However, the manoeuvres had to go on. We were entrenched on the edge of this wheatfield, and this time our attackers were an airborne unit and we had to stop them claiming the 'airfield'. At the same time, the farmer was harvesting his wheat using a combine harvester – the first one we had seen, so we took an interest in this great machine. Our leisure ceased all at once when great flames of fire landed on the

Landing-craft at Walmer beach hard. Although initially constructed as part of Operation Fortitude South, the four hards at Deal and Walmer were tested at least once in the autumn of 1943 in case they were required for Operation Overlord. Here jerry-cans of petrol loaded onto trucks are being landed from the USS *James Harrold*, at the hard opposite Cambridge Road, Walmer.

field and set the wheat on fire. It was mortar shells that the 'enemy' had thrown over our heads on to the field. Now there was an outcry from the senior officers, including the brigadier who was in command of the operations. He went hopping mad and ordered operations to cease, and we had to go and help put the fires out.

Monday 6 September
22.16hrs: One HE fell in the garden of Eastry House (2 seriously damaged; 100 slightly damaged; 2 slightly injured).

This single bomb caused damage to Clark's grocery stores in High Street, Eastry, as Mrs Finnis recalls:

There was a bomb which fell on a group of trees in the grounds of Eastry House and exploded behind our shop, after a bomber was caught in the local searchlight. The aircraft must have had only the one bomb left, but the pilot dropped it over our village, and it caught in the branches of a tree and so exploded in the air, rather than on the ground.

I was in bed, as it was about 10 o'clock in the evening. Mum was having a bath, as I think we had all been out hop-picking, but she got me up, and I can remember seeing the ceiling coming down as we made our way to the shelter.

Wednesday 8 September
Douglas B-26 41-34970 of 386th Medium Bomb Group USAAF ditched off the Goodwin Sands after a raid on Boulogne; crew of five rescued by ASR launch (aircraft shot up by mistake).

Sunday 19 September
Spitfire XII MB799 of No. 91 Sqn was abandoned over the sea off Deal, but F/Sgt Bulmer (RAAF) was picked up.

Sunday 26 September
A civic service was held for the third anniversary of the 'Battle of Britain' at the Methodist Church in West Street.

LAC WAAF Patricia Parker was posted to RAF Hawkshill Down as a radar operator for about one year, working on the 'Oboe' site. She was billeted in Dover Road, Walmer:

> My memories of 'The Croft' was that it must have been a very beautiful residence, but to us it certainly was not a 'Home-from-Home'. We ignored the warnings about shelling from France – we were supposed to go to the shelters, but never did. We would look through binoculars and watch the Germans patrolling on the cliffs across the other side when weather was clear and sunny.
>
> We went swimming from that very stony beach which shelved so steeply. The sea was very rough, and we had a terrible time trying to get back again. We practically had to form a human chain to get everybody out, and when we found we could do this, we all went back in the sea again!
>
> We had parties up at the Drum Inn on the main road, and I went on some dates with Royal Marines who we met with at the canteen over the road. We would go to a café on the seafront in Deal, when we had any money, to have bacon, eggs and generous portions of chips. I was even invited to a Burns Supper in Deal when they marched the haggis in to the sound of bagpipes!

Mrs Barbara Leigh also recalls that things were very civilized in Deal at this time, and that as far as possible the pre-war niceties were maintained, at least at one eating establishment:

> When we came up to Deal to see Grandpa, mother and I would visit Tapping's Tea Rooms, on the corner of Victoria Road and South Street, where they still had waitresses in black dresses, white aprons and headdresses. I used to think that this place was beautiful, and we could have tea and cakes. When the plate of cakes arrived, it always had a chocolate eclair on the top of the pile, but it would not have been filled with 'real' cream.
>
> After this, Mother and I would walk up to the seafront and chat to the men manning the Coastal Defence guns, and then make our way along to 'The For'sel' bait shop opposite Deal Pier. This shop was the only sea-front premises which stayed open all through the war, and it still had pre-war picture postcards of Deal Pier on sale. Mother would buy some of them to send to her friends in

Gloucester. She would write such things as 'You will never believe this, but we have just had tea and cream cakes!'

By October 1943 the fire block point at St Andrew's Rectory had been closed, and the town's Stalingrad Hospital Appeal had raised some £525 5s 11d. The local education committee had decided to reopen Deal parochial school, but before repair work could be completed, a shell fell on Deal station, and damaged it yet again.

Sunday 3 October
22.00hrs–02.00hrs: Two cross-Channel gun duels with a one hour break while RAF bombers attacked Calais and Boulogne. The British guns opened fire at 10.00 p.m.; the enemy at 10.15 p.m. One shell landed near Deal Castle, hitting Prince of Wales Terrace, a second fell on the goods sidings at Deal station at the rear of the Eagle Tavern, while two more fell in the marshes beyond the Northwall Road level crossing; another nine fell in the sea. 15 SHs (3 seriously damaged; 17 slightly damaged). There was also some damage in Beach Street; on The Strand (Col Barker's house); in Marine Road; Sondes Road; Southwall Road; and in the South Street area. British guns sank a 3,094-ton ship off the French coast.

During daylight shelling across the Channel, the Royal Marines manning 'Winnie' at St Margaret's, had the assistance of spotters who would report the fall of shot. As the Army Co-operation aircraft allocated to this task were often attacked by enemy fighters, another method was used, according to Stan Blacker:

> Instead of aircraft always spotting for us, sometimes we had an RAF barrage balloon with a basket underneath, with two airmen in it. It used to go up to a height of

Having attempted to obliterate Deal station on several occasions, the Luftwaffe managed to damage the freight sidings and goods office in October 1942 so that operations had been transferred to Walmer by the time it was demolished by a shell a year later.

Shell damage at West Cliffe Farm, St Margaret's. Constantly bombarded by shells, West Cliffe Farm at St Margaret's was damaged again in the spring of 1943. Harry Curling, landlord of the Swingate Inn, is pointing shown out the latest incident to Land Army girls Margaret Robinson, Mary Rogers, Mary Evans and Florrie Bell.

300ft, but nine times out of ten, when it was sent up (always in daylight) the Germans over at Cap Gris Nez would 'air bracket' it, with shells passing either side of the balloon, trying to shoot it down. When this happened, we could hear the two airmen shouting at the tops of their voices to be hauled down. The winch crew on the lorry flying the balloon used to haul it down like lightning, with the wire hawser becoming nearly red hot. As soon as their basket was near the ground, the two men would jump out and run like hell. If we met them later, they used to say 'Blow that for a lark', but next day, or a couple of days later, up they would go again!

Monday 4 October
Hot midday meals for schools introduced, from five feeding centres throughout the town at a charge of 3d each.

The catering arrangements at the Deal RM barracks had to be kept flexible as personnel were constantly on the move, as Wren Cook Eva Turton found out one morning:

While we were at 'Brunswick House', we used to have an arrangement with the telephone switchboard at the barracks to give us an early morning alarm call if we were on early shift, and I would then go round and wake up the other girls. I can remember that one morning we had to step over sleeping bodies in the drill hall on our way to the galley as a draft had come in overnight.

We worked in three shifts, starting at 04.30hrs on every third day, and would cook and prepare breakfast before having a break to get our own. Then the next shift came on at 08.00hrs to start preparing dinner for anything up to 200–250 men, then prepare the suppers, and get things ready for the next day.

Wren Cook Thelma Mansell was not very happy at having to 'turn to' for her early morning shift, but enjoyed her work in the galley:

> It was really quite daunting to leave the 'Fair Maid of Kent' or 'Brunswick House' before dawn, all alone as a rule, to walk through the streets of empty houses, where the damaged doors and windows slammed and crashed in the wind. We would be challenged at the depot gates, and having given the pass-word we were ordered to 'Advance and be recognized'! On one occasion, while on our way to work, a half-drunk soldier lurched out of a house, but we were safer then than we are these days. There was a camaraderie not seen since.

Friday 8 October

Two HEs fell at Beaconhill Cottages, Great Mongeham and at Little Mongeham (4 slightly damaged).
   20.10hrs: Eighteen HEs and IBs landed at Sutton (2 slightly injured).

One of the main results of incendiaries being dropped in country areas was the damage to straw-stacks and crops, combined with the lack of readily available sources of water for the fire brigade. Stuart Harlow recalls that he had the willing co-operation of two local men:

> In country areas fire-fighting was very different to Deal, and the manager of the Hammill Brickworks (Mr Parker) was a great help, as he knew where all his static water was located. He had all the rivers, streams and ponds marked up on a large Ordnance Survey map in his office. At Wingham, an estate agent and part-time NFS Company Officer, Mr George Petley, was also a useful contact when we were called in to deal with stack fires in country areas, all of which he knew well as he also farmed locally. Most of the stack fires we were called to had been caused by incendiary bombs dropped by aircraft making their way back to their home airfields from raids made further inland.

Saturday 9 October

De Havilland Mosquito HK120 of No. 85 Sqn was hit by Dover ack-ack when closing with an enemy aircraft; it crashed into the sea 2 miles off St Margaret's Bay; Lt Thoren (RNorAF) and P/O Benge both missing.

The Women's Land Army girls could be sent to any of the farms in the area, and Mary Evans recalls some of their many and varied jobs:

> One of the crops we worked on was sugar beet, which was taken to Martin Mill station by lorry. We rounded up the sheep and bullocks, which always wanted

to go anywhere but where we were supposed to take them. Sometimes we would be taken on the back of a lorry to work at threshing on Sandwich Flats. The corn was cut either by combine harvester or by reaper/binder and thrashed at the farms by thrashing machines driven by steam engines, but it was mainly manual labour. There were times when we got soaked to the skin, and black from harvesting flax or peas, but it was all a great experience!

One of the local farmers, according to the rumours heard by Stan Blacker, was suspected of being a German citizen, or perhaps it was simply another case of deliberately spread 'black propaganda' to keep people alert and on their toes:

> This was very upsetting to all ranks as we could not understand why he had not been interned. It was stated that the reason he was not interned, but allowed to continue farming, was that he had come to this country, and settled in the East Kent area long before the war started, and that he was considered to be 'one of us'.
>
> When the German shells fell nearby, although never seeing this mysterious German, we always blamed him, saying that somehow he must be passing information across the Channel to the enemy, as we thought 'Once a German, always a German!' Whether there ever really was a German farming in the vicinity we never found out, nor did we ever see him, so we never knew if the story was true or not.

Monday 25 October
Three SHs landed in Victoria Road, Wellington Road, The Strand, York Road and Campbell Road; sixteen properties slightly damaged.

WLA girls digging potatoes in winter. Even when wrapped up well against the cold, life for WLA girls was not always the most pleasant, especially when 'spudding' thistles, harvesting flax or, as shown here, digging potatoes on a chill winter's morning at Westmarsh.

Monday 1 November
18.25hrs: Eleven HEs landed at Worth.

Monday 8 November
North American Mitchell II FV939 of No. 226 Sqn crash-landed near Eastry; W/C C.E. Tait (Canadian) and crew all safe.

Sunday 28 November
12.02hrs: Three HEs near Sandwich.

Wednesday 1 December
Spitfire NJ122 of No. 401 Sqn abandoned in the sea 1 mile off Kingsdown; it ran out of fuel on a sweep and had to ditch.

Sunday 4 December
15.30hrs–16.00hrs: Germans shelled in retaliation after British guns attacked a convoy; shells fell in High Street, Golf Road near the gas works and near Sandown Castle. 3 SHs (1 demolished; 2 slightly damaged; 48 slightly damaged; 2 slightly injured). One shell hit 'Comarques' in High Street; Brown & Browns and the Congregational Church opposite were damaged; and tree trunks in front of the 'Central Mission' were severed; windows on the northern side of St George's Church, and the glass shop-fronts in the High Street were shattered.

Sunday 16 December
20.00hrs–21.00hrs: Shells landed in Victoria Road and Cannon Street; 7 SHs (26 slightly damaged; 2 killed; 13 seriously injured; 23 slightly injured). One shell landed at the rear of 'Hawthorn Villa' and 'Mayo Villa' in Victoria Road; there was damage to 'Woodbine Cottage' and 'Roseleigh' in Wellington Road; and another landed in the back garden of 11 Cannon Street.

Wren Eva Turton found herself involved in this shelling and was saved from injury by an unknown Royal Marine when one of the shells landed:

> I remember one shell which fell on a house in Stanley Road about 9.15 p.m. a few days before Christmas. I had just got off the train from Folkestone, and was walking up Victoria Road, when I was thrown to the ground by a Royal Marine who was following me when this shell exploded nearby. I never did see who he was, but I arrived back in quarters with my stockings torn and knees bleeding, but I told everybody I was OK. The next day, though, I was in the sick bay, suffering from shock; but one reason I was feeling very annoyed was that I hadn't finished my Christmas shopping!

Monday 23 December
22.00hrs–22.30hrs: Eight shells landed at Eastry.

Shell damage, Central Mission, Deal High Street. As well as demolishing brickwork at 'Comarques', a shell which fell in the Deal High Street early in December caused considerable damage to surrounding properties, stripping roofs, breaking windows and tearing the weather-boarding from walls.

Bernard Kimpton recalls that the main difference between bombs and shells was the size of the holes they caused. A case in point was the huge shell crater which appeared in the back garden of 11 Cannon Street just before Christmas, 1943.

Stan Blacker left the Royal Marine Siege Regt just before Christmas 1943, having reached the age of nineteen, to train on landing craft, ready for the Normandy invasion. As far as is known, despite shelling and bombing, he was not injured during his stint at St Margaret's, but if he had been, he would have been treated on site:

> We were told – and believed – that there was a small hospital and casualty unit some 60ft underground somewhere near our camp. I did not see it, but I understand that whenever the Germans started shelling, one Sergeant Major was so frightened that he always took cover there. As we always had to 'close up' to the guns whenever the Germans started shelling, in order to be ready to retaliate, I never witnessed this.
>
> One day some people from the BBC arrived to record 'Winnie' firing. They had placed their recording equipment much too close to the gun, and as a result when 'Winnie' was fired the sound was so loud that the equipment could not handle it, and regrettably disintegrated – without any recording being made!

Friday 31 December
B-24 Liberator 42-63975 of 389th HBG force-landed at Goodnestone after returning from a raid on the Colombes area of Paris.

As this particular aircraft had simply run out of fuel and had not been too badly damaged, the USAAF decided that it could be safely flown out of the fields near the south-west corner of Goodnestone Park estate, rather than being dismantled. This operation involved the construction of a temporary runway across the fields towards Rowling House, much to the interest of the local schoolchildren, including John Rolfe and Rodney Betts:

> It remained there for several weeks, while it was repaired and a runway was laid across the fields. The overhead electricity wires had to be removed and the 'anti-glider' poles taken down, and the runway was constructed using a caterpillar tractor and a bulldozer. This was the first time this type of heavy earth-moving equipment had been seen in the district. The engines were run up for an hour at the time, and the Eastry Fire Brigade used to stand by while it was being refuelled. (Rodney Betts)
>
> I went up there several times when the engines were being tested – the noise was just terrific; it could be heard in Eastry, as it echoed from the surrounding trees. We had heard that on some particular day it was due to be flown out but we were in school; however, we heard the engines start up, and we all looked out of the windows and saw it flying low over towards Staple. (John Rolfe)

By the end of 1943 shortened parade services were being held each Sunday afternoon at St George's Church, because of the large numbers of troops now training in the area.

CHAPTER SEVEN

January–December 1944

The start of the year saw a period of prolonged shelling as the British artillery sought to 'soften up' the enemy positions prior to the D-Day landings. The enemy gunners retaliated by trying to knock out our artillery positions, railway guns and radar installations on the coast which could aid both our reprisal raids, and convoys passing through The Downs. The local residents became used to the nightly gun duels, and domestic routines had to be adjusted, as remembered by Mrs Helen Ward:

> When the shelling restarted, I had a Morrison shelter in our living room. Like a table made of steel angle irons, with wire mesh sides, it could take a full-sized mattress, and could be used for sleeping in if required. The shells fell in salvoes, so once you had noted the pattern, such as the number of shells and the seconds between each salvo, it was possible to count the seconds between explosions. You could then pop out of the shelter to put on the kettle, brew a cup of tea or make up the fire, and then pop back under the shelter before the next round dropped.

Substantial reinforcement of personnel from other NFS districts were sent to the Deal area in readiness to deal with reprisal raids in the aftermath of D-Day. Fortunately these did not occur, but troops and equipment did increase in numbers prior to D-Day, and many a quiet copse and wood contained hundreds of soldiers or weapons. Some of these troops were Americans, and at St Margaret's Bay, Cynthia Turner rushed home to tell her mother 'the Germans have landed!' after meeting soldiers wearing differently shaped steel helmets at the top of Bay Hill. Another effect of the sudden influx of American troops into the area was a morale boost for local young ladies, but Roy Catherick recalls that it put a stop to courting expeditions into Deal as suddenly all the local 'talent' seemed to disappear.

The success that the micro-wave early warning system radar site at Sandwich was enjoying with the ground control interception of enemy raiders, led the authorities to suspect that the Germans might attempt to mount a commando-style raid across the marshes, via the River Stour. Thus, in early 1944 Sgt C.P. Turl, then serving in the Royal Marines Combined Operations Section, found himself at Sandwich:

> One day the 906th LC flotilla were ordered to move by train, and we arrived at 10.00 p.m. that night at Sandwich, and found ourselves marching along the main road towards Ramsgate to finish up in a wooden shed. The next morning we had to dig trenches on the south side of Richborough Castle and soon found out that we were to guard a radar site about ¾ mile away, using our Bren guns firing on fixed lines.
>
> After the war was over we found out that in March 1944 the Dutch Underground movement had discovered that German paratroops were being trained to drop over Richborough Castle, and attack that radar unit and then

make their withdrawal across the golf course to board waiting E-boats and thus return to the Dutch coast.

This arrival of the Royal Marines at 'Robertson' puzzled Mr J.G. Martin as there seemed to be a distinct lack of activity on their part while at Richborough Port:

> The Navy had gradually left 'Robertson', except for catering and medical services, and RM Landing Craft flotillas were moved in. They were trained before arrival, but I have never heard of them conducting any operations. Perhaps we were part of the big bluff we put up against the Germans to convince Hitler that Normandy was only a feint and that we had a Second Army under US General Patton waiting to invade in the Calais area.

Tuesday 4 January
Approx. 23.55hrs: FW190 of I/SKG10 engaged by Dover HAA at 16,000ft and shot down; it crashed at Oxney Court, the pilot's [either Uffz Martin Gunther or Erwin Hanke] fate unknown.

The coastal gun batteries, including 'Winnie' and 'Pooh' were now in constant duels with the enemy gunners, and sometimes it wasn't only the enemy shells which caused casualties, as Marine Wyatt remembers:

> When we opened up it really shook the area. I personally had to go round to certain houses and tell the occupants to open their windows before we fired.

Entrance gate to HMS *Robertson* at Stonar. The First World War port complex on the River Stour, north of Sandwich, was used by RM landing craft, RN motor launches and torpedo boats, Army railway repair parties and civilians constructing the Mulberry Harbour units. The naval part of this complex was known as HMS *Robertson*.

But one old fellow looked at me and said, 'Open my windows! I haven't any b...y windows left,' and burst out laughing. There were a few casualties, and I once saw two young boys standing in the road opposite the mess as we opened fire. Danny, the eldest, was paralysed in his left hip by the blast.

Tuesday 18 January
HMML25 was driven on to the far side of the Goodwins at speed, and the propeller shaft was forced through the bottom of the hull. The Walmer lifeboat crossed the Goodwin Sands, in rain and rough sea, to rescue thirteen of the crew.

Thursday 20 January
Prolonged shelling; warning sounded at 5.00 a.m. At 05.30hrs shells fell on the Park Tavern in Park Street; one demolished a street shelter in Robert Street; others fell on the golf course and in Golf Road. 4 SHs (10 demolished; 23 seriously damaged; 65 slightly damaged; 12 killed; 7 seriously injured; 13 slightly injured).
   08.45hrs: Two SHs landed at St Margaret's and another at Oxney.
   23.00hrs–00.01hrs: Four SHs at Sholden.

One of the worst shelling incidents in Deal happened in January 1944 when one of a pair of street shelters in Robert Street received a direct hit, killing everyone inside. The remaining shelter still stands, with the emergency exit through which the occupants had been rescued visible although covered with a sheet of tin.

The shell which demolished the Park Tavern early on the morning of 20 January 1944 also severely damaged the Deal Library and Mr Ellesmere's fish and chip saloon. This was one of the favourite places for supper and a nightcap for Bernie Kimpton and his pals. Both properties were so badly damaged they were later demolished.

One of the worst shelling incidents occurred in Robert Street, when one of the surface shelters was demolished. Vic Skinner recalls:

> One of the bad incidents was in Robert Street. We had quite a lot of brick-built street shelters all over the town, built back to back with entrances at opposite ends. This particular day it was decided that all the men would go into one shelter [according to Mary Osbourn this was so the men could smoke] and the women and children would go into the other. Unfortunately the blast of the explosion killed all the women and children – there was not a mark on the bodies – but the men were untouched.

The Park Tavern was a sad loss to many in the town as it was a very popular drinking place, and Mr Ellesmere's fish and chip shop opposite was convenient for a late supper to eat on the way home. Mr Oatridge seems to have been a pretty phlegmatic character, but his daughter recalls even he was upset by this incident:

> One shattering thing for my father was that he owned quite a number of properties about the town, and in nearly every bomb or shell incident, one of them would be hit. But the first time I saw him affected by the shelling was after the little Park Tavern, which stood opposite the Deal Library in Park Street, had been hit. Father used to go in there every morning for a drink, and he went off down there the morning after it had been hit, and came back with an ashen face! His favourite pub just wasn't there any longer.

The Park Tavern in Park Street was damaged by a shell on 4 January 1944. 'Suddenly his favourite pub wasn't there any more', recalls Peggy Oatridge of her father's favourite watering hole. The landlord and his wife were both killed, but their baby daughter and the family dog survived the direct hit on the property.

Another property to suffer when the shell demolished the Park Tavern in Park Street was the Co-Operative Stores next door. Unlike the adjacent public house, the Deal Library and Ellesmere's fish and chip saloon opposite, this building was eventually rebuilt after the war.

After this shelling, units of the Kent Mobile Rescue unit were summoned from Minster and Bridge, to assist local ARP rescue squads, while Dr James Hall and his medical team at Deal Hospital worked for some eight hours to treat the injured.

Friday 21 January
Prolonged shelling again. Eight SHs caused severe damage at the rear of Clarabut's and Marks & Spencer's shops in the High Street; others fell in Oak Street; in Western Road; in Golf Road, damaging the water pumping station; in College Road; Marine Road; Victoria Parade and Beech Street (2 demolished; 13 seriously damaged; 63 slightly damaged).

Monday 24 January
Spitfire MH375 of No. 122 Sqn abandoned 6 miles off Deal after its engine cut out; F/O P. Goods missing.

Friday 28 January
22.45hrs: One HE dropped at Coldred.

Saturday 29 January
20.40hrs: One HE dropped at Holt Street Farm, Nonington, and two IB containers at Wingham; IBs also dropped at Great Bossington Farm, Adisham.
   21.00hrs: Three shells fell in open ground at Bere Farm, two more at St Margaret's and another at West Cliffe Farm; others landed in the sea. One shell at Longlane Farm, Shepherdswell.

Sunday 30 January
B-17G Fortress 42-31021 of the 389th Heavy Bomb Group USAAF force-landed at Overland Farm, Ash.

This aircraft was returning from a raid on Brunswick and at least one local youngster was intrigued by some of the damage it suffered:

> This B-17 crash-landed in a field by Little Knell Farm, and had torn out its engines as it slid across the field. I noticed one wingtip was missing, and upon enquiring the reason a member of the crew told me that it had been cut off in a collision with a Messerschmitt fighter while over Germany.

During February hundreds of bombers and fighters were to be seen passing over the district on raids during the softening-up process before D-Day, attacking the V1 launching sites before they could be used. One helpful change for strangers to the town was that the road-signs removed in 1940 were now replaced. Furthermore any war-damaged property could now be restored if the cost was less than £500. By 20 February Sandwich GCI radar station had claimed thirty-seven successful interceptions; they were working mostly with No. 85 Squadron Mosquito night-fighters at RAF West Malling. F/O Tom Hackney recalls visiting Sandwich, with

The B-17 Fortress that crash-landed at Worth. Many of the American heavy bombers which passed over this district en route to raid Germany struggled back badly damaged and short of fuel, to crash-land in open fields. Mostly they were dismantled and taken away on lorries, although one American bomber was flown out from a termporary runway laid down over fields near Goodnestone.

some fellow pilots, to watch their colleagues intercepting on the radar screen, and see how incoming enemy shells could be tracked.

Friday 4 February
05.00hrs: Ten HEs dropped at Wingham.
  05.45hrs: IBs fell on dutch barn, and set Guilton House alight; one HE at Moat Farm and one Phosphorus IB at Mount Ephraim, all at Ash. Three HEs and four UX Phos. IBs dropped at Each Manor Farm, Woodnesborough.

Sunday 6 February
Two HEs fell on Church Lane, Sholden, but caused no damage and no injuries.

Wednesday 23 February
Five SHs fell in open ground at St Margaret's (nil casualties).

Saturday 26 February
Civil Defence standards presented to Deal and Sandwich ARP.

Tuesday 2 March
03.00hrs: One HE dropped at Eythorne.

On one of my family's annual visits to Eythorne Baptist Chapel for their anniversary services on Good Friday, I can remember seeing one large railway-gun, well camouflaged with a tarpaulin, parked on the siding by the level crossing when we walked down to catch the bus to Deal at the White Horse pub after the evening service. Colonel Edgar E. Gee recalls that the 8th Super Heavy Regt was still there at this time:

> I remember going to Dover one evening for a meal at 'The Crypt', and on my return I could hardly get back to my battery because there was a 'snap' exercise by the Corps, in conjunction with the Home Guard. The trouble was that I was supposed to be there commanding my troops; but I had a good captain, who explained my absence by telling the Corps officers that I was 'inspecting the outposts' – so I managed to get away with it!
>
> I attended the Eythorne Baptist Chapel every Sunday morning, where the pastor was the Revd A.C. Miller, a very nice man. At one time I had many requests to change religion from non-conformist to Roman Catholic. The reason for this was that there was no Catholic church nearby, so Roman Catholics did not have to go on church parade. I found a Catholic priest whose church was about 6 miles away. When I asked him if he could arrange for my chaps to have a service at 7.30 a.m. at his church, he said that he would be delighted to oblige. So the next Sunday I ordered a church parade for the 'Catholics' at 7.00 a.m. – and I did not get any more applications for change of religion.

Monday 20 March
21.35hrs–00.21hrs: Eleven SHs fell at St Margaret's; (1 Mil. slightly injured).

Tuesday 21 March
21.28hrs: Forty-four shells fell during the day in the St Margaret's area – only thirteen of them falling on land.

Roy Stout was posted to RAF Hawkshill Down in the spring of 1944, and recalls that because of the nature of the work being undertaken there, access to the site wasn't very easy. By this time there were several types of radar on the site, one of which Roy remembers as being a bit 'Heath Robinson':

> As I recall this was a Mk 1 station, but adjacent to it was a bunker which contained a TRF hand-built modified 'Oboe' set, what we these days would call a 'lash-up'. The Mk 1 'Oboe' was as well, to some extent, but the adjacent one was worse, but if I remember, from what I was told and shown, it was none the less very successful. The Germans were effectively jamming the Mk 1 but it was kept going as a blind, whilst the adjacent 'lash-up' did the job!
>
> I also seem to remember being shown another semi-underground bunker on this site, which contained the very latest 'Oboe' set – a huge complex with a massive Magnetron TX, and I believe at least ten control consoles; it was the very latest Mk III made by Cossor.

Tuesday 25 April
03.30hrs: Lancaster JB278 of No. 103 Sqn ditched in Sandwich Bay returning from Karlsruhr, after being attacked by a night fighter. Crew rescued from the Goodwin Sands.

The above account does not reveal the whole story. Having ditched safely, F/Lt Ogden and his crew boarded their dinghy, then set off to paddle towards what they thought was the coastline, having seen the breakers on the Goodwin Sands. They struggled against wind and tide to reach them, only to be disappointed that it was only an isolated sandbank. However, they had been spotted by the coastguards, and at 11.00 a.m. Joe Mercer and his crew set out in the Walmer lifeboat to pluck them from their fast diminishing refuge. As time was now of the essence he ran the *Charles Dibden* right across the sands, and he was later awarded the RNLI's Bronze Medal for his bravery.

At St Margaret's Bay, the build-up for D-Day was also watched by Private Albert Daniels:

> It all started in the spring of 1944, with these great concrete structures, entered in my logbooks as 'bridge sections', being towed past our battery, day and night; they turned out to be the caissons for the Mulberry Harbours. There was also the giant 'bobbin' which we later found out carried the pipeline that was to become PLUTO.

Monday 1 May
Tempest JN771 of No. 486 Sqn crashed in force-landing at Staple; P/O J.G. Wilson uninjured.

Friday 5 May
The start of Deal and Sandwich Salute the Soldier Week in which Deal raised some £89,794; and Sandwich £66,688 4s.

The soldiers I remember best were in Victoria Park, a Canadian Bofors gun crew living in the single-storey pavilion, perched up on the bank alongside the railway line by 'The Dip'. Marilyn Hayward and myself made friends with the gunners, as Marilyn's mother Mrs Joan Islemonger, recalls:

> One of the Canadians, Johnny Kozachenko, sent a letter back home to his folks in Canada telling them all about you two. One of his family decided that they would like to send you something, and eventually a parcel arrived, but when it was opened they had sent two pairs of boys' grey woolly socks as they thought you were both little boys. Marilyn was not very happy about this especially as you were given both of the pairs. After this I took a photograph of you two for Johnny to send to his folks.

Tuesday 9 May
Deal was shaken shortly after midnight by earth tremors from seven waves of bombers pounding the defences on the French coast.

Johnny Kozachenko with Marilyn Hayward and the author. The Canadian Bofors gunners at the site in 'The Dip' at Victoria Park befriended the only local children still living in the area – Marilyn Hayward and myself. 'Bruce' and 'Johnny' watch from their sand-bagged gun pit in the background.

Sunday 21 May
02.35hrs: One HE at West Langdon.

Tuesday/Wednesday 23/24 May
Three shells landed on Victoria Parade, and at Walmer, but caused no damage and no casualties.

The local boatmen's predictions about the difficulties of keeping concrete 'hards' free from shingle were proved to be accurate, and bulldozers were constantly busy on this work. A group of Yorkshire NFS firemen were drafted into Deal this month and were accommodated in the Caxton Home. Among the troops that were posted into the area prior to D-Day were some Canadians, and Sergeant Bob Waugh recalls them visiting his searchlight site at West Studdal, to barter cigarettes:

> They were staying in tents in the woods, and they used to come over to our site and offer to swap their cigarettes for ours. They liked our 'Players' and 'Capstan' and we liked their 'Sweet Caporal'. During our conversations, I happened to mention that we could never have chips because we could not get cooking fat, so after that they kept us supplied – by the bucketful.

Somebody else who recalls the Canadian troops stationed in Willow Woods is ex-Wren Thelma Mansell, who enjoyed a tea party with them:

> Large numbers of Canadian soldiers were drafted into the area before D-Day, nice young lads. One Sunday afternoon a few of us were out walking and met some of them and were given a luxury tea in the woods, where they stayed until the big day.
>
> Just before D-Day all the craft were off Deal for us to see (but we were not to mention them in our letters home). It was an awe-inspiring sight, and we knew something very special was afoot.

Tuesday 6 June: D-DAY

There were great convoys of shipping passing through The Downs with escorting destroyers and MTBs; liners, cattle-boats, cargo steamers, tankers and coasters, sometimes stretching from The Gulls to South Foreland; smoke-screens were being laid before they reached Hope Point, with each vessel carrying a barrage balloon.

This vast panorama of shipping passing down the Channel was witnessed by Albert Daniels from his 410th Battery BOP on the cliffs above St Margaret's Bay:

> At dawn on D-Day a whole parade of American Liberty Ships sailed past our battery, carrying men, armour, ammunition, etc. to be landed at Normandy later in the day after the bridgehead had been established. All these US ships were named after forts; I saw *Fort Huron*, *Fort Lauderdale* and several others, with our RN destroyers fussing around them, laying smoke, and making quite an impressive sight.

Wednesday/Thursday 7/8 June

Five shell warnings during the night; but Deal escaped without damage.

Tuesday 13 June

First V1s seen; heavy gunfire was heard and the air raid alert was on for 12 hours – a record.

Albert Daniels was on Observation Post duty at St Margaret's on this night, and was in a perfect position to watch the launch of the preliminary attack by Hitler's 'secret weapon', the Vergeltungswaffwen 1 or V1 (better known as the 'doodle-bug', 'buzz-bomb', or other less salubrious nicknames):

> About 2.00 a.m. on the morning of the 13th, I saw this light in the sky approaching the coast between us and Deal. I reported this to our HQ, but didn't know exactly what it was then. I knew it wasn't an aeroplane because of the light, and then as it came nearer, I could hear a sort of 'chug-chug' noise, like a two-stroke motor-cycle engine. Anyway, it was a sound I was to get very used to in the next few weeks in 'Buzz Bomb Alley' or 'Doodle Bug Alley', as it became known. I've seen our fighters meet them over the Channel and fly alongside

them, and then tip the Bug's wings with their own to turn them back over France many a time, and just occasionally shoot them down over the Channel.

The first night that V1s were launched is remembered by many as the night that parachutists were supposed to have landed in this area. Mrs Olive Harlow recalls that when she arrived at the Denne's Yard fire station to start her turn of duty that evening, she was warned that enemy parachutists had dropped at the bottom of Drum Hill:

> I told them, 'Well, I've just cycled up Drum Hill and I didn't see any parachutists!'

In Lower Walmer, nurse Zena Hambrook was on duty at the Forester's Hall FAP:

> The ARP control centre rang through with a report that some parachutists had been landed at St Margaret's Bay. That really frightened all of us, and there was lots of activity down on The Strand below our restroom, with soldiers running about in the road. About half-an-hour later control rang back again to tell us it had all been a mistake!

My Uncle Leslie also remembers that there were other rumours – about an enemy landing even nearer Deal – circulating at the Deal gas works that night:

> At first we couldn't make out what this noise was, and various reports started coming in, and 'we heard everything'. One story was that the Germans had landed on Kingsdown beach and the Royal Marines were fighting them off by pushing the ready-fused shells over the cliffs to detonate at the bottom (that's all we had to protect us). However, by 7.30 a.m. everything had cleared up so I was able to go home, despite the alert still being on, as I had my security pass.

The noise of the V1's motor could also be mistaken for a motor-boat cruising off Deal, as Pte M.W. Cole of the Royal Warwickshire Regt recalls:

> I was doing a night patrol, which involved looking out for the enemy landing on the beaches, or even an invasion, during which patrol we covered the sea-front from 'Seagirt' to Walmer Castle. This patrol involved two sentries, one starting from either end and meeting in the middle, usually near Deal Pier.
> On this particular night, we had met up, and were looking out across the sea as it was bright moonlight, when we heard what appeared to be the engine of a motor-boat, but we could not see anything. By now we were getting a bit edgy, as the noise came nearer, then we spotted a flame up in the sky. This turned out to be the first 'Doodle Bug' to come over Deal.

Friday 16 June
Start of the regular bombardment by V1s.

Serving at Kingsdown, LAC Len Hale remembers the first night of the V1 bombardment for another and perhaps more sinister reason, the final outcome of which was a general stand-to over the whole of south-east England, or so he was told by the flight sergeant of his RAF Regt ack-ack squadron. Having spotted some suspicious lights flashing from the old Walmer UDC rubbish dump, Len and his sergeant had investigated, but to no avail:

> It was too dark to make a proper investigation, so we started to make our way back to camp, but were interrupted when a light appeared in the bedroom window of a house at the corner of Upper Street. There were no curtains in the bedroom window, and we had been told it had been unoccupied since the beginning of the war. We made our way stealthily to this house, but after a good search, we could find nothing, and nobody. We returned to camp to find an irate flight sergeant, who had only heard about our 'spy-seeking' mission second-hand from the new crew brought in to man the gun. By then, the whole camp was on stand-to, and we were not stood down until dawn of the following day
>
> That day, Paddy and I were instructed to relate the incident to two civilians [possibly MI5 men] who pocketed various pieces of paper, and other miscellaneous items from both sites. On both occasions the lights seen were of a definite 'on/off' type and at the house, which was some 300 yds from the tip, it illuminated the whole of the window area.

Spontaneous fire breaking out on the rubbish tip would appear to be the most logical explanation, and reflections in the bedroom window from another source, but both these explanations are discounted by Len, who reflects that the real explanation of this will probably never be known. Roy Catherick recalls that he had a narrow escape when working near Hawkshill MOD Listening Post on the lower cliffs towards Kingsdown when an extra low-flying V1 appeared:

> I was haymaking, with 'Joey' on a horse rake, when this V1 came over a bit lower than usual. The troops on the beach opened up with every weapon they had, machine-guns as well, and most of the fire was going over our heads. So 'Joey' just bolted, with me trying to turn him in a circle, and at the same time stay on the iron seat of the rake. Every time I put my foot on the trip pedal, the rake came flying upwards. Then I knew what it must have been like to be a Roman charioteer in 'Ben Hur'. The noise did not last very long, as the Doodle Bug was fast for that time, but the rake needed some attention afterwards.

The bomb officer of Eastry Rural District Council organized his own V1 plotting system to back up the Royal Observer Corps spotters; John Wilson of Ash remembers that his system involved some of the lads from the local Air Training Corps. They were told to report to the searchlight site at Foxborough Hill, Woodnesborough:

> When we arrived there was great excitement, with the searchlight crew standing-to with rifles and fixed bayonets, even the chap from the cookhouse had his rifle with him. There were also some RAF Regt chaps there with Bren-guns, and they also had the 30mm Hispano cannon. We were to go on duty at 19.00hrs, but had to wait until after midnight before anything started to happen.

However, by this time there were lots of low clouds drifting in from Sandwich Bay over the top of the hill, so all we could see were these twinkling lights passing over above it. Mr Ovenden, who lived nearby, came out in [Home Guard] uniform with his rifle, and everybody started firing away at these Buzz Bombs, together with the Bren guns and the Hispano cannon, so the amount of noise was terrific. However, it was soon decided that we ought to get down into the trench shelter, and we were able to observe from a somewhat safer distance. The sergeant promised to keep us informed. Their searchlight was off and on all the time, but the cloud was so low, it was just like 'lighting up a brick wall'. As the V1s went over they were only about 100ft up, and we could see the flames coming out the back, but could not pick up their silhouettes.

Tuesday 20 June
Convoy of twenty landing craft, each with two balloons, passed through The Downs, behind a smoke-screen; they were not shelled.

Thursday 29 June
Three shells landed on The Beach, Walmer; Granville Road; and in the sea off Deal Castle (12 slightly damaged; 1 slightly injured).
   15.50hrs: Two shells fell in open ground at Reach Road, St Margaret's.

In July 1944 Deal was created a 'special area' where women were no longer required to do fire-watching duties at their places of work, but they could still volunteer. Personnel from the Deal sub-division of the NFS were sent to assist in Dover, and to other areas during the V1 raids.

Saturday 8 July
07.46hrs: RAF four-engined bomber came down 2¾ miles east of Walmer lifeboat station – wreckage was found but no crew members.
   Capt Peterson landed his B-17 Fortress 42-97855 of 398th Heavy Bomb Group on a sandbank between the minefields at Sandwich Bay with flak-crippled engines after returning from a tactical mission over France.

Sunday 23 July
15.19hrs–16.28hrs: Four SHs at St Margaret's; one in Reach Meadow; one at 'Kilmarie', The Droveway; one at 'Sark Cottage' and 'South Lawn', Bay Hill; and one at the Dover Patrol Memorial.

Friday 28 July
Wreckage of a four-engined bomber found off Walmer.

In mid–August a change in tactics was ordered, as every available anti-aircraft gun was moved down to the south-east coast, leaving the aircraft to patrol over the Channel and inland as far as the balloon barrage around London. Some of the ack-ack units moved into the Deal area were from the American Anti-Aircraft Corps with their long-barrelled 90mm guns, SCR 584 radar sets, searchlights and 'Bonzo' proximity-fused shells. One such battery was stationed on Walmer Green, by the lifeboat house, and Stuart Harlow encountered this unit en route to their new location:

> I had been allocated a motor-cycle to get around our area, which at the time reached as far as Waldershare, Preston and Wingham. The first motor-cycle I was given had a hand-change gear lever, but then I was allocated a more modern 250cc BSA, with a foot-change gear lever. I thought I would have a run to try it out, and so set off on the quiet back way to Dover via Coldblow to Martin and East Langdon. I had just reached the little narrow railway bridge between East Langdon and Guston when I met a Jeep. In it were a driver, a sergeant and possibly an officer. I managed to stop my new motor-cycle some distance from them, and then pushed it up to their Jeep to be greeted with, 'Say! Buddy! What outfit do you belong to?' Behind the Jeep was a lorry, and behind that was a whole string of large ack-ack guns. The next question I was asked was, 'Are we on the right road to Walmer?'

Harry Adnitt was serving with No. 2852 Sqn RAF Regt when it was posted to Deal to further 'beef up' the ack-ack defences against the V1s:

> In particular I remember our site in Walmer, I believe it was called Hawkshill Down. Our armament was based on the Hispano cannon, twin Browning machine-guns — and good aircraft recognition ability. Part of our duty was not to draw attention to the radar sites, but we endured our share of shellfire, and the occasional scurry when we thought that we were threatened. When fired upon we blasted everything in sight!
>
> I also remember being sent out, with four of my squad to guard a Liberator that had crashed after being badly shot up. Despite the obvious blood in the nose compartment, the main thing that I recall is that it had taken out a complete line of the posts that were supposed to prevent aircraft landing.

Saturday 12 August
01.30hrs: V1 brought down by AA fire at Barfreston.

Wednesday 16 August
16.00hrs–17.16hrs: Registration bombardment by 'Winnie' and 'Pooh' on a German gun battery.
     17.22hrs: V1 brought down at Little Knell Farm, at Ash.

When this V1 fell at Little Knell Farm, Westmarsh, the Women's Land Army girls were helping with the harvesting: Kathleen Upton was atop a haystack, while her room-mate Connie was fruit-picking in an orchard at Overland Farm:

> When we saw this Doodle Bug coming towards us, we dashed down to the ground from the top of the haystack, and it exploded a field or two away.

Connie was up a ladder in an apple tree and she looked up and saw it right above her. Her colleague and she slid to the ground, and she wanted to run one way, while the other girl said the other, so in the end they both lay down flat on the ground. She told me later that when the V1 exploded the shock had lifted them both off the ground. All the farm chickens were blown up in the air, and when they came down again, they hadn't any feathers left; while in the next field all that remained of the rows of cabbages were just the stalks!

19.03hrs–19.43hrs: RM guns undertook another bombardment: twelve rounds were fired at enemy gun positions.

19.45hrs: V1 fell at Kittington Farm, Nonington (CC Type).

Thursday 17 August
07.09hrs: V1 landed in a field at Easole Street, Nonington.

09.55–11.25hrs: Both 'Winnie' and 'Pooh' were firing at enemy batteries. At 11.30hrs their target was changed to another enemy battery. Between 11.45hrs and 12.17hrs both guns fired fourteen rounds but scored no hits. From 16.00hrs to 18.45hrs their original target was engaged again, obtaining seven hits.

Most of the V1s which came across Deal had been diverted by ack–ack fire or aircraft attack over the Channel. I remember seeing 'my' Buzz Bomb spluttering along just above the roofs of the houses in Mill Road as mother and I emerged from our back door at 19 Park Avenue. I was thrilled that at last I had seen a real live Doodle Bug and I can remember pointing it out to mother, who was close behind me. 'Get down into that shelter!' was the response, accompanied by a shove in the back to get me to move faster – she was not impressed! Elsewhere in Walmer, Mrs Helen Ward had decided to take shelter in a somewhat more unconventional location when V1s appeared:

> My daughter Carole was born in 1943, and that summer and in the following year I worked part-time for Fred Friminger on his smallholding behind Cornwall Road [now James Hall Gardens]. I was 'side-shooting' tomato plants and tying them to stakes for 1s an hour. During the second summer, the Doodle Bugs started to appear. When one was coming near, I'd pick Carole up out of her pram, and run with her away from the greenhouse into a little brick build-ing where the pig-swill was cooked – the pig-swill being preferable to flying glass – but none of these V1s fell near Deal, so we were always OK.

Saturday 19 August
11.12hrs–15.46hrs: Both 'Winnie' and 'Pooh' in action again, some twenty-five rounds being fired. At 12.08hrs the AOP spotter plane reported 'Both guns direct hit, large explosion followed'. [This was probably an ammunition dump, and the force of the blast was felt on this side of the Channel.]

Sunday 20 August
11.00hrs–13.42hrs: Last day of operations by 'Winnie' and 'Pooh'; forty-two rounds were

fired on a close-range target. When all available ammunition had been expended, firing ceased and the AOP observer's last message heard was 'Congratulations to gun crews on excellent shooting.'

Monday 21 August
Tempest EJ602 of No. 501 Sqn flew into the ground in fog at Woodnesborough; F/Lt C.B. Thornton was killed.

Wednesday 23 August
09.20hrs: V1 fell at Womenswold.

Tuesday 29 August
Nine SHs on Walmer beach and Kingsdown (1 slightly damaged; 1 slightly injured).
  18.50hrs–19.52hrs: Three SHs at Bere Farm and Bere Wood, St Margaret's.

Fortunately the V2 long-range rocket attacks were aimed directly at London, the nearest one to Deal falling at Minster. However, they could be spotted at night as quick flashes across the sky, as Charles Grant recalls, but there was some sort of defence against them. Serving at Kingsdown at this time was RAF radar operator LAC H. Williams, who arrived with No. 43 Mobile Signals Unit, having been kept in reserve for the D-Day landings:

> When it was found later that we were not required 'over there' we were sent to Kingsdown to augment the unit already there on a hastily erected fixed site. This site consisted of about a dozen wooden huts surrounded by blast walls, and near each hut were three 20–30ft high aerials. The unit was set up to provide radio counter-measures to any German radio activity.
>
> It was thought that the planned V-weapons might be radio-controlled; hence the need for counter-measures. There were receivers on site, plus transmitters at the ready to jam any signals from the enemy. During the period I was there the transmitters were not used operationally.

Wednesday 30 August
Seven British destroyers anchored in The Downs all day.

Thursday 31 August
Spitfire IX PL222 of No. 504 Sqn dived into the ground on air-test near Sandwich; F/Lt K. Bishop was killed.

This was probably the Spitfire which John Rolfe remembers seeing after his family had moved from Millbank to Boitler Cottages, towards the northern end of the village. The circumstances he describes suggest that this aircraft developed a sudden engine fault which caused it to crash, so it might well have been on a test flight.

One evening we were playing at the back of F.A. Butcher's yard, when these three Spitfires flew over, and just as they were passing over the other side of the railway line, the engine of the middle Spitfire gave a puff of smoke. It then turned over on to its back, and crashed in Mr Cook's field at Wells Farm, Selson.

In the field where it fell, Mr Revell was hoeing cabbages, having laid his coat and 'snap' [miner's slang for a sandwich tin] on the ground; one wing of this Spitfire pinned his coat to the ground when it landed, but the pilot baled out too low for his parachute to open completely, it just flapped behind him as he fell, and so he was killed. When I had walked round the plane, I spotted that Mr Revell had covered the pilot's body with his parachute.

Friday 1 September
04.30hrs: One shell at St Margaret's.

14.00hrs–19.00hrs: Five hours continuous shell warning in Deal and surrounding area. Eleven shells landed: one on the beach at the top of Clanwilliam Road, badly damaging 'Deal House' and 'St Pierre'; others fell at the rear of 'The Antwerp' on the site of the Olde Victory pub; one on Catt's restaurant in Market Street; one at the rear of Little's Restaurant in Queen Street, damaging the café; one on the roadway in front of 48/50 Sandown Road – both houses were wrecked; one in a field across the road from Deal gas works in Golf Road, which damaged the gas works and showered Westfield Cottages with shrapnel; there was damage in Harold Road, on Victoria Parade, also in Ranelagh Road, Stanley Road and Queen Street. All this took place while the enemy was attempting to evacuate the Channel ports. (14 demolished; 85 seriously damaged; 109 slightly damaged; 7 slightly injured.)

Thelma Mansell, and her WRNS colleagues made frequent expeditions into the town, and had a fortunate escape this afternoon, when several of their favourite haunts suffered damage:

> There was a small cinema near the barracks; I don't recall its name [The Kings Hall] but it was always full. The fish restaurant in Deal [Catt's] was shelled, not long after we left it, with loss of life, I believe. Also the quaint 'Golden Hind' café on the sea-front, and Allen's the hairdressers in Broad Street . . . I was having a perm there one day, all tied up in the old type of machine, when the shell warning sounded! I remember Little's Café in Queen Street, which served raspberries in season, and even managed half a spoonful of sugar, and the Deal Victoria Baptist Church, where some pleasant ladies served diced beetroot and cheese sandwiches for 1½d each, and also gave us a Christmas Party.

Peggy Oatridge was on duty with the WVS tea van on this day:

> I can remember going to the shell incident at 'St Pierre' on the sea-front, and to another incident in Sandown Road. I wasn't on duty the time that Comfort's shop was hit; Mrs Wakeham was on the tea car that day, and told me the rescue squad brought a little girl out of the rubble, she was terribly sick, and then she just died; awful things happened, but you got used to them.

Another incident that we attended was at Mr Hunnisett's shop, and I can remember seeing the old man, with his white beard, picking things over from the wreckage of his shop in the High Street. When the Park Street library was hit, I can recall seeing the girls knocking all the dust out of the books as they picked them out of the rubble.

Saturday 2 September
23.33hrs–03.20hrs: One SH north of Winkland Oaks Road, Ripple.

Sunday 3 September
There was British shelling in the morning, then a cross-Channel gun duel later. One shell landed on 'Fairlight' in Park Lane, and caused damage to Deal parochial school.
    15.00hrs: Further shell bombardment in the afternoon, causing damage to the northern end of Blenheim Road; Alfred Square; the South Eastern Hotel; the Royal Marines swimming-baths; and on the foreshore at Walmer, shrapnel burst through the windows of St Saviour's and marked the choir stalls. 6 SHs (1 demolished; 12 seriously damaged; 48 slightly damaged; 2 seriously injured; 1 slightly injured).

Wednesday 6 September
20.55hrs: One SH south of East Studdal.

Saturday 9 September
11.15hrs: One shell exploded in the air over Sutton.

Sunday 10 September
02.15hrs: Two SHs landed at St Margaret's, killing one person. Later four shells landed, on Kennels Farm, in Golf Road; in Northwall Road near the North Deal level crossing; and at the pier head (29 seriously damaged; 48 slightly damaged; 3 slightly injured).
    05.45hrs: One shell landed at Worth.
    10.22hrs: One shell exploded in the air over Sutton.

Ron Warren, who served with the Royal Engineers on searchlight sites around Dover Harbour, recalls that an American B-17 'Flying Fortress' crash-landed near the village of Worth:

It came down at the back of the house where my parents were then living, and skidded into the fence which acted as a break, just a few hundred yards from the farmhouse which was in its path. It had been on a bombing mission and was badly damaged. Some of the crew stayed with local people until they were picked up by their own people. The aircraft was dismantled and taken away on lorries.

Monday 11 September
One shell (nil damage/injury).

Tuesday 12 September

Four shells at Sandwich Bay, others landing on Beach Street and The Marina (28 seriously damaged; 49 slightly damaged).

   19.15hrs: One shell fell at Coldred.

   19.53hrs: Three SHs fell at Worth.

Wednesday 13 September

16.05hrs–03.00hrs: Sixteen shells fell at St Margaret's village.

   17.50hrs: Shells fell inland as far as Waldershare. One damaged the water-tower at Lambert's Laundry, which had only recently been repaired; another landed at 'Blue Pigeons' at Worth; and one on the Deal–Sandwich railway line at the back of Sholden (2 seriously damaged; 24 slightly damaged; I seriously injured; 3 slightly injured).

Thursday 14 September

03.00hrs: Three SHs at Sholden.

   16.06hrs–16.13hrs: Three SHs at Worth.

Friday 15 September

Nine SHs landed in Ringwould Road at Kingsdown (I demolished; 39 seriously damaged; 54 slightly damaged).

Sunday 17 September

18.53hrs: Two SHs fell in Reach Road and at West Cliffe at St Margaret's; six fell on North Deal and Kingsdown.

This day something new was seen in the air over Deal and district – streams of aircraft towing gliders; as Ron Read recalls, they could be seen heading out towards the coast 'in separate streams just before they all linked up to cross the Channel together'. This airborne armada was en route to Arnhem, and just in case of accidents, former RAF Air Sea Rescue HSL crew member Terry Pattinson remembers, their launches were moored at a buoy off the South Foreland to rescue crews who might be forced down into the Channel.

Tuesday 19 September

Police announced that access limitations to coastal towns would now cease, and the anti-aircraft guns on the roofs of Clarabut's and the Odeon are to be removed, as well as the guns on the foreshore in front of 'Beach House'.

Thursday 21 September

Lancaster LM277 of No. 514 Sqn crashed in the sea off Walmer; only wreckage was found.

Sunday 24 September
A Westland Lysander was seen to crash into the sea at Walmer.
  Today saw the last leaflet balloon launch by 'M' Balloon Unit from Walmer.

Tuesday 26 September
02.00hrs–03.00hrs: Shells fell in Wellington Road, Northcote Road, The Marina, The
Strand, and in the back gardens of 'Redlands' in Blenheim Road. Damage was caused to
'Blenheim Villas' and the *East Kent Mercury* printing works. 6 SHs (37 seriously damaged; 64
slightly damaged; 1 slightly injured).

Bert Curling, then working at the *East Kent Mercury* printing works behind their
offices in Queen Street, recalls that the incident fortunately happened when the
composing room, which had a glazed roof, was unoccupied.

> When I arrived for work next morning there was type everywhere; we still used this
> although we had two Linotype machines; but the ARP chaps helped sift through
> the rubble and sort it all out into boxes. In the Linotype room, Ernie Graves took
> one week to bring out an eight-page 'Emergency Edition' of the *Mercury*. The type
> was made up for two sides of the two folded sheets and then printed off while the
> type for the reverse side was made up and then that side was printed.

Friday 29 September
Operations by 'M' Balloon Unit from Walmer suspended.

Sunday 8 October
An open air Service of Thanksgiving was held in Alfred Square to mark the end of the
shelling bombardment of north Deal.

Another benefit of the capture of the Pas de Calais area was that the launching sites
for the V1 flying bombs were also overrun, and these weapons were not seen on a
regular basis in this area thereafter. This in turn led to a 'stand down' of the anti-
aircraft artillery units along the coast and life was also more relaxed over at HMS
Robertson, after the enemy had been cleared from the Channel Ports. WRNS rating
Mrs R.G. Wells, remembered:

> I was later based at HMS *Robertson* at Stonar, and towards the end of the war,
> after the shelling and the V1s had ceased, a group of about nine of us Wrens
> were offered a trip round to Dover on one of the Royal Marines' landing craft.
> The captain was reputed to be the brother of James Mason, the film actor, so we
> were very enthusiastic about this trip, but when we got on board we found that
> there was nothing for us to sit on apart from the deck. After we arrived at
> Dover we were taken back to *Robertson* by lorry.

Across the road from *Robertson* the sidings of the 'New Salvage Yard' were now
occupied by imported rolling stock assembled for shipping to the Continent. These

included American flat-beds (wagons) and box-cars (covered vans) as well as huge 2–8–0 locomotives. This area came under the responsibility of 'D' Division NFS and Stuart Harlow recalls the US operating crews caused him some problems:

> Before Richborough was hived off to the Thanet Division we had to lay 6in steel pipes to supply their hydrants. However, the Americans had some half-track vehicles which they regularly drove over our pipes and thus squashed them. I would have to organize a repair party, usually at weekends, to replace those damaged pipes; the replacement pipes were supplied in random lengths, so this involved us in having to sort out the appropriate lengths for replacement.

Wednesday 25 October
Five hundred local elementary schoolchildren left for holidays in Brighton, paid for by a donation of £500 from New Zealand.

In November the military authorities approved the removal of the various defence works along the shoreline and on the beaches, so the services of the Royal Marine Engineers, the Civil Defence Rescue Squad and Deal Borough Council workmen were requisitioned for this task. A steam roller was used to crush the coils of barbed wire, and after the minefields had been cleared from local beaches, fishing was again allowed. Unfortunately access to the pier was now impossible, thanks to the breach caused by the *Nora*!

Assorted shipping had started to re-use The Downs anchorage and this involved Dr James Hall in additional emergency calls, including a trip to the US generator ship *Sea Power* to treat the 2nd Engineer for an abcess; a trip to the US Liberty ship USS *Shoemaker* and a visit to the US Army tug SR742 to treat an Army private who had injured his face. Many ships could now be seen passing The Downs, and most of those which fell foul of the infamous 'Shippe Swallower' (the Goodwin Sands) were American, because their navigation standards sometimes left a lot to be desired. Dr Hall's son Martin recalls:

> The frequency and intensity of the trips during this second period – 404 patients were treated on 152 ships – was due very largely to the great number of US Liberty and Victory ships on passage to war-torn Europe. They carried every conceivable cargo from petroleum to horses and other livestock, and foodstuffs ranging from bananas to 5lb tins of jam – which were occasionally washed ashore, to our (and other beachcombers') advantage when some of these ships came to grief. The ships rarely carried an MO and Father told us that sometimes no pilot was taken on board when proceeding into The Downs because the Master had to pay the pilotage out of his own pocket. Hence the significant number of wrecks on and around the Goodwins.

Early in November an assault was mounted on Walcheren Island and Flushing; it involved the RN monitors *Roberts* and *Erebus*, the destroyers *Garth* and *Cottesmore*, and the old battleship HMS *Warspite* supported by minesweepers, and all of them were seen in The Downs prior to departure.

Monday 6 November
US Liberty ship *Abraham Baldwin* ran aground on the Goodwins at night. The Walmer lifeboat, under the command of 2nd Cox'n Fred Upton, was afloat for seven hours, rescuing half the crew. Thirty-one men were taken off. The ship was later refloated and left the following Sunday.

Tuesday 7 November
Trawler *Grethe Mortensen* stranded on the Goodwins.

Wednesday 8 November
Dr Hall was called to a small Dutch tanker – it had rescued airmen aboard who were transferred to Ramsgate by MGB.
   20.24hrs: A V1 fell near Northbourne School after skimming over The Downs.

On 15 November 'M' Balloon Unit was transferred to 2nd TAF, prior to their move to France. Alice Bond, then serving at Sandwich radar station, recalls the successes the radar station had enjoyed over the previous five months against enemy missiles:

> From 13 June to 20 November 1944 the board showed 212 V1s. I also remem-ber we once got three good plots on shells at ten second intervals on their way across the Channel, but no V2s.

In December 1944 the Hon J.J. Astor informed Deal Borough Council that he wished to donate the Winter Gardens Theatre in Stanhope Road to the town. Deal's other theatre was at the Royal Marines barracks off Canada Road and Thelma Mansell recalls that the depot WRNS once mounted their own production there:

> The appropriately named Globe Theatre, was in North Barracks where we queued for ENSA concerts and plays. We also did our own thing there once, all suffering from stage fright, and our audience disappeared a few at a time. The director of the WRNS, Mrs Vera Laughton Matthews, came several times. I had lost my brother in Italy in May 1944, and she gave me her condolences. Hearing I was to marry, she told me to apply for a wedding dress given by American women [for hire to Service brides] so I did. I was lucky to have such a lovely creation in the midst of wartime economy.

During December 1944 Dr Hall took his eldest son Martin with him on the lifeboat to the Liberty ship *James D. Havilland* where he treated a fireman with angina, and a seaman with tonsillitis. Martin Hall recalls this trip took place during his school holidays, that it was late in the evening, and that it must have been one of the last trips which 'Old Joe' Mercer made as coxswain of Walmer lifeboat before he retired:

> I nagged father to take me along, and father in turn persuaded Joe to let me come aboard, much against the coxswain's inclination and certainly against the rules. The US Liberty ship had an urgent medical case on board and because the weath-er outlook was unfavourable, the lifeboat was rostered to make the trip instead of

one of the more usual motor-boats, such as Freddie Upton's *Rose Marie*.

The sheer excitement of the boat's launch down the steep shingle beach, once the shackle-pin securing her to the winch had been knocked out, speeding over the greased 'woods' laid to the water's edge, was an experience I'll never forget. The nearest shore-based comparison might be found on board a fire-engine racing downhill at top speed.

This turned out to be one of father's more dangerous trips, since as we approached the ship's location in The Downs, the weather had deteriorated considerably. By this time I was wet through, freezing cold and desperately sea-sick. I was tucked out of the way under the engine-room combing, where fuel fumes and Perce's 'Naval shag' tobacco added to my discomfort. Eventually father made it back to the lifeboat, thanks to incredible timing on the part of the crew, since the last part of his descent necessitated a jump into the boat – a fearfully risky move since he could so easily have fallen between the ship and the lifeboat, with more than a sporting chance of being crushed between them. As it was, the spouting waves hid him from the view of the crew as he slowly descended the rope-ladder, making it even more difficult for them to judge the correct manoeuvring of the lifeboat.

The return trip was hampered by the fact that during one of the lifeboat's 'bounces' up the side of the Liberty ship whilst 'standing-by' serious damage had been sustained to the lifeboat's rudder. However, Perce Cavell's brilliant handling of the engines, the experience, judgement and instincts of the coxswain, Joe Mercer, and the outstanding teamwork of the whole crew brought her home safely. Keeping direction would have been even more difficult if the lifeboat had had only one engine.

Saturday 23 December
Two Lancaster IIIs, PB683 and PB678, of No. 35 Sqn collided off the South Foreland en route to Cologne; both crews were killed.

CHAPTER EIGHT

January–August 1945

By the turn of the year, war activity had moved to the Continent and troops were now almost non-existent in the area as the need for Coastal Defence diminished. However, off-shore an ever-increasing number of vessels were to be seen making up Channel as the various Continental ports were liberated and supplies poured in to support the Allied armies advancing through Europe. Aerial activity in the main was almost continuous, both in support of the land forces and in bombing Germany. Long-range fighters such as Spitfire XIVs and Mustangs accompanied the bombers, many of which struggled back after suffering battle damage.

The V2 rockets continued to bombard London, supported by air-launched V1s from over the Thames Estuary and North Sea. The assault lasted until March 1945, and a 'last ditch' suicide mission to bomb London or towns in the south east could not be ruled out. Therefore it was necessary for No. 80 Wing RAF to maintain their radio surveillance duties up on the cliffs at Hawkshill Down. One of those involved in this was LAC Arthur McAughty:

> I was billeted with a Mr and Mrs Fordham at No. 3 Owen Square. We took our main meals there, but when working our shifts at Walmer it may have been that our meals were brought in by RAF transport. I do remember that there were also frequent visits to the site by a mobile NAAFI. Mr Fordham was a steward at the Royal Marine barracks, and it was there we went, when off-duty, to dances in the NAAFI. The man of the house was also a keen fisherman, and often took us to fish off the beach at high tide.

Recruit training continued at Deal, and one trainee who arrived at the RM depot was Jim Sutherland:

> It was in January 1945 that I joined up and spent most of that year doing my training at the North Barracks, then at Kingsdown Camp. Many a cold and frosty morning's run we had along the beach on the sea-front, right along the road past Walmer Castle.
>
> I also remember a lady who lived in a house by the South Gates who used to take in our washing. I have happy memories of those days when we were happy to have tuppence in our pockets for a packet of five Woodbines.

During January 1945 the daily convoys of Liberty ships could be seen passing The Downs, and occasionally picking up pilots to guide them through, or past The Goodwins. With a severe shortage of petrol and few mechanical farming implements in use throughout war-ravaged Europe, horses and mules were shipped in from across the Atlantic in large numbers. Not all animals survived the journey and one hazard encountered by Dr James Hall, when approaching the vessels which carried horses,

NAAFI tea van with 80 Wing RAF personnel. The RAF wireless operators at Hawkshill Down always welcomed the sight of the NAAFI tea van and the two ladies who manned it, as their site was very isolated and they had to work twelve-hour shifts listening out for German radio signals.

was the crews' disconcerting habit of just dropping carcasses overboard on arrival off Deal.

Since the enemy minefields were now cleared, miniature submarines posed the greatest threat to these vessels. Minesweeping operations were backed up by local coastguards who undertook 'mine watching' duties, reporting any that were adrift and floating into the shipping lanes.

Saturday 8 January
B-17 Fortress 43-39068 of 487th Heavy Bomb Group force-landed at Westcliffe Farm, St Margaret's-at Cliffe.

Friday 14 January
Dr Hall visits US Army tug *LT492* to treat seaman with acute appendicitis; he was landed and taken to hospital with Perce Cavell who was injured ashore.

Saturday 15 January
Call to cargo vessel *Dan-y-Bryn*, with a cargo of explosives on board, in Trinity Bay, moored near the *James Harrold*, which was also flying the explosives flag.

Sunday 16 January
02.00hrs: A loud explosion was heard; the crew of the *James Harrold* was rescued by the lifeboat and some drifters. Dr Hall was called to visit the Liberty ship *Edward E. Spafford*, where seven crewmen were injured in the collision with *James Harrold*. He was later called to the GWR Mail-steamer *Sambur* – 3rd Engineer had a high temperature.

The collision between these two Liberty ships occurred in The Downs, and caused the *James Harrold* to catch fire. After all the crew had been rescued, efforts to extinguish the fire and discharge her deck cargo of tanks and jeeps occupied an assortment of services over the next few days. She was towed inshore near Deal Castle, and eventually the fire was put out, and most of the cargo salvaged, but her back was broken. Her stern remained firmly jammed on the Malmes Rocks, while her forward and centre sections were towed away for a new stern to be built on. Bernie Kimpton recalls the tragic aftermath of the incident:

> The *James Harrold* had been loaded with petrol in four-gallon jerry cans, and after this was landed it was transferred to Walmer Station. Some American troops [US Labour Corps] based in huts at Oxney Bottom were loading the petrol into rail-tankers in the sidings at Walmer when there was an explosion, probably from a discarded cigarette end, and five of them were killed.

Monday 17 January
Dr Hall on morning call to *Edward P. Mitchell* in a gale to treat a cook with bronchitis, a fireman with burns and another with fibrositis.

Tuesday 18 January
Dr Hall called to the British Liberty ship *Sammex*; carpenter with a broken leg landed to hospital.
   P.m.: Dr Hall called to *Montevideo* (Nor); young mess boy with appendicitis was landed to hospital.

The timber jetties constructed at the beach 'hards' at Deal and Walmer to serve as loading points for oil tankers in an emergency were not needed. Here an Army DUKW amphibious vehicle departs for the stranded *James Harrold* after the fire on board had eventually been extinguished.

Wednesday 19 January
00.01hrs: A call came in from the US tug *LT492* requesting the return of their patient from Deal Hospital; Nursing Sister accompanied Dr Hall.

Saturday 22 January
The US Liberty ship *Helen Hunt Jackson* arrived with a suspected case of diphtheria; Dr Hall visited in bad weather but could not confirm the diagnosis. The lifeboat was damaged when it collided with the vessel.

On 14 February the 'Freedom of Deal' was granted to the Royal Marines in a ceremony at The Odeon cinema. A parade of Royal Marines and Wrens marched around the town led by the band of the RN School of Music, while the band from the RM Chatham Division entertained a vast crowd of Deal residents watching the event in Queen Street.

> I stood with my family opposite the Odeon, lifted up on my father's shoulders to see over the crowd. The Mayor, and the Town Clerk, with aldermen and councillors, accompanied by the RM Commandant, walked up Queen Street, where the 'Honour Guard' were waiting to be inspected. We were not privileged to be invited to attend the presentation of the Freedom Scroll, which took place inside the cinema, but this event is one of my most vivid wartime memories.

Friday 25 February
GPO cable ship *Alert* was lost off the North Goodwins.

Monday 28 February
B-17 Fortress of 457th Heavy Bomb Group ditched in the sea off South Foreland; four of the crew were killed.

There were more emergency calls during the months of March and April. Dr Hall was called out at 8.30 p.m. one evening to the US vessel *Stanton H. King*, taking one of the Deal hospital nursing sisters along. A negro fireman with severe constipation was treated. Then a call was received to visit the Liberty ship USS *Edward L. Grant*. A couple of days later he visited the cattle-boat *Robert W. Hart* to treat a cattleman with a broken foot, and two other medical cases – and discovered that she had a girl stowaway on board.

Sunday 8 May: VE Day
Much celebration, including many street parties.

To celebrate the end of the war in Europe, a dance was held in the former static water tank across the road from the Royal Marines swimming-baths on Walmer Green, now drained of water and with a gap broken through one end. There must have been some other activities during the day, as I can remember my parents and I gazing down at the group of dancers down below performing what I discovered later was square-dancing. During the evening the scene was illuminated by a couple of floodlights, and a string of fairy lights, rigged up on scaffold poles around the edges of the pool, with music from a gramophone via loudspeakers provided by Mr Walder, who had a radio shop along The Strand. Another spectator of the scene that evening was Marilyn Hayward, who had a better view of these celebrations:

> I would have been leaning out of a window above my Grandfather Bullock's greengrocery shop along the Strand, overlooking the Walmer Green water tank. I remember that after dark, this was the first time that I had ever seen fireworks like Catherine wheels and 'sparklers', being held by Canadian soldiers. The one tune that I can still remember being played that evening was 'And let the rest of the world go by'.

For some reason, Martin Hall had not returned to his school for the first day of term, so when Sir Winston Churchill announced that there was to be a two-day holiday to celebrate 'Victory in Europe' he was still at home in Walmer:

> My recollections are a bit vague, but I do remember seeing an informal parade in the streets of Deal, with everyone — informally dressed servicemen and cheerful civilians — linking arms and singing behind an even more informal band. Unlike my future wife, who enjoyed a street party outside her house in Gladstone Road, I don't recall being involved in the public jollifications but I do remember getting back to school and finding that all the wartime blackout precautions had been dismantled and the whole building was full of light after nearly six years of war.

The end of hostilities saw a start on the reconstruction and the rehousing of families made homeless during the previous six years. In St Richard's Road, the Patterson family saw some changes:

> My school was moved to 'Warden House', where my mother continued working as the caretaker, and the old Isolation Hospital was burned down at the same time. The Anderson shelter was unearthed, and became our garden shed. Before the pre-fabs were built in St Richard's Road and Marlborough Avenue, German POWs worked as labourers, laying the foundation slabs, and I remember seeing them being marched up St Richard's Road each day, carrying their tools.

Sunday 14 August: VJ Day
Today marks the end of all hostilities.

Martin Hall remembers that his father decided to celebrate this event in a suitably 'nautical' way:

> I recall that this was a much more low-key celebration in Deal than VE Day had been. In the early evening Father decided that he would make his own private contribution. He had acquired, at some time during the war, a large lifeboat flare, which I remember was kept in the airing-cupboard at home. The traffic in Dover

There were plenty of local people to line Deal's streets in February 1945 when the Royal Marines received the Freedom of Deal; the march past included this group of Wrens from the Deal Depot, being watched by their Royal Marine drill instructor (left) to see they kept in step.

Road was minimal, compared with the endless traffic jam found there today. So we went out into the middle of the road and Father with his usual aplomb set the flare alight. It made a spectacular bang and illuminated the area with a brilliant red flash.

But what was it like, living and working in the Deal area during the Second World War? Everybody will have their own memories, just as I have, but some things seemed somehow better then, despite what was happening each day. Peggy Oatridge summed up her feelings thus:

The war seemed to go on so long that you got used to it. Private life went on despite bombs, shells, machine-gunning, and you got 'desensitized' to it I suppose. There would be an air raid, and you would hear that somebody you knew had been killed, and you were sorry, but after a raid your reaction would be, 'Well, I'm still here', which seemed awfully selfish. You were sorry about those people who 'copped it' but grateful that you hadn't.

Nobody grumbled about things, they just got on and did it – that spirit has somehow gone nowadays. I cannot remember anyone being unpleasant, people were all willing to help. I don't know what has happened to that spirit today.

The people of Deal have always had a great love and respect for the Royal Marines, and thus were granted the 'Freedom of the Borough' in February 1945. So it is fitting that a member of that Corps, Peter Stewart, who 'took the King's shilling and enlisted' at the depot should pay his tribute to the fortitude and endurance of the local people during the six years of war:

What I have left in my memory is the great fight the people of Deal put up during the last conflict with the German nation. Big guns, fighters and bomber planes – they took it all, and not once did they flinch.

Appendix

The War Record for Deal
Bombardments and Air Raids:

High Explosive bombs dropped in and around Deal	173
Shells	127
Incendiary Bombs	118
Parachute Mines	2
Flying Bombs	nil
Machine-gun attacks	many

Alerts:

General Alerts	2,521
Immediate Danger Alerts	1,056
Shell Warnings	99

Casualties:

Killed	65
Seriously injured	59
Slightly injured	197

Deal Civil Defence Officials

Chairman, Emergency Committee: His Worship the Mayor, (Alderman E.J. Dobson JP, OBE)

Sub-Controller: The Town Clerk and Clerk of the Peace (Mr D.A. Daniels OBE)

ARP Officers: Col W. Sinclair OBE, RM (Rtd) 1935–1939
   Lt Col C.H. Congdon RM (Rtd) 1939–1940
   Mr G.A.M. Gentry AMICE, MIM, & CyE 1940–1945

Deputy ARP Officers: Mr G.E. Ford AMCDI, ARPS 1938–1942
   Mr S.E. Coe LARP 1943–1945

Casualty Service, Medical Officer of Health: Dr D.W. Kirk MB, ChB

Chief Warden: Lt Col H.W.F. Paterson CIE 1939–1941
   Lt Col Buchanan-Dunlop CMG, DSO 1941–1942
   Councillor G. Brenchley 1943–1945

Training Officer: Major K.D. O'Callaghan 1939–1942

Bomb Reconnaissance Officer: Major K.D. O'Callaghan 1941–1942
   Mr A. Sutton 1942–1944
   Mr S.E. Coe 1943–1945

Decontamination Officer/Sanitary Officer: Mr J.P. Byng Cert. SIB, AR San I, MSIA

Fire Guard Officer: Mr G.E. Ford 1941–1942
   Mr R.H. Fisher 1942–1945

WVS Hon Central Organizer: Mrs L.K. Bethell 1939
   Mrs E.A. Dobson 1939–1940
   Mrs M.F. Brown 1940–1941
   Miss Lushington-Taylor JP 1941–1945
   (Mrs L.H Shelvey)

Main Wardens' Posts
(Before Amalgamation)
No. 1: Mayfair Court, The Marina, Deal (later 3 College Road)
No. 2: 163 Beach Street, Deal
No. 3: Deal Castle (later 1a Victoria Road, Deal)
No. 4: 'Beachwood', Albert Road, Deal (later 'Cherry Orchard', London Road, Deal)
No. 5: 'The Hut', Walmer Green, Walmer (later 4 Canada Road, Walmer)
No. 6: 'The Lawn', Lawn Road, Walmer (later Wellington House, Dover Road, Walmer)
No. 7: Cemetery Lodge, Cemetery Road, Deal
No. 8: Beach Court, Park Road, Upper Deal (later 296 St Richard's Road, Deal)
No. 9: 165 Mill Hill, Deal (later 99 St Richard's Road, Deal)
'K': Dial House, Kingsdown

(After Amalgamation)
Nos 1 and 2, 'A': 3 College Road, Deal
No. 3, 'B': 1a Victoria Road, Deal
No. 5, 'C': 4 Canada Road, Walmer
No. 6, 'D': Wellington House, Dover Road, Walmer
Nos 4 and 7, 'E': 'Cherry Orchard', London Road, Deal
Nos 8 and 9, 'F': 99 St Richard's Road, Deal
Kingsdown, 'K': Dial House, Kingsdown

Main Depots
Rescue Service and First Aid Posts:
No. 1: Cemetery Road Depot, Cemetery Road, Deal
No. 2: Foresters' Hall, North Barrack Road, Walmer (later South Deal Infants' School, Mill Road, Deal)
No. 3: Nelson Hall, Nelson Street, Deal (later 'Rosway', Middle Deal Road, Deal)

Ambulance Service:
No. 1: Foresters' Hall, North Barrack Road, Walmer (later South Deal Infants' School, Mill Road, Deal)
No. 2: Nelson Hall, Nelson Street, Deal (later 'Rosway', Middle Deal Road, Deal)

First Aid Post and Mobile Unit: Park Centre, Victoria Road, Deal

Repair Service:
No. 1: Cemetery Road Depot, Cemetery Road, Deal
No. 2: West Street Depot, West Street, Deal

Bibliography

Aircraft Casualties in Kent, 1939–40, KAHRS, Meresborough Books (1990)

The Battle of Britain – Then and Now, Winston G. Ramsey, Plaistow Pictorial (1980)

Battle over Britain, Francis K. Mason, Aston Publications Limited (1990)

The Blitz on Canterbury, Paul Crampton, Meresborough Books (1989)

The Blitz – Then and Now, Vols I–IV, Winston G. Ramsey, Battle of Britain Prints Ltd (1987–92)

Buzz Bomb Diary, KAHRS (1994)

Confound and Destroy, Martin Streetly, Macdonalds and Janes (1978)

Deal and The Downs in the War of Liberation, 1939–45, E.C. Pain, T.F. Pain & Sons (1948?)

Forgotten Shipwrecks of The Downs, David Chamberlain (1993)

Goodwin Sands Shipwrecks, Richard Larn, David & Charles (1979)

A Heritage from The Goodwins, David Chamberlain (1994)

History of Sandwich, Helen C. Bentwich (1971)

Kent County War Diary, Kent County Archives

Mighty Eighth War Diary, Roger A. Freeman, Janes Publishing (1981)

Royal Air Force Serials, various vols, James J. Halley, Air Britain Historians Ltd

Sea Surgeon, James Hall OBE, T.F. Pain & Sons (1962)

Ships of the Royal Navy, J.J. Colledge, David & Charles (1970)

The Lifeboat Service, Oliver Warner, Cassell (1974)

Victoria Baptist Church Centenary Booklet, R.J. Monckton, R.J. Monckton (1981)

Walmer Baptist Church, 1908–1983, Rodney Pearce, Rodney Pearce (1983)

Various issues:
Bygone Kent
East Kent Mercury
Kent Messenger
Kentish Gazette

Index